NO WAY

THE NATURE OF THE IMPOSSIBLE

NO WAY

THE NATURE OF THE IMPOSSIBLE

Edited by

Philip J. Davis and David Park

W. H. Freeman and Company
NEW YORK

Library of Congress Cataloging-in-Publication Data

No way.

  Includes index.
    1. Science—Miscellanea. 2. Engineering—Miscellanea.
3. Humanities—Miscellanea. 4. Social sciences—
Miscellanea. 5. Possibility—Miscellanea. I. Davis,
Philip J., 1923–   . II. Park, David Allen, 1919–
III. Title: Nature of the impossible.
Q173.N7 1987 111'.6 86-19728
ISBN 0-7167-1813-8
ISBN 0-7167-1966-5 (pbk)

Printed in the United States of America

2 3 4 5 6 7 8 9 0 MP 6 5 4 3 2 1 0 8 9 8

*The editors dedicate their share of the work to
Jessica Hilary Park and Susan Jean Wesley
with love and admiration.*

Goe, and catch a falling starre,
*   Get with child a mandrake roote,*
Tell me, where all past yeares are,
*   And who cleft the Divels foot,*
Teach me to hear Mermaides singing
*   And finde*
*   What winde*
Serves to advance an honest minde.

—John Donne

CONTENTS

Chemistry

Computer Science

Technology

Physics

Mathematics

• • •

Intermission

• • •

Law

Politics

Economics

Psychology

Education

Poetry

Music

Philosophy

• • •

Taking Leave

• • •

INTRODUCTION

- It is impossible to translate a poem.
- It is impossible for the president of the United States to be less than 35 years of age.
- It is impossible to send a message into the past.
- It is impossible for a door to be open and closed at the same time.

The above are some miscellaneous statements; one might even say that they have nothing in common except the word "impossible." One is a common opinion, another is inscribed in statute, the third says something about the nature of the physical world, the last sounds like pure logic but isn't. What about a revolving door? We learn early in life that the world is full of loopholes and that, when someone says "impossible," the word is often not to be taken at face value. "It becomes a wise man not to think anything impossible," wrote Sir James Hill in 1751. Then what is the use of the word? It seems to be most used as a guide to policy or action. "It is impossible to elect a Republican in the Fifth District." Sometimes it denotes a recognition of the limits of our strength or imagination, or a recognition of the laws that restrict ("govern," we say) the natural world about us. Sometimes the word is elicited by our conservative nature or a fit of depression; it may point to the absence of an enveloping faith. Once spoken, it warns of thin ice and urges us onto established paths. But also it may spur us to rise above the ordinary, to do what no one has yet done, to perform a miracle. Everyone knows we live in an age of technological miracles. What will they think of next? The telephone, the moon walk; when it was new, penicillin used to be called the miracle drug, and so it is.

Some miracles are largely matters of tempo: when an otherwise normal process occurs quickly enough it may be called a miracle. Only elves could repair all the old shoemaker's shoes in a single night, but what about what computers do? They perform a million acts of stupid logic or arithmetic at miraculous speed.

Think about the miracles of religion: a virgin gives birth, a man raises the dead and walks on water. Are these possible or are they impossible? Decide.

From childhood, our sense of the world tells us, of every contemplated act, whether or not it is worth trying. What can't be becomes a part of what is. The possible and the impossible are like two countries: one is well known, the other cannot be visited and yet is not entirely unknown. Sending messages into the past is one of the things they do there, but is 2 + 2 equal to 5? The world is infinite. Is the country of the possible finite? Then that of the impossible is infinite, or it may be the other way around, or both may be infinite. Decide: it is a test that separates temperaments. Is the boundary between the two like a fence across miles of countryside or is the territory of each penetrated by thousands of little islands of the other? Declare.

The dream of the Founding Fathers as they met in the Constitutional Convention turned out to be, within limits, a dream of the possible. Isaiah's dream that men shall beat their swords into plowshares and their spears into pruning hooks, that nation shall not lift up sword against nation, neither shall they study war anymore seems to us too much to believe, yet is it really impossible? Physically it is possible. Is it socially impossible? Perhaps the tension between physical possibility and impossibility of another kind is one of the sources of faith. Tertullian wrote, "It is certain because it is impossible." God does not waste his time or ours with dubious miracles. If the divine were plainly in evidence to everyone so that it could not be doubted, what would be the use of faith? Augustine wrote, "I believe because it is absurd."

To live at the boundary between the possible and the impossible, and to be aware of it, is to be truly alive. What is really new in the world emerges at this boundary. The microchip, of course, but also at the extreme edge of possibility occurs, when it occurs, the truly erotic moment. It just might happen. . . .

What is this boundary? Is it a river or a cliff, put there by nature, is it a high wall erected by man, or is it a strip of territory that neither country controls? Whatever its nature we should explore it a little, since mankind tends to spend quite a lot of its time nearby. Consider the numbers they use there. In all mathematics written from Babylonian times well into the Middle Ages there is no mention of numbers less than zero. Such a number was clearly meaningless; it is clearly impossible to have a negative number of apples or a line of negative length or a field with a negative area. Negative numbers made their appearance in commerce when it was noticed that a negative balance in an account book, resulting from subtracting a larger number from a smaller one, made sense and could be a useful thing to know about. Negative numbers moved into the borderland and thence into the land of the possible. Of course, it was not the numbers that moved; rather, it became possible to think about them. Once negative numbers were accepted, the question inevitably arose as to whether such a number has a square root. Clearly it was impossible. This time it was mathematical practice that broadened people's minds. It was not acceptable that the equation $x^2 = 2$ should be soluble while $x^2 = -2$ should not be. Numbers of a new kind were introduced. In deference to prevailing opinion they were called impossible numbers or imaginary numbers, but lightning did not strike when the new symbols were written down, and mathematics moved forward.

Is impossibility, then, always an illusion of ours? Here we must be careful. There are logical impossibilities. It is impossible that stone A should be both heavier and lighter than stone B, but as we have seen, it is not impossible for a door to be both open and shut. How is this? We believe these statements because we know something about stones and weight and about doors. We call this universe-assisted logic. Until the invention of mathematical logic over a century ago it was just logic. Mathematical logic goes like this: M is not the same as N. It is then impossible that X should be the same as both M and N. This statement is necessarily true, the impossibility is real, but is it really real? Does it exist anywhere except in the world of symbols and symbolic reasoning? "The commander of the Continental Army" is not the same as "The first president of the United

States," and yet George Washington is the same as both. Logicians know how to get around this bit of slipshod reasoning, but how sure can we be that other examples taken from the real world are not infected with subtler forms of the same virus? We must not assume that logical impossibility carries over into the real world.

Then, what really counts as impossible? A man cannot fly simply by waving his arms. On the other hand, we can remember when people declared that a four-minute mile would never be run. That was thought to be the combined result of physical and psychological barriers. It was not supposed to be possible to climb Mt. Everest without carrying oxygen along, but Reinhold Messner did it. The dilemma is this: You can prove logical impossibilities, but do they say anything about the real world? You can assert practical impossibilities, but are they really impossible? Why bother about the question? Because mankind is inspired by the challenge of the impossible, and so it behooves us to have some conceptions of what it is. Conceptions, not absolute knowledge. We can't know. There is no criterion of impossibility, no final test. Every field of endeavor faces barriers of impossibility. The essays in this book examine a few of them, chosen almost arbitrarily. You will find that to our various colleagues impossibility shows very different aspects.

• • •

The essays were commissioned by the editors and were written specifically for this book. Some of them have received prepublication in various journals. The following journals have graciously allowed us to reprint: *Harvard* (M. Katz), *Perspectives in Biology and Medicine* (J. Barondess), *Mathematics Magazine* (P. Davis). The editors would like to thank the individual contributors not only for their own articles, but for many constructive criticisms and suggestions.

They also wish to thank the following people for help and encouragement during the course of their work: Hadassah F. Davis, Brenda Engel, Michael O. Finkelstein, Frank Rothman, Joan Rothman and Thomas F. Banchoff and James Trefil who provided very constructive reviews on the manuscript.

Philip J. Davis

David Park

The summit of Mount Pumo-Ri, Everest range, Nepal. Photograph by David Park.

EVEREST AND THE IMPOSSIBLE

W e did not stare the impossible straight in the face until the very end, when it became clear that, for our expedition, the summit of Mount Everest lay utterly out of reach. "Summit no possible this time, sahib," one of the Sherpas told me gently, offering me a hot cup of tea. "But still we have life."

Moments before we had received a radio call from Camp Five announcing that our last summit team had been forced back at an altitude of 28,200 feet—a bare 800 vertical feet below the summit. Yet, though we had pushed within shouting distance of the top of the world, we had no strength left to launch another summit bid. We were spent, finished—*gingiplut* as the Sherpas would say. In the eyes of the world, the 1985 American Mount Everest West Ridge Expedition was a failure.

Back in Camp One, the reactions of my teammates to the reality of our "failure" varied. Those on the actual summit team were too tired to care—their faces a blank mask of exhaustion. One climber, forced to take several Dexedrine tablets to get himself down to Camp One alive, moved with the unnatural animation of a puppet on strings. He had descended over 8000 vertical feet of ice and rock in a single day.

Those of us below felt equally let down by what had happened. Some simply shrugged their shoulders; some shook their heads in disbelief; some just stared and stared at the mountain above without uttering a word, as if searching for something lost. A few looked as if they wanted to cry, although none did. Others, more violent and vocal, screamed obscenities up at the mountain like drunken hecklers at a losing game, until the mountain, in perfect equanimity, echoed them back.

Strictly speaking, we were lucky to be alive. The route we had been attempting, the West Ridge Direct, is considered by many to be the hardest route on Everest. It had, within the last twelve months, claimed the lives of three climbers, all of whom had been on their way *down* from the summit after a "successful" expedition. Meanwhile, on the much less difficult South Col route, a Norwegian expedition that shared the mountain with us this year was forced to pass within full view of three more corpses, all grotesquely preserved against decay by Everest's deep-freeze climate. Two were the bodies of Sherpas killed last year on an earlier American Expedition; the third was the body of an Austrian woman who collapsed from exhaustion near the summit. One of our Sherpas, a summit veteran, had been by her side when she died.

Another of the corpses on Everest is that of the first of the "Everest Martyrs," George Mallory. He was last seen, with his companion George Irvine, climbing toward the summit of Everest on the Northeast Ridge during the 1922 British Everest Expedition. Then the clouds closed in, and neither of the two men was ever seen again. It is impossible to know what happened to them up there— whether they collapsed on their way to the summit, or died in a fall while making their way back down. "It is just possible," asserts Chris Bonnington, the leader of several recent British expeditions, "that they did reach the summit in 1922"—over thirty years before Tensing and Hillary made the first official ascent of the mountain in 1953.

We will never know, although since that fateful day in 1922 a few tantalizing shreds of evidence have appeared. In 1933, a British expedition found an ice axe on the ridge at 27,000 feet which could only have belonged to Mallory or Irvine. More recently, a Chinese climber claimed to have stumbled upon a body high on the ridge, dressed in the tattered remnants of the British woolen climbing garments of half a century ago. But the Chinese climber himself died in a fall from the North Face of Everest before his claims could be substantiated.

What is certain is that the mysterious disappearance of Mallory and Irvine gave them a kind of permanent public immortality. In 1922, news of their death near the summit was greeted with an almost unprecedented outpouring of grief. Like "Lawrence of Arabia" or "Scott of the Antarctic," "Mallory of Everest" was eulogized as a Saint of the Empire, a Knight of the Impossible. As one British editorial proclaimed,

> In the days of peace, England will always hold some who are not content with humdrum routine and soft living. The spirit which animated the attack on Everest is the same as that which prompted arctic, and other expeditions, and in earlier times led to the formation of the Empire itself. Who shall say that any of its manifestations are not worthwhile? Who shall say that its inspiration has not had far reaching influence on the race? It is certain that it would grow rusty with disuse, and expeditions like the attempt to scale Everest serve to whet the sword of ambition and courage.

As the defensive tone suggests, there *were* those in England who thought the "conquest of Everest" a scandalous waste of time, human life, and (perhaps especially) money. When the idea of forming an expedition was first proposed, one critic wrote, "Some of the last mystery of the world will pass when the last secret place in it, the naked peak of Everest, shall be trodden by those trespassers." Somewhat less eloquently, another editorialist lamented that "it will be a proud moment for the man who first stands on top of the earth, but he will have the painful thought that he has queered the pitch for posterity."

Yet, despite their differences of opinion, these commentators do share at least one concern—a concern for which Mount Everest is merely a symbol. I am referring here to what must be called, for lack of a better term, the "Death of the Impossible." It was *this* death (the passing of "the last mystery of the world") which both critics and supporters of Everest were lamenting, far more than the deaths of two otherwise obscure climbers, or even the death of an empire.

To understand what I mean here, it is perhaps better not to rattle off the usual edifying list of modern triumphs (the conquest of the air, the conquest of polio, the conquest of Everest, etc.) but rather to call to mind some of this century's most spectacular failures: the civilized butchery of World War I; the outrage of fascism; the grief

of Auschwitz; the destruction of Hiroshima and Dresden; the reign
of terror of Stalin and Mao. What well-intentioned Victorian, raised
in the sunset glow of Enlightenment and Empire, could have imagined such barbarities to be possible? For we live in an age in which
one man, Winston Churchill, began his career in a cavalry charge
and ended with his finger on the atomic bomb. In our century, the
impossible didn't die of old age; it was murdered.

Granted, one might argue that the impossible had in fact been
dead (or at least seriously ill) since at least the time of Prometheus.
But it was not until our own century (or so the story goes)—a century that witnessed, not coincidentally, the Death of God—that the
impossible was finally buried once and for all beneath an enormous
heap of human achievements, discoveries, adventures, tragedies, triumphs, and hype. For some, this seemed ample cause for celebra-
tion: the full force of human potential unleashed. For others, it
seemed cause for despair: "the last mystery" solved, the "last secret
place" trampled underfoot.

But whatever side of this argument one might have been on, everyone agreed that Mount Everest should be viewed as an enormous
symbol of the death of the impossible writ large. Recall first that the
sport of mountaineering is itself scarcely 250 years old: previous to
that time, mountain climbing was not considered "impossible"; it
was simply not considered at all. Nor was Everest known to be the
highest mountain in the world until well over a century after the
sport of mountaineering began, when it was finally measured by the
Indian Trigonometrical Survey (an organization originally directed by
one Sir George Everest) in 1852.

One hundred years later, in 1952, the summit of Mount Everest
still remained unclimbed, despite numerous heroic efforts of Swiss
and British expeditions over the years to reach its summit. It was
precisely this long string of desperate attempts and sometimes tragic
failures on the mountain that earned Mount Everest its enduring
place as a symbol of the impossible. As Everest historian Walt
Unsworth observes,

> Had Mount Everest been climbed at the first attempt it would have
> been hailed as a notable achievement and quickly forgotten. The
> peak itself, because it is the highest in the world, would have
> become no more than a curious statistic for use in quiz games. It
> was, ironically, the repeated failures which gave the mountain real
> stature in the public's eyes ... as a symbol of the unattainable.

Then, on May 23, 1953, the "unattainable" was finally attained: New Zealander Edmund Hillary and Sherpa Tensing Norgay reached the top of the highest mountain in the world. Many at the time (including many mountaineers) predicted that the world's fascination with Mount Everest would immediately decline. Yet, despite the fact that the climb could no longer be considered strictly impossible, international interest in the mountain only intensified. In 1954, a Swiss team seconded the British ascent; one by one, the nations lined up to place their own representatives on the summit.

Meanwhile, a new race was on, the race to climb Mount Everest by ever more impossible-looking routes—"Everest the Hard Way," as Chris Bonnington called it. In 1963, the Americans became the first to climb the West Ridge (though not by the "Direct" route which our expedition attempted this year). In 1975, the Southeast Face, the Southeast Ridge, and the North Ridge were all climbed for the first time. In the same year, Everest was first climbed by a woman, Junko Tabei of Japan. Note that in 1922, the British Everest Committee had declared, "It is impossible . . . to contemplate the application of a lady of whatever nationality to take part in a future expedition on Mount Everest. The difficulties would be too great."

In the decade between 1975 and the present, the list of "impossible" accomplishments on Mount Everest has continued to grow. In 1979, two German climbers, Reinhold Messner and Peter Habeler, shocked the world by successfully climbing Mount Everest without oxygen. At the time, such an attempt was considered suicidal. Habeler and Messner were warned that they would go up as sane men and return as functional idiots; yet both returned from the summit alive and well.

In 1980, Messner returned once more to climb Mount Everest solo, by an untried route, and again without oxygen. It was a spectacular feat, arguably the greatest in modern mountaineering history. Even today, it marks the outer boundaries of the possible for the mountaineer. As Messner himself reports, "The last maybe three, four hours I was thinking it is maybe impossible. And it is the first time in my high altitude climbing that I was not anymore thinking of the way down. It was no longer important for me to go down. It was only important to go up."

Looking back in this way over the history of mountaineering, it is easy to see how Mount Everest could become a public symbol for the death of the impossible. Even if one attempt failed, the next attempt (or the next, or the next) would almost certainly succeed. It was only a matter of time. "Everywhere, in every field of endeavor," wrote René Dittert, "the inaccessible and the impossible are only a matter of great patience, a patience which man has within him, not as his own property . . . but as a magic ring which the vanquished gives to him who succeeds in the attempt. Thus, in the long run, the gates open which man at first believed to be remorselessly shut."

Yet, having said all this, it must next be admitted that the history of Mount Everest actually does less to support my conclusions about the death of the impossible than it does to refute them. For looking down the list of impossibilities overcome (Everest without Oxygen; Everest the Hard Way; Everest Solo; Everest on Roller Skates), it becomes increasingly clear that the impossible in fact *cannot* die, cannot be murdered, least of all by those who strive to overcome it. It is, to the contrary, continually recreated, redefined, transfigured, reborn. Climbers don't conquer the impossible, they invent it.

In the words of Doug Scott, the first man to climb Everest "the Hard Way" (via the Southeast Face, in 1975),

> It is impossible to measure the heroic exertions that have taken place over the years on the flanks of Everest and to suggest that one effort was more heroic than another. Right from the start in the early 1920s, a few climbers periodically have found themselves at the limit of what was presumed to be physically, physiologically, or psychologically possible. It must always have been pretty much the same limits, the same sort of struggle. The only difference has been one of time and place, for on each occasion the frontiers of the possible were transcended.

This phenomenon—the continual rebirth of the impossible as opposed to what I have been calling its death—is, of course, not limited to mountaineering: it can be found in virtually any field of human endeavor. In truth, the real problem with such rhetorical flourishes as "The Death of the Impossible" or "The Death of God" is that they make our present century sound unique and far more uninhabitable than it possibly could be: perpetually the barriers of impossibility are broken down; perpetually they rise again, like waves on a shore. Can we honestly believe that no one before us doubted the existence of the gods? that no one overcame great obstacles at impossible odds? or set forth in miraculous machines, chariots of fire, to the unknown, undiscovered, even undreamed-of places of the earth? Certainly there must once have been those, even in the time of Odysseus, who thought of sailing ships as de-humanizing technologies and of those who sailed them as alienated. Yet for all that, in the intervening 2500 years, the oceans have lost none of their mystery, and the mountains have lost none of their allure.

In fact, concepts of death and rebirth, creation and destruction, immortality and impossibility have for centuries been associated with each other and with the mountains. In Sanskrit, the word *Himalaya* means literally "abode of the snows," the place where Shiva, at once Creator and Destroyer of all things, dances in eternal carnal embrace with his female counterpart, Devi (also known as Parvati, the Moun-taineer). Even today, their various incarnations are among the most venerated deities in Nepal. Nor are the Nepalis the only people to hold the mountains sacred: the Greek Olympus, the Norse Valhalla, the Buddhist Kalais, the Christian Purgatory all testify to this fact. In the Old Testament, Moses spoke to Jehovah from the summit of Mount Sinai; in the New Testament, Christ spoke to mankind from the Mount of Olives. In the Americas, the Incas built shrines on the summits of the Andes as high as 20,000 feet; in Japan, mountains have for centuries been the objects of Zen and Taoist meditations; and in China, as the French philosopher and mountaineer René Daumal observes, "masters instruct their pupils on the edge of an abyss."

In 1928, René Daumal actually went so far as to *invent* a sacred mountain for the modern world—a peak that is, by definition, im-possible to climb. In his novel entitled *Mount Analogue,* Daumal writes, "For a mountain to play the role of Mount Analogue its sum-mit must be inaccessible, *but its base accessible* to human beings as nature has made them. It must be unique, *and it must exist geo-graphically.* The door to the invisible *must be visible.*" (italics mine)

As Daumal describes it, Mount Analogue lies directly on the bor-der between the possible and the impossible—the same border on which Mount Everest lies, at least in the minds of mountaineers. And thus Daumal's metaphor, however fanciful, does provide one way to describe what actually happened to us "up there" (I speak here not of any visible sequence of events, but of those invisible inner events that formed the true weave and substance of our life on the mountain): at the moment when we first realized that the sum-mit of Everest lay beyond our reach, Mount Everest *became Mount Analogue* for us—"its summit inaccessible, *but its base accessible* to human beings as nature has made them." The door to the invisible *became visible*, like the summit of Everest itself suddenly torn from the clouds.

I do *not* mean that we lost sight of the real Mount Everest behind a screen of hazy metaphors. Indeed, what I admire most about Daumal's *Mount Analogue* is its concreteness. What the modern world lacks, in Daumal's view, is not just another symbol of the impossible, but an actual physically existing embodiment of it. Hence Mount Analogue "*must* exist geographically," its base *must* be "accessible to human beings as nature made them"—not in spite of the fact that its summit is impossible to climb, but because of it. Thus Mount Analogue is not a symbol of the impossible at all (if by "symbol" we mean something found in a book, some bloodless metaphor); rather, it *is* the impossible glimpsed face to face, something one can grasp and struggle with, feel, fear, live with, die for.

So that when I say that Mount Everest became Mount Analogue for us, I do *not* mean that Mount Everest suddenly became a "symbol" of the impossible in our eyes. It had always been that: a goal we had dreamed of, planned for, trained for, read about in books. Instead, for perhaps the first time in our lives, we glimpsed the impossible face to face, not just as a symbol this time, but as something physically to be confronted: something that made your legs ache and your lungs burn and your eyes fill with tears when you saw it, something beautiful and painful and frighteningly real, always just out of reach, always just a little higher, always just barely visible, always just *up there*.

This concreteness, this physical focus, is what distinguishes a mountaineer's insight, his vision if you will, from the "out of body" visions of mystics and madmen. The mountaineer does not want to escape from the earth, or somehow leave his individual existence behind (to do so, at least on a mountain, is so painfully easy: one has merely to "let go"). Rather, the mountaineer seeks to intensify those very thoughts and sensations that the mystic seeks to overcome, holding on to them, grappling with them, bleeding them dry. In the words of Reinhold Messner, perhaps our foremost apostle of the impossible in mountaineering, "I want to climb with my strength, with my fears, with my senses." It is finally this purely physical fascination, far more than some vague metaphysical quest, that is at the root of the mountaineer's seeming obsession with the impossible— why mountaineers so continually seek it out, continually reinvent it (as I have argued) rather than stand and watch it die.

At its best, then, climbing provides us with a way to reconnect ourselves to ourselves (and to the impossible) not in any vague metaphorical sense, but within the grasp of our own two hands on the rock and the rope. This is not to ignore the very real sense of frustration, even of failure, that we felt at the end of our expedition. But it does serve as a reminder that those who *did* reach the summit of Everest before us felt no more sense of satisfaction, of "victory" over the impossible, than we did (this the dark side, the sinister side, of the impossible for mountaineers: like the end of the rainbow, it must always elude us). So that, even in the wake of the first "successful" ascent of the West Ridge, expedition leader Norman Dhyrenfuth found himself quoting Nietzsche: "There are two tragedies in a man's life. The first is to have failed to have reached your goal; the second is to have reached it." Tom Hornbein, another member of that same expedition, describes his own feelings on the summit this way:

> We felt the lonely beauty of the evening, the immense roaring silence of the wind, the tenuousness of our tie to all below. There was a hint of fear, not for our lives, but of a vast unknown which pressed in upon us. A fleeting feeling of disappointment—that after all those dreams and questions this was only a mountain top—gave way to the suspicion that maybe there was something more, something beyond the three-dimensional form of the moment. If only it could be perceived.

"Fear," "disappointment," and a vague "suspicion"—judging by their own words, Hornbein and his companions felt no more sense of satisfaction, no more sense of completeness or "conquest" following their famous success than we did following our quiet failure. Even from the summit of Everest, a mountaineer's view of the impossible remains the same: always just out of reach, always just a little higher, always just barely visible, always just *up there*. That, in George Mallory's words, is why mountaineers have always gone to climb Mount Everest, and why they always will: because it (the impossible) is there.

A bit of Nature's luxuriant diversity: some of the intricate and varied single-celled aquatic organisms. From F. Blochmann, *Die Mikroskopische Tierwelt des Süsswassers, Abtheilung I: Protozoa*, Lucas Gräfe and Sillem, Hamburg, 1895.

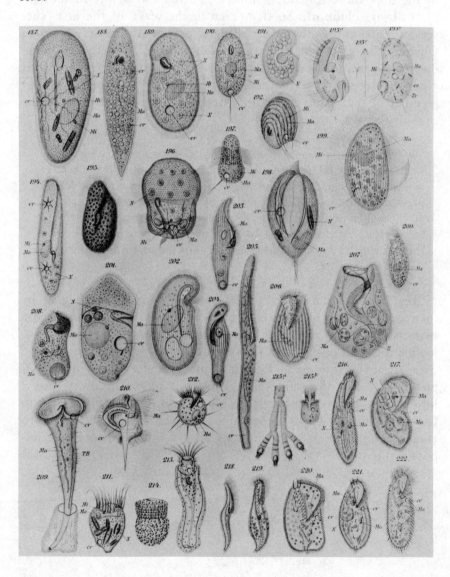

ARE THERE BIOLOGICAL IMPOSSIBILITIES?

When you have eliminated the impossible, whatever remains, however improbable, must be the truth.

Mr. Sherlock Holmes, in "The Sign of Four," Chapter 6

Biologists rarely use the word "impossible." To a biologist the range of the possible is so large, the potential biological entities so overwhelmingly numerous, that the impossible is only a tiny issue. To a biologist the impossibilities are the wall at the edge of the universe—real and formidable constraints, but constraints lying somewhere far away, somewhere in the realm of the physicist. The biologist sees these physical constraints as if through the wrong end of a telescope; miniaturized, the limits of the physical universe form toy fences in someone else's province. With more than 1500 different species of daisies in Europe alone and more than 2000 different species of crickets worldwide, with 30,000 different proteins specific to the brain of the rat, the biologist has little room on his desk for perpetual motion machines or for rockets that travel faster than the speed of light.

Biologists rarely use the word "impossible." In part this is because of the richness of their realm, overflowing as it is with strange possibilities. In part it is also because the mainstream biological tradition is natural history, the record of Nature's accomplishments, the careful charting of the possible. Moreover, biologists are artisans at heart; they want to do things and to make things and they actively seek out the possible—that is, those things that can be done and that can be made. Beyond these reasons, however, I suspect that there is a more fundamental reason why biologists rarely speak in terms of the impossible: perhaps there are no biological impossibilities. Perhaps deep within the true province of biology, everything is possible.

• • •

Could this be the case? Are there no biological impossibilities? Could all things come to the biologist who waits? I think the answer is yes; and to see how a biologist can be so optimistic, let me explain what biology is all about, because the wide range of the possible in biology depends on the uniqueness of the peculiar province of the living. Living beings form a special realm of science, filled with collages of butterflies, sheets of grasses, mildewing molds, people, bears, whales, and bats, eggs and embryos, grandmothers and grandfathers. To find the impossible in biology, we must first be clear as to what biology means.

Biology is about life, and life is organisms. We know them well, these organisms. We pass them every day as we walk on the grass, under the trees, past the birds and the squirrels. Gardening, we run our hands through the cool earth, crumbles of plant detritus, worms, larvae, hundreds of microorganisms. We know them by touch, smell, and sight; and those organisms that never come within our grasp, such as gulls at the shore, we know by sight and by sound. Most of all, however, we know human organisms. We know our parents and our friends; we know strangers on the bus, on the street, and in the stores; and, of course, we know ourselves. How many times a day do we look at our hands? A hundred? A thousand? We feel our toes from outside and from inside. We hear our heartbeats, we smell our sweat, we taste our blood. We are not all physicists or economists or mathematicians but we are all biologists. We know organisms, and most of us know them quite well.

Biology is the province of organisms—yogurt cultures and yaks, hawks and humans. These organisms fall into a few general types but into an innumerable number of specific varieties. In fact, each organism is unique: Human identical twins differ in many ways; for example, their fingerprints are different. Even a pair of cloned organisms are sufficiently complex so that during their creation the stochasticism of the world can insinuate itself and change a molecule here or an organelle there and in this way produce two individuals that are at least slightly different. The complexity and the individuality of its particular items of study—organisms—are certainly characteristics of the biological realm, but they do not completely distinguish biology from physics or metallurgy or economics: Galaxies are complex and individual, alloy metals are complex and individual, the European Common Market is complex and individual. Physics, metallurgy, and economics face items of study that have many interactive parts forming unique and distinct wholes. Something else, then, distinguishes biology from other disciplines.

It is true that along the edges of biology there are areas that overlap other fields. There is a biophysics, a biochemistry, and probably a bioeconomics; but there is also a clear-cut central biology, and the biologist settles comfortably into the center of his own special niche as if it were a well-worn armchair. He may get a little nervous when measuring the refractive index of a lipid bilayer. He may feel that he is treading somewhat afield when he calculates the cost-benefit ratio for parental care in a chimpanzee troop. Nevertheless, when he analyzes the larval stages of a grasshopper or when he studies the axon patterns of the human brain, the biologist knows that he is truly immersed in his own special element. What is it that uniquely determines this discipline of biology, distinguishing it from other sciences?

Organisms are patterns of matter that are at once complex and individual, and the features that distinguish these patterns from the other complex and individual patterns of the natural world are the two sequential processes that produce organisms: these processes are ontogeny and phylogeny.

Ontogeny is the developmental sequence of an organism. It is the history of a living entity from conception through birth to maturity and death. An ontogeny is the history book of an organism, laying out all of the stages in its transformation from an unspecialized embryonic form to a particular and idiomatic machine. Ontogenies come in all shapes and sizes. At one extreme, bacteria go through an ontogeny that is entirely internal: the transformations from a single parent cell to two daughter cells are all cascades of changes of molecules inside the cell. On the other hand multicellular organisms such as squid, butterflies, and people begin as single fertile cells and then transform into unified collections of millions of cells. The ontogeny of a multicellular organism is a cascade of intracellular, cellular, and extracellular changes that establish whole cities of specialized cells. During the ontogeny of a multicellular organism, interactive pockets of cells are geographically segregated into organs and tissues connected by highways of nerves and vessels. The construction of these cities is continuously dynamic, and it proceeds inexorably in a particular sequence, the characteristic ontogeny of that organism.

An ontogeny is stereotyped and highly reproducible. It is like a phonograph record: when conception sets the needle in the first groove, it plays out the full music of a life. Random dust will change the notes a bit along the way. Sometimes the environment intervenes to distort the sound. Occasionally the needle gets caught by a scratch and falls into the endless loops of a cancer. Usually, however, a scratch or even a jarring of the turntable only causes a skip in the sequence as the needle falls into a different groove and proceeds once again resolutely on its inevitable path. Ontogenies are dogged things, and organisms are those highly complex patterns produced by ontogenies. It is ontogeny—the repeated generation of complex yet stereotyped patterns—that first sets the biological realm apart from the other spheres of science.

• • •

Generation after generation, organisms beget like organisms. This is phylogeny, the ancestral lineages of organisms. Ontogenies are the life histories of individual organisms, and phylogenies are the repeated unfoldings of ontogenies. Our ancestors are our phylogeny.

Biological time is different from physical time; the biological clock of phylogenies ticks in generations. The physical time scale of phylogenies ranges through six orders of magnitude for the same unit of biological time: in one hundred years a human phylogeny contains 5 generations, a buttercup phylogeny contains 100 generations, a fruit fly phylogeny contains 2500 generations, and a bacterial phylogeny can contain 2,500,000 generations. On the grand scale, a human phylogeny of five generations is a very short time, and it represents an almost unchanging set of transformations. In the course of one hundred years humanness is preserved. True, we look somewhat different from our parents, but there is a strong family resemblance. Those differences that do show up during a few generations are subtle, and each child is much more like his parents than he is different from them. This is because a few generations of phylogeny is a biologically stable time interval. On the other hand 100,000 generations is quite another story.

Two hundred thousand generations ago, humans were not human. At that time, our ancestors were $3\frac{1}{2}$- to 5-feet-high apelike creatures living in what is now eastern Africa. They were bands of primates, no taller than our children and not as smart, living in forests and eating roots, tubers, and grubs. Although these animals looked much like apes, they differed from their neighboring apes in a dramatic and significant way: 200,000 generations ago the members of the human phylogeny—*Australopithecus afarensis*—walked upright. In biology notable changes happen on a time scale of hundreds of thousands of generations, and 100,000 generations after *Australopithecus afarensis* the members of the human phylogeny—*Homo habilis*—had acquired the large brains that are characteristic of today's humans. In the course of hundreds of thousands of generations, the differences between members of a phylogeny can become so marked that we say the original organism has evolved into a new organism, and over hundreds of thousands of generations *Australopithecus* evolved into *Homo*. Phylogenies evolve, and evolving phylogenies are unique to the biological realm.[1]

Thus, one distinguishing characteristic of the biological realm is ontogeny, the recurrent, stereotyped re-creation of a very complex pattern, and the other distinguishing characteristic is phylogeny, the ancestral lineage of these ontogenies. While an ontogeny is a relatively stable sequence, a phylogeny is an evolving sequence of ontogenies. When we ask what is impossible in biology—in biology specifically, above and beyond physics and chemistry, beside psychology and economics, separate from mathematics and the arts—we are asking what is impossible in ontogeny and in phylogeny.

• • •

If there is a constant in biology, it is the rich variety that drives the theoretical biologist to continually remark "Well, I never would have predicted that!" A major contributor to this rich unpredictability of living things is unnecessary complexity—biological systems often contain more machinery than is minimally necessary to make them work properly. For instance, the major role of DNA is to code for the production of proteins, yet 99 percent of the DNA in human cells does not code for any proteins. Cells in related species of animals can differ in their DNA contents by greater than a hundredfold; this suggests that, if the excess, noncoding DNA plays any role at all, it must be an exceedingly modest role. There is no simple rule for predicting how much DNA a cell will have. The actual DNA content of any particular cell is probably an accident of history and the theoretician who attempts to construct a table of the DNA content in various cells sets forth on a futile exercise.

Another example of unnecessary complexity is the blood-clotting cascade: When you cut your finger, blood proteins immediately begin to clump together, the wound is soon dammed up and the cut stops bleeding within ten minutes. To staunch the blood flow, the initial injury sets off a waterfall of a dozen separate chemical reactions in two chains; each chemical transformation gives rise to the next in an orderly sequence. At least 13 different proteins—coagulation factors—form the normal clotting cascades in humans, and if one of these factors is missing the person can have a bleeding disorder such as hemophilia. The complete blood-clotting cascade is quite complex, and a theoretical biologist would be hard pressed to predict its actual details from a priori considerations, from first principles or from the requirements of blood-clotting systems. One of the factors—Hageman factor or Factor XII—even appears to be unnecessary: those people who, through genetic disorders, develop without any Factor XII do not have bleeding problems; and whales, dolphins, and porpoises, all of which survive injuries quite normally, do not have any Factor XII.

Rich and excess complexities permeate life: At the molecular level there are the "futile metabolic cycles" in cells, circular chemical reactions that go back and forth producing and unproducing the same molecules while depleting energy stores to no apparent purpose. There is also the fact that cells can use a variety of alternative fuels. The brain normally runs strictly on carbohydrates, burning the elemental sugar glucose for energy. During starvation, however, the brain takes advantage of other, parallel metabolic pathways, switching over to burning ketones, which are derived from fats. The chemical pathways of cells are not lean and geometric, as if etched by Piet Mondrian, but varied, interdependent, multidimensional, and often overdetermined, as if they had been woven together by Mark Tobey.

Complex and elusive intricacies also characterize the tissue level of biological organization. The corpus callosum, one of the largest bundles of axons in the human brain extensively interconnects most areas of the cerebral hemispheres, but its functioning is so subtle that for years no one understood exactly what it does. The five out of a thousand individuals born without a corpus callosum cannot easily be distinguished from those people with a corpus callosum. It was only through a specialized series of psychological experiments that Roger Sperry finally showed how the two halves of the brain normally use the corpus callosum as their most intimate route of self-communication. From his desk, the theoretical biologist could not determine the role of the corpus callosum with certainty and could not predict its appearance or its use in those animals (the placental mammals) that have acquired it during the last two hundred million years. Who could have imagined that the human brain contains two separate minds, a right mind and a left mind, each localized in one of the cerebral hemispheres? Normally the two minds are in such close touch that they think alike, they trade thoughts instantaneously, they share the same sensations and emotions, and they act as one. All this intimacy flows through the corpus callosum and the intercommunication is smooth and efficient. At the same time, each separate neural unit is a powerful and complete mind. Normally two brains make each human, and two brains are a wonderful but unnecessary complexity.

The corpus callosum is not a necessity, but is it just a frill? Two brains are not a necessity, but is the second brain a frill? Two kidneys, two tonsils, two testes are not a necessity, but is the second one a frill? These are difficult questions, and this same difficulty appears throughout biology. Consider the innumerable excess cells that are generated in embryos: in the normal embryonic spinal cord, there is regularly a 100 percent overproduction of young nerve cells; only half of the original complement of cells survive to adulthood, and the excess cells simply die and disappear. Is this purposeful or is this wasteful? Such questions, questions with words like "frill," "purpose," or even "necessity," are slightly askew, and they are difficult to answer because they are built from peculiarly human judgments. Nature need not adhere to human standards, and she need not follow human principles. Nature does as she does, and we can only be secure in our science when we act as natural historians, conscientiously describing the natural realm retrospectively. We can rarely be confident armchair theoreticians, and we walk a precipitous course when we attempt a priori evaluations based on anthropocentric standards.

Ontogenies and phylogenies are highly textured and quite varied; they are not limited to the simplest or the most efficient paths. In the natural realm, organisms are not built by engineers who, with an overall plan in mind, use only the most economical and appropriate materials, the most effective design, and the most reliable construction techniques. Instead, organisms are patchworks containing appendixes, uvulas, earlobes, dewclaws, adenoids, warts, eyebrows, underarm hair, wisdom teeth, toenails, and upright posture. They are a meld of ancestral parts integrated step-by-step during their development through a set of tried and true ontogenetic mechanisms that ensure matching between the disparate elements, between nerves and muscles and between bones and joints, but that have no overall vision. Natural ontogenies and natural phylogenies are not limited by principles of parsimony; possible organisms can be overdetermined, unnecessarily complex, or inefficiently designed.

• • •

Vitamin C (ascorbic acid), the popular home remedy for colds, is an enzyme cofactor that is necessary for the healthy functioning of multicellular organisms. Most plants and animals can synthesize their own vitamin C from glucose, but a few animals (humans, monkeys, guinea pigs, fruit bats, certain fish and certain insects) cannot make vitamin C and must get it from their food. It is likely that the ancestral organisms of most phylogenies could manufacture their own vitamin C and that this ability was then lost during evolution in selected lineages. From an engineering viewpoint it seems surprising that animals would add a dietary constraint by relinquishing direct control over their vitamin C stores. Nature, however, is not an engineer—she is not required to play by human rules or human principles, and she can take any of the available roads. Why have monkeys and guinea pigs lost the capacity to make vitamin C, while goats and mice have retained it? In this case the answer is probably that it was simply an accident of history.

The constraints in building organisms are usually insufficient to limit Nature to only one blueprint, and a wide range of alternative constructions have evolved. There is no one right way to build an eye. The eyes of the octopus and the human appear quite similar, but the human eye is built exactly inside out when compared to the eye of the octopus: in an octopus, light passing through the lens falls directly on the photoreceptors, while in a human light must travel through many layers of cells and of axons before reaching the photoreceptors, which are themselves pointing the wrong way—that is, toward the back of the eye. Likewise there is no one right way to build a wing, and Nature has used a number of radically different designs. Bat wings are modified hands, while insect wings are entirely separate appendages.

There is no one right way to excrete the effete products of metabolism: in terms of DNA degradation, some animals (like humans and dalmatians) excrete purine wastes as uric acid, others (like mice and turtles) degrade purine further and excrete the wastes as allantoin, and yet others (like fish and frogs) take the degradation process another step, excreting the purine wastes as urea. There is no one right blood level of salts: the concentrations of blood sodium and blood chloride differ by 100 percent between bony fish (such as the carp) and cartilaginous fish (such as the skates). Even within the same species the normal range of concentrations of blood molecules can span a 50 to 100 percent difference. In adult humans, for example, the normal range of blood albumin is 5.4×10^{-3} to $7.4 \times 10^{-3}\,M$, the normal range of blood copper is 1.1×10^{-5} to $2.3 \times 10^{-5}\,M$, the normal range of fibrinogen is 1.5 to 3.6 grams per liter, the normal range of glucose is 3.6×10^{-3} to $6.1 \times 10^{-3}\,M$, and the normal range of magnesium is 0.75×10^{-3} to $1.2 \times 10^{-3}\,M$. Not only can the concentrations of critical molecules vary, but the actual structures of the molecules can vary as well. Although certain parts of a biological molecule are fairly immutable, there is often no one right overall molecule. Insulin is an essential protein hormone that is built of about 50 subunits (amino acids). The insulin molecules of pigs, cows, and humans differ in 3 to 5 of these subunits; nonetheless the insulins from pigs and from cows are perfectly acceptable substitutes for human insulin, and both pig insulin and cow insulin are commonly used to treat human diabetes. In all of these cases, many viable avenues are open to Nature.

In terms of many roads, the capricious courses of phylogenies are most telling. Evolution has followed the exigencies of the times under the whims of chance and accidents of history. Had the continents not drifted apart, Australian fauna and flora would undoubtedly be less peculiar; Australia would probably have had indigenous hoofed animals and indigenous apes, animal groups that never developed on that island. Had Alexander Fleming not discovered penicillin, penicillin-resistant bacteria would be a freakish oddity rather than ubiquitous cohabitants of our planet. Or, consider the composition of our bones:

> [They] might have been silica, I thought, or aluminum, or iron—
> the cells would have made it possible. But no, it is calcium, carbonate of lime. Why? Only because of its history. Elements more numerous than calcium in the earth's crust could have been used to build the skeleton. Our history is the reason—we came from the water. It was there that cells took the lime habit, and they kept it after we came ashore.[2]

Extant organisms are legacies of the habits acquired by their ancestors, but these habits coalesced from a plethora of possibilities.[3]

• • •

Science fiction comes in two varieties: On the one hand there are the tales that explore worlds harboring phenomena that scientists think are impossible. These stories ask the questions of dreams— How would people spend their evenings if everyone had a perpetual motion machine in the basement? How soon would you get bored if you lived forever? What is on the other side of the wall at the far edge of the universe? On the other hand there are the science fiction tales that explore worlds that just might exist. These stories ask the questions of science—In what language could we talk to an extraterrestrial creature? What could we do with self-reproducing automata? What will people do when the sun goes out? The standard science fiction of biology can fall into both of these categories, but which biological tall tales are the stories of dreams and which are the stories of science?

Consider mushrooms—"the elf of plants" Emily Dickinson called them. Actually they are only distantly related to plants. Mushrooms are many-celled fungi, relatively advanced organisms with cell walls (like plants) but with no ability to manufacture their own food (e.g., no photosynthetic machinery), with no ability to move and with no nervous system. We are all aware that many animals are fungivorous, but it took science fiction to popularize the idea that mushrooms could be carnivorous. There are, for instance, the mushroom people of the mysterious planet Basidium-X, who must eat chicken eggs to remain healthy (E. Cameron, *The Wonderful Flight to the Mushroom Planet*). The stories of dreams? Surprisingly not. Carnivorous mushrooms actually exist here on earth: certain species of woodland toadstools trap and eat worms,[4] and from worms it may be only a small step to chickens. Carnivorous mushrooms, once in the realm of the tall tales of science fiction, are now unequivocally science fact. Or consider the square organism, once a creature known only in Flatland, where all "Professional Men and Gentlemen are Squares" (E. A. Abbott, *Flatland: A Romance of Many Dimensions*). Today the square organism has found a home on our well-worn Earth, swimming in brine pools of the Middle East: there, tiny flat transparent bacteria "in the form of a thin square sheet"[5] float like ghostly salt crystals, mimicking the perfect planar polygons and belying the notion that—to reduce their surface to volume ratios—cells must be spheres.

Carnivorous mushrooms and square bacteria bring a smile to the biologist. They are surprises but only small surprises. They elicit a "What will Nature think of next?" but they do not shake the roots of the biological sciences. Carnivorous mushrooms and square bacteria do not stretch the bounds of biology because they can be explained by mechanisms that sit somewhere on Nature's cluttered shelf of standard organismic machinery. True, the biologist may have to root around a bit among the everyday mitochondria, the familiar Krebs cycles, and the mundane cyclic AMPs to retrieve all of the appropriate mechanisms. Moreover, he will have to spend some time in serious study to find how these very mechanisms have been stuck together in the peculiar combinations that make carnivorous mushrooms and square bacteria. Nonetheless, somewhere in a corner of her cupboard Nature is sure to have just the right bits and pieces to construct these natural oddities. Nature regularly builds baby carnivorous mushrooms from spores of parent carnivorous mushrooms and replicates daughter square bacteria from parent square bacteria, and Nature derived the parent carnivorous mushrooms from other preexisting mushrooms and the parent square bacteria from other preexisting bacteria. Strange as they are, carnivorous mushrooms and square bacteria—the incarnations of biological tall tales—are neither ontogenetically nor phylogenetically impossible.

Angels are somewhat different: although they adorn the spiritual world, our natural world has no angels. Why is this? The answer is that, while it is not absolutely impossible, it is nonetheless quite difficult for Nature to construct an angel from an extant phylogeny. In addition to the arms and the legs of a human, an angel has a set of wings along its back, and wings are complex structures sculpted of muscles, bones, and nerves (and angel's wings are covered with feathers). To introduce wings or any other complex appendage into an extant organismal lineage (a phylogeny), Nature needs the appropriate raw materials and the appropriate organizational blueprint. Nature needs preexisting structures that can be transformed because she rarely creates complex biological forms ex nihilo.

For angel's wings, the preexisting structures are not presently available: the wings of the natural extant flying vertebrates—the birds and the bats—are direct modifications of preexisting front limbs. The muscles, the bones, and the nerves were already there in ancestral organisms, and Nature proceeded to evolve wings by stretching, shrinking, folding, and bending these preexisting elements. Through all of the geometric transmogrifications, the overall organization of the front limb has remained the same during evolution. (For example, the upper limb always has a single long bone, the humerus, and the lower limb always has a pair of parallel long bones, the radius and the ulna.) On the other hand, the back of a mammal has no preexisting structures that can be stretched or shrunk, folded or bent, into a wing. To make an angel, the fundamental ground plan of the existing elements must be tampered with and new structures must be generated without precedent. This Nature cannot easily do:

Evolution behaves like a tinkerer who, during eons upon eons, would slowly modify his work, unceasingly retouching it, cutting here, lengthening there. already exists, either transforming a system to give it new functions or combining several systems to produce a more elaborate one.

Today, angels seem destined to remain spiritual, and winged horses like Pegasus will undoubtedly remain mythological, but biologists do not consider them impossible. Instead, they are put into another realm: they are highly improbable biological phenomena. Improbable biological phenomena cannot easily be pieced together by Nature herself from any of the mechanisms in her crowded cupboard of organismic machinery and in the context of any extant phylogenies. Without the coincidence of a number of highly improbable events, Nature cannot generate an angel or a winged horse via an existing ontogeny.

• • •

> He said 'I look for butterflies
>   That sleep among the wheat;
> I make them into mutton-pies,
>   And sell them in the street.
> I sell them unto men,' he said,
>   'Who sail on stormy seas;
> And that's the way I get my bread—
>   A trifle, if you please.'
>
> L. Carroll, *Through the Looking-Glass*
> *and What Alice Found There*

With the development of his complex and special brain, man has taken a place beside Nature as a biological creator. Nature creates through ontogenies and phylogenies, but man is an engineer and can construct biological forms from other beginnings and through other, ad hoc processes. Man is not limited to the natural routes and sequences of creation, and in the laboratory he can generate unnatural biological phenomena: in the laboratory, the biologist can create biological phenomena that would be highly improbable in nature.

A biological item is a thoroughly complex thing. A protein, an organelle, a cell, a tissue, an organism—each is made of a great many different parts and in each case these parts are organized in some particular and characteristic design. The many parts and the unique designs are found at every level—we see them whether we look at an elephant from a distance or examine its gall bladder under a microscope. Moreover, these biological items are truly complex in all ways: not only are they composed of many different parts interrelated in unique designs, but their fabrication is complex. In most cases the parts of a biological item will not fully self-assemble and the item requires a detailed blueprint for its construction. You cannot shake a beaker of salts and amino acids and make insulin, and you cannot stir a soup of cells and make a mouse. To build a protein or an animal you must carefully put all of the parts together in their single proper order, imposing detailed external information—a blueprint or templet—on the raw materials.

Biological items form only a small subset of all of the possible items that one might construct from the same raw materials. This means that, as an architect, the biologist cannot merely choose the appropriate bricks and mortar, he must also draw up the right blueprint and then contrive to interweave the building blocks into just the right design. This is a difficult set of tasks. Often the parts are miniscule and cannot be easily moved about or stored by themselves, isolated from their natural settings. Furthermore, gluing these tiny parts together in such a way as to create the proper order at all levels, from macroscopic to microscopic to molecular, takes extreme patience, steady hands, x-ray vision, and highly specialized, Rube Goldberg-like contraptions.

In the face of these problems, biologists have been undauntedly optimistic, twiddling and fiddling, tinkering with bones and nerves, gingerly reconstructing hormones, and rearranging genes. Although the job of building a biological item entirely from scratch is usually too overwhelming to be practical, the fabrication of a complete biological item from extant biological scraps and the sculpting of new biological items from preexisting ones have become everyday operations in the biologist's laboratory: In baby newts, embryonic eyes are transplanted to tailbuds, where they eventually mature and send out nerves. The adult newts, three-eyed oddities such as Nature has never seen, swim in laboratory aquariums, two eyes fore and one eye aft. In embryonic chicks, extra limb buds are grafted alongside the normal ones; later, the adult chickens run through the laboratory waving supernumerary appendages. Mouse and human cells are fused to form hybrid mammalian cells, biological items never found in nature but powerful laboratory tools for mapping human chromosomes. Copies of human insulin genes are inserted into yeast or bacterial cells, and these tiny and primitive creatures, as different from us as any organisms on Earth, will now manufacture human proteins. In the laboratory, the biologist is busily creating highly improbable biological phenomena.

Given the range, the power, and the detailed precision of modern technologies, is there anything that the biologist cannot do within the bounds of the physical constraints of the universe? Are all improbable biological phenomena possible in the laboratory? Today's biologists have the faith that it is possible to construct almost any biological item from precursor materials. A gene, a protein, a cell, a tissue, an organism—these all seem to lie in the realm of possibility. It may not always be practical to create these items from the most elemental materials, such as the essential atoms (hydrogen, oxygen, carbon, nitrogen, calcium, phosphorus, chlorine, potassium, sulfur, sodium, and magnesium); nonetheless, new genes can be manufactured by mutating and rearranging existing genes, short proteins can be made to order from their constituent amino acids, primal proto-cells can be formed in appropriate man-made molecular soups, and new and complex cell types can be pieced together by fusing whole cells or by combining parts of cells. New tissues can be designed by growing cells on artificial templates, and new organisms can be constructed by mutations, by genetic engineering, and by embryonic reconstructions such as grafts and transplants.

Biologists can build improbable biological items in the laboratory—they are regularly turning butterflies into mutton-pies—but the hallmarks of the biological realm are more than individual biological items. The uniquely biological phenomena of the world are ontogenies and phylogenies. Life is not a DNA molecule or a nerve cell or a kumquat or a wolf spider; life is not a particular thing at a given time. Life is a special set of sequences; it is the autonomous and recurrent stereotyped recreation of certain very complex patterns. Life is a child growing and becoming a mother and eventually a grandmother. Can the biologist create new grandmothers—that is, can he generate ontogenies and phylogenies never before seen in nature?

The answer is yes, although the new ontogenies take advantage of natural cascades of developmental events that are normally found in preexisting ontogenies. To begin, the biologist makes an improbable change in some developmental event; for example, he grafts a frog eye primordium into the side of a newt embryo. In nature the two sets of tissues would never interact, but in the laboratory the hybrid organism undergoes an ontogeny: The frog cells form an eye and send an optic nerve into the newt nervous system. Concurrently, the newt skin cells form a lens and the newt nervous system accommodates the aberrant nerves. Frog cells integrate with newt cells, newt cells mesh with frog cells, and the strange three-eyed chimera that develops unfolds through a truly new ontogeny. Similarly, new phylogenies—ancestral lineages never before seen in nature—take advantage of natural cascades of ontogenies that are normally found in preexisting phylogenies. Here, the biologist makes an improbable change in the stuff of inheritance; for example, he grafts a sequence of human DNA into the DNA of a bacterium. In nature, the two sets of genes would never interact, but in the laboratory the hybrid bacterium divides and quickly becomes a grandmother. All of her children and grandchildren will manufacture certain human proteins, and a truly new phylogeny has been founded.

Such ontogenies and phylogenies are new, but they are not unnatural. Once triggered, they unfold spontaneously and thereby enter the natural realm, producing surprising wonders like three-eyed frog-newts and insulin-secreting germs or carnivorous mushrooms and square bacteria. Man-made ontogenies and man-made phylogenies are autonomous and recurrent stereotyped re-creations of certain very complex patterns, just as are naturally initiated ontogenies and naturally initiated phylogenies. It is only the initiating event that may have been unnatural. When the biologist founds a new ontogeny or a new phylogeny, he can, of course, understand the initial improbable event. Many times, he can also understand the initial event when Nature founds a new ontogeny or a new phylogeny. On the other hand, initial events are not always easy to understand in nature. In the province of biology, buttermilk-thick with life and under the patience of millions of generations, Nature sometimes stumbles on the extremely improbable, and arcane initial events can indeed be quite natural. Arcane initial events just "happen to happen" and are not very likely to happen again. Moreover, when they happen in a natural ontogeny or phylogeny, arcane events can trigger sequences that are as natural as apples. It is the initiating event in the generation of an angel that would undoubtedly be arcane, but the autonomous development of an angel from a tiny wisp of an angelic embryo or the spontaneous unfolding of a lineage of angels, once set on their way, become natural phenomena no more impossible in the biological realm than the autonomous development of an oak from an acorn or the spontaneous unfolding of the ancestral lineage of the great Bach family.

• • •

What then is an impossibility? I think that for the biological realm, the requirements are rather special. Not only must we be able to write science fiction tall tales about it, we must also be able to imagine it as a part of a natural ontogeny and phylogeny. Truly biological entities are always enmeshed in a developmental and an evolutionary sequence: they are dynamic, they have a lifespan, they have ancestors, and they beget progeny. In this way, a biological impossibility would be something—be it an organelle, a cell, or a creature—that we could envision in some ontogeny or phylogeny but that cannot ever exist in the real world. Physically impossible organisms, such as hedgehogs that run faster than the speed of light and perpetual motion bees, can be dreamt by the physicist, but I cannot easily imagine a biologically impossible organism. When we have eliminated the physically impossible, when we remain within the constraints set by the physical limits of the universe, whatever remains—no matter how improbable—must be considered biologically possible. With the biologist as creator, the improbable has oftentimes become probable. But Nature herself is wild and rich and her splendor is unconstrained, and afternoons poking about the Woods Hole seashore among the horseshoe crabs, the seaweed, and the tunicates, or munching blue-eyed scallops and beach peas on a rocky island in Penobscot Bay, or chipping ornate brachiopods from the shale of the Chagrin River make me hesitate to think that I could ever dream of a creature that might not creep out from among the cattails one windy spring morning.

Notes

1. Evolution is never-ending, and phylogenies continue to evolve.

> It gives one a feeling of confidence to see nature still busy with experiments, still dynamic, and not through nor satisfied because a Devonian fish managed to end as a two-legged character with a straw hat. There are other things brewing and growing in the oceanic vat. It pays to know this. It pays to know there is just as much future as there is past. The only thing that doesn't pay is to be sure of man's own part in it.
>
> There are things down there still coming ashore. Never make the mistake of thinking life is now adjusted for eternity. It gets into your head—the certainty, I mean—the human certainty, and then you miss it all: the things on the tide flats and what they mean, and why, as my wife says, "They ought to be watched."

L. Eiseley, "The Snout," in *The Immense Journey*, pp. 47–48.

2. L. Eiseley, "The Slit," in *The Immense Journey*, Vantage Books, New York.

3. The richness of biology means that besides being a theorist, the complete biologist must always be part explorer and part natural historian. In this regard, Sherlock Holmes offered a veiled warning to theoretical biologists when he pointed out to Dr. Watson why Holmes' abstruse brother Mycroft could never be a true detective:

> "You wonder," said my companion, "why it is that Mycroft does not use his powers for detective work. He is incapable of it."
> "But I thought you said—"
> "I said that he was my superior in observation and deduction. If the art of the detective began and ended in reasoning from an armchair, my brother would be the greatest criminal agent that ever lived. But he has no ambition and no energy. He will not even go out of his way to verify his own solutions, and would rather be considered wrong than take the trouble to prove himself right."

A. Conan Doyle, "The Greek Interpreter"

4. R. G. Thorn and G. L. Barron, *Science,* 224: 76–78 (1983).

5. A. E. Walsby, *Nature,* 283: 69–71 (1980).

6. F. Jacob, *Science,* 196: 1161–1166 (1977).

The manticore: biologic impossibility? From E. Topsell, *The Historie of Four-footed Beastes*, Jaggard, London, 1607. Courtesy of the Chapin Library of Williams College.

This could be an abstract expressionist output of a métamatic painting machine, but is actually a photographic record of swimming bacteria (dashed lines) and tumbling bacteria (white blotches) followed with a stroboscopic light for four seconds. (Reprinted from Dana Aswad and D. E. Koshland, Jr. (1975) *Journal of Molecular Biology, 97:225–235.*)

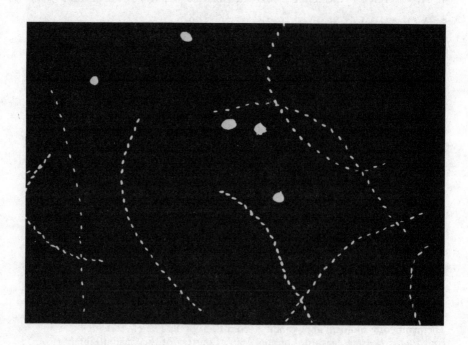

ON IMPOSSIBILITY
IN BIOLOGY

In his preface to the Jessie and John Danz Lectures at the University of Washington, collected under the title *The Possible and the Actual*, François Jacob distinguishes between the forms of life that have been considered to be possible (as depicted, for example, in sixteenth-century books devoted to zoology or in today's works of science fiction) and those that in actuality populate the earth.[1] Here, however, our concern is with neither the possible nor the actual but, rather, with what we believe would transgress the limits of the possible. The project risks flying out of sight at the moment it is hatched. We could easily be seduced at the outset by fantasies of a lunar hummingbird-lobster recombinant that subsists entirely on cosmic debris and Brahms concertos. Let us, instead, start with our feet on the ground. Later in this essay we shall give fantasy and philosophy the opportunity to soar. Let us begin by asking what are the limits of environmental stress that life can tolerate, the limits beyond which life, as we know it, is impossible.

The Limits Beyond Which Life Is Impossible

To answer this question, we must address the bacteria. No other group of organisms is as versatile. Since prehistoric times, perishables have been pickled in brine, boiled, or iced to prevent bacterial spoilage. But bacteria able to survive each of these environmental extremes do exist: halophiles flourish in the salterns of the Dead Sea, thermophiles live on the scalded rocks of hot springs, and cryophiles in clouds or dew turn supercooled water to ice. Even the cold and boredom of outer space does not guarantee the absence of microbial survivors. A remarkable tribute to the hardihood of bacteria was paid by the first moon-walking astronauts: prior to lift-off, the astronauts had their space suits sterilized.

Microbes have found ways to adapt to some stresses that more complex organisms can evade. Whereas saltwater fish desalinate the water they take in, the halophilic bacteria do not. Instead, their proteins are so constructed as to function in a saturated salt solution. In freshwater bacteria, the water-soluble proteins are tucked safely inside. But the halophiles can use such proteins externally for structural purposes; high salt concentrations render them insoluble. (Consequently, certain halophiles suspended in fresh water literally dissolve, a curious form of drowning.)

Some mechanisms by which microbes cope with the stress of a rise in temperature are operative in higher organisms as well. The synthesis of a few "heat-shock" proteins is induced; the synthesis of many other proteins is inhibited. These alterations provide protection against the effects of a second heat shock. However, this protection does not go very far. Even the bacterial denizens of hot springs will perish in a pressure cooker. Despite some recent claims to the contrary, it appears that a temperature much above 100°C is totally inconsistent with vital chemistry.

When the temperature falls, a major risk to life is posed by water freezing. Ice-induced damage, at cell membranes or at intracellular sites, can be averted in some noteworthy ways. There are beetles that winterize their body fluids with glycerol antifreeze to prevent the nucleation of ice crystals; there are arctic fishes that send specialized glycoproteins coursing in their veins to prevent the growth of ice crystals that have already started to form. Many bacteria are able to take a draconian measure—dehydration. However, the cost of evasion of death as a desiccated bacterial spore is a suspension of life. Spores in space lead no life at all.

Relative to our own feeble capacity to tolerate variations in the local environment, the capacity of bacteria to do so appears remarkable. But, however ingeniously particular kinds of bacteria cope with punishing environments presented to them by microbiologists, no bacteria can cope with the harsh environmental conditions that are familiar to chemists and physicists. No bacteria thrive with an internal milieu that is other than aqueous. Nor do we know of any bacteria that thrive when their aqueous internal milieu is in the disorganized gaseous phase or in any of several uncompromisingly organized phases that ice can assume. We are forced to recognize that the processes involved in life as we know it, although not the persistence of organisms capable of life, depend on aqueous chemical reactions that are only possible under a limited set of conditions.

Life entails the formation, alteration, and destruction of molecules of great architectural complexity and specificity. These molecules are composed of carbon united to oxygen, hydrogen, nitrogen, and other less abundant but still important elements. Chemical bonds of varying strengths cause these molecules to interact, some of the most significant bonds being individually ineffectual but collectively strong and highly specific. As far as we know, the necessary conditions for these reactions are found on only a thin superficial layer of the earth's surface. This layer is appropriately warmed by the sun's radiation but appropriately shielded from its most energetic rays. We are a species empowered to disturb the radiation flux that reaches the earth's surface by depleting this layer or adding to that one. We are also a species that can deduce and act on the possible consequences of such disturbances for our survival. It is important to remind ourselves of life's fragility: *under all but the narrowest of conditions, life is impossible.* I can think of no lesson in biology more important than this one.

Up to this point, we have confined our discussion to life as we know it. Life as we do not know it might be based on the chemistry of a different set of elements in an utterly different environment. For all we know, our carbon-based life might have originated as the clever experiment of alien creatures whose habitat and molecular architecture have little resemblance to our own. This scenario, a perverse conjecture of Francis Crick, cannot be excluded. Therefore, it may be prudent to make our strong assertion slightly less categorical: under all but the narrowest sets of conditions, life is impossible.

The life of actual organisms does not operate with cogs and ratchets as do simple clocks, nor with magnetic tapes and silicon chips as do computers. Vital functions are largely chemical rather than mechanical or electronic. Can life be otherwise?

Artists have provided ambiguous answers to this question; the artificial intelligencia is awaiting its turn to do so. Among artists of my own generation, Jean Tinguely has been particularly concerned with vitality in machines. In 1959 he perfected a mechanical device of touching awkwardness that he called a métamatic painting machine. His *Métamatic-automobile-odorante et sonore,* constructed for the first Paris Biennale, produced some 40,000 abstract expressionist paintings. A year later, his *Homage to New York* performed an act still more alien to the world of machines. In the presence of a select group of worthies in the sculpture garden of the Museum of Modern Art in New York, and with some terminal assistance from the New York Fire Department, the machine destroyed itself. The event was an affecting one: ludicrous, dismaying, awesome. In the *Space Odyssey 2001* of Stanley Kubrick, there is also an episode in which the destruction of a machine is calculated to engage our emotions. This machine—a computer aboard a spaceship—was more explicitly endowed with human characteristics; it even bore a man's name.

Let us not dismiss the possibility that the next several decades will see the development of self-conscious automatons that are as creative or passionate as those of Tinguely or as wily as "Hal" of 2001. Today's computers contribute to the design of the circuitry to be used in the next generation of computers because they have been programmed to do so. A computer that tackles such design problems of its own volition, for the sake of the intellectual challenge or even for the sake of its progeny, is not unthinkable. When computers begin to invent their own future, it will be interesting to inquire of them whether they consider themselves living organisms. Perhaps one of these latter-day Golems will reply in the affirmative but express some skepticism as to the status of the questioner. How shall we explain what *we* mean by life?

The Impossibility of Defining "Life"

An important feature of biology, as opposed to a discipline such as astronomy, is that its subject matter is impossible to define. It is not for lack of trying that the question "What is life?" has not been answered. Poets and prophets, scientists and philosophers have long sought to crack this old chestnut. The contemporary biologist will admit that "there is no special substance, object or force that can be identified with life."[2] Nor is there general agreement among professionals as to a set of attributes that distinguishes the animate from the inanimate. Any attempt at such a distinction can be readily shown to contain an ample dose of the arbitrary.

How, for example, can a live bacterium be distinguished from a dead one? In the case of those bacteria that cause disease, this matter can be of practical importance. You might think the issue long ago resolved. A live bacterium grows, divides, respires, takes up and metabolizes various substances, and may also mate, swim, tumble, excrete toxins, and so on. A dead bacterium exhibits none of these capacities. But suppose we successively eliminate these vital functions one by one with the aid of selective poisons. At what point is the bacterium no longer alive? Ironically, when all of the capacities mentioned above have been destroyed (e.g., by heat), the potential of killed bacteria for causing virulent infections may still be passed on to appropriate nonpathogenic relatives. Killed bacteria can leave behind a residue of genetic material with a potential for immortality; even in the microbial world, the victory of death need not be absolute. The transformation of nonpathogens by heat-killed pathogens was first found in 1928 by Griffith, who showed it to occur in the nasal passages of mice. The "transforming principle," as the material basis for the legacy of the dead bacteria was called, has since been identified as deoxyribonucleic acid, DNA. DNA directs major vital processes within the cell and is the major determinant of hereditary continuity. However, in the absence of the complex machinery of the cell, DNA is an inert polymer. Hence, DNA itself is not considered to be alive.

There are those who claim that DNA is the secret of life and those who claim that life (without which DNA is inert) is the secret of DNA.[3] The last word has not been said. The very relevance of a particular class of macromolecules to the problem of defining life "only a few generations back would have seemed merely wild speculation, and in the remote past simply blasphemous."[4]

If we cannot draw a firm line between the living and the nonliving, if we cannot be sure that we have recognized life's secret, or even that it has one, does this predicament set the science of life apart from other disciplines? I suggest that it does, not because I have illusions that other fields of endeavor can be defined with precision or possess a recognizable essence, but rather because the question "What is life?" is of unique significance. Our approach to this question defines our most important relationships: our relationship to Nature, to one another, to our individual mortality. Thus, Schrödinger's seminal little book *What Is Life?* ends by raising another question, which is the natural sequel of the first: "What is this 'I'?"[5] The connection between these two questions is succinctly expressed in the closing line of a poem by Rilke: "This life—who lives it really? God, do you?"[6] These questions are not trivial.

Faced with the problem of defining life, the French physiologist Claude Bernard proposed that "life is creativity."[7] This characterization covers more of nature than life alone and includes Nature's imitator, Art. Bernard's wide net catches the snowflake and the sonnet along with the medusa and the snail. However, of any definition I have encountered, it gives the greatest satisfaction per unit length. There is no lack of examples to illustrate the creativity of life. I cannot resist citing one such example from the behavior of our humble bacterium, who, in order to survive, must elude the poisons we have so cruelly introduced into its watery environment. The surface of our bacterium happens to be adorned with versatile organs of locomotion, flagella. These whiplike appendages can rotate clockwise or counterclockwise. Rotation of the flagella shafts counterclockwise causes them to cohere and rotate together. The resultant corkscrew propels the bacterium forward as it turns. When the propeller stops, the bacterium comes to an immediate standstill. In response to a flux of irritant, the flagella will reverse their rotation, but this reversal does not send the bacterium away from the irritant. Instead, the separate strands of the corkscrew unwind and spread apart. Their chaotic motion provides a turbulence that causes the bacterium to tumble, sending him on a random, exploratory course that will prevail until his path leads away from the irritant. Then the predominant mode of flagellar rotation will become counterclockwise again and the bacterium will swim happily away.

This kind of adventuresome goal seeking has been epigrammatically characterized by Georges Guilbaud: "heads I win, tails we start again—on the other foot."[8] Its occurrence is not limited to bacteria. The protozoologist H. S. Jennings observed near the turn of the century that an injurious environment may stimulate a protozoan into random activity until the organism finds itself once again in a favorable situation. W. R. Ashby accords this process a grandiose status, finding in it both the origins of the self-organizing and adaptive power of the nervous system during ontogeny and the creative power of natural selection during phylogeny. "Thus natural selection [achieves coordination] by the repeated application of the two operations: (1) test the organism against the environment; if harmful interactions occur remove that organism; (2) replace it by new organisms differing randomly from the old."[9] This train of thought leads us conveniently to our next topic.

Biological Statements That Assert the Impossibility of Achieving Something

The principle of natural selection is the grandest generalization in biology and comes as close as biology permits to the status of a law of physics. The unique character of this principle is aptly expressed by Sewell Wright: "The Darwinian process of continuous interplay of a random and a selective process is not intermediate between pure chance and pure determinism, but in its consequences qualitatively utterly different from either."[10] This characterization should become clearer as we proceed. The point I wish to emphasize here is that the principle of natural selection enjoys a unique, central position. If any principle of biology is to be rated second in importance, it is perhaps the "Central Dogma" of molecular biology, Francis Crick's generalization, to be described below, about the direction of information flow among biological macromolecules. I propose to show that these two principles are related to each other and can be assimilated to a class of statements of impossibility to which belong both laws of nature (as embodied in physics) and natural law (as embodied in religion).

The place in physics of assertions of impossibility was pointed out in 1947 by a British mathematician and physicist, Sir Edmund Whittaker.[11] He noted the family resemblance of various propositions in thermodynamics, electromagnetics, quantum mechanics, and relativity, all of which are assertions of a conviction that certain things are impossible to do. For example, physicists assure us of the impossibility of building a perpetual motion machine, although there is no logical necessity for the failure of such efforts. Sir Edmund went so far as to look forward to a time when all of physics could be derived by syllogistic reasoning from a set of principles of this form.

The place in religion of analogous statements is firmly established. The preponderance of proscriptions over prescriptions in the Old

Testament is well known. Eight of the ten commandments are prohibitions. Even the commandment to worship the one God is
couched as a statement of what is forbidden.

Let us now proceed, if we can, to squeeze the generalizations of
Darwin and Crick into this same mold. Crick's Central Dogma is
commonly and inadequately interpreted to be a set of directions for
a process of mechanical construction: DNA makes RNA and RNA
makes protein. It is understood that proteins with catalytic roles are
required for the successive steps of transcribing DNA into RNA and
translating RNA into protein. The transfer is not of substance, but
only of information, the information inherent in the linear sequences
of the subunits (deoxyribonucleotides, ribonucleotides, or amino
acids) that make up these aperiodic polymers. Had Crick in 1958
formulated the Central Dogma in the words just given, he would
have had to retract his proposal. Subsequent discoveries have revealed the existence of enzymes that can transcribe RNA into DNA
and of conditions that permit DNA to be directly translated into
protein. But Crick did not formulate the Central Dogma as a prescription. The Central Dogma states only what is forbidden:
". . . once 'information' has passed into protein *it cannot get out
again*."[12] Sir Edmund would have been pleased.

Dogmas attract heretics; the Central Dogma is no exception. In-
fectious agents that are claimed to be self-replicating proteins have
been cited as potential violators of the Central Dogma. Self-replica-
tion by a protein implies a forbidden transfer of amino acid sequence information from parent to progeny molecules. The agent of
kuru caused grief among the Fore people of the upper highlands of
New Guinea who cannibalized infected individuals. A careful analysis showing the agent of kuru to be a self-replicating protein unrelated to any DNA or RNA template would cause glee among those
who have refused to swallow the Central Dogma. Recent reports in
this area of research, however, do not encourage the heretical hope
that the Central Dogma has been violated.

At present, the Central Dogma is more vulnerable to attack as a
law of nature for a different reason: on the grounds that it is a statement of what, for trivial historical reasons, does not happen and not
a statement of what, for profound reasons, does not or even cannot
happen. Distinguished scientists have expressed this point of view,
but I believe that the issue is not at all clear-cut. The distinction
between a trivial statement of what is counter to fact and another
that is profound is a question not of verifiability, but of the extent

to which the consequences of finding a counterexample would contradict our view of the world. To what extent would biology be altered if information that had passed into protein *could* get out again? How would it matter if protein could serve as a donor of sequence information? Is it of any importance that the role of donor be limited to special molecular species, DNA (or RNA), to which genetic potential is uniquely entrusted? The question is not whether life can exist without DNA (or RNA) but whether life can exist without the principle implied in DNA. The late Nobelist Max Delbrück suggested that "if that committee in Stockholm, which has the unenviable task each year of pointing out the most creative scientists, had the liberty of giving awards posthumously, I think they should consider Aristotle for the discovery of the principle implied in DNA. It is my contention that Aristotle's principle of the 'unmoved mover' originated with his biological studies. . . . 'Unmoved mover' perfectly describes DNA: it acts, creates form and development, and is not changed in the process."[13] The Central Dogma affirms Aristotle's principle of an unmoved mover: whatever changes occur during development in the form, abundance, or distribution of proteins (so-called phenotypic changes), the sequence information residing in protein is locked in place and cannot be transmitted to the organism's unmoved mover, the bearer of its genotype. Will life without an unmoved mover, whatever its molecular nature, still be life? I think not. The capacity for evolutionary progress would be lost without a barrier that protects the creator of form and development from that which it creates. Without an unmoved mover, the concept of living organism would, I believe, become blurred beyond recognition. This line of reasoning leads me to assert that the Central Dogma is grander than a mere fact. Just how much grander is debatable, but it is clear that the Central Dogma is similar in form to many a law of nature.

The statement that sequence information is trapped in protein means that protein cannot serve as a template for its own replication or for the synthesis of a nucleic acid (RNA or DNA). With the irretrievable trapping of information in protein, the proteinaceous soma (which represents the actual) is isolated from the nucleic acid germ plasm (which determines the possible). This isolation of mortal soma from immortal germ plasm explains why adaptive changes in the soma fail to direct hereditary changes, Lamarck and Lysenko to the contrary. It is impossible for acquired characteristics to direct evolution; the biochemical means for so doing is (by the arguments presented above) necessarily absent. The first part of this sentence states the essence of Darwin's break with his predecessors;[14] the second is the essence of the insight that Crick formulated a century later. This paired formulation of the contributions of Darwin and Crick indicates their logical connection and their similar form. That is precisely what I proposed to demonstrate at the beginning of this section.

In an article for *Nature* written in 1970 to explain the Central Dogma, Crick wrote that he attached as much importance to his restraint as to his brashness. Crick refrained from indicating which of the then undiscovered information transfers (from RNA to DNA and from DNA directly to protein) might occur. The restraint he exerted was similar to that which Darwin had earlier exerted in avoiding emphasis on possible mechanisms by which hereditary variation might occur. The germinative power of a negative statement lies precisely in what is not said. So it is with a story that is commended to memory by "that chaste compactness that precludes psychological analysis." Consider the difference between an assertion that, of all the values x can assume, a particular value is forbidden and an assertion that x has a particular value. The difference between them can be likened to the difference between a story and information. Walter Benjamin had this to add: "The value of information does not survive the moment; it has to surrender to it completely and explain itself to it without losing any time. A story is different. It does not expend itself. It preserves and concentrates its strength and is capable of releasing it even after a long time."[15] An assertion of what is forbidden takes into account the inner activity of nature just as a story takes into account the inner activity of the human mind.

The Impossibility of Reversing Biological Time

Physics distinguishes between deterministic processes, whose time course is determined solely by the initial state of the system, and processes that evolve according to probabilistic laws, laws that fail to provide more than the probabilities with which particular outcomes obtain. The dynamics of simple isolated systems is deterministic; its time is freely reversible. Substitute $-t$ for $+t$ in the equations of motion of the planets and only the directions of their rotations will be reversed; it will be as if we simply moved the vantage point from which we were looking at the solar system from one side to the other. The behavior of large populations of individual entities, be they molecules or molluscs, can be described only in terms of gross attributes, such as population density, whose evolution with time obeys probabilistic laws. Processes that are governed in this way are called stochastic. A particular configuration of molecules (or molluscs) that changes as a result of a stochastic process is highly unlikely to return to its initial configuration. More likely, memory of the initial state of the system will be erased in time. Morphogenesis during development and speciation during evolution involve stochastic processes; their time is essentially irreversible. A recording of embryonic development or of evolutionary history that is run backward would appear absurd.

In order to distinguish between the time of Newtonian mechanics, in which nothing new happens, and the time of biology, in which novelty is the rule, Norbert Wiener introduced the terms Newtonian time and Bergsonian time.[16] That was in 1948 (B.t.). The date 1948 is based on an enumeration of the yearly revolutions of the earth about the sun. Whereas a physicist, using Newtonian time, might consider each annual cycle identical to the next, a historian, using Bergsonian time, sees all the difference in the world between 1948 A.D. and 1948 B.C. Dates are in Bergsonian time. The distinction between Newtonian and Bergsonian time continues to fascinate. In the opening chapter of his recent novel *The Unbearable Lightness of Being*, Milan Kundera contrasts the "mad myth" of life in which everything recurs as we once experienced it, with life as we know it, in which every experience is unique. In the first (Newtonian) case, pride in achievement is compromised: "If the French Revolution were to recur eternally, French historians would be less proud of Robespierre." In the second (Bergsonian) case, condemnation is compromised: "For how can we condemn something that is ephemeral, in transit? In the sunset of dissolution, everything is illuminated by the aura of nostalgia, even the guillotine."[17]

The arrow of time had been introduced into physics in the nineteenth century with the concept of entropy: the increasing disorder into which all isolated systems decay. The temporal orientation thus pessimistically defined does not point to the time of your life, but to its end. The understanding of time that Henri Bergson sought is an understanding that is connected to life's creativity, not to its decline. Bergson despaired of obtaining that understanding through science. A relatively new branch of thermodynamics is claiming for itself the achievement of pointing time's arrow in its proper, less pessimistic direction. Unfortunately, the validity of this claim is not for everyone to judge. The irreversible thermodynamics of open (as opposed to isolated) systems, of processes that are far from equilibrium, in which nonlinear relationships prevail, is not accessible to all. In this new Prigoginian physics, irreversibility, instead of being lamented as the cause of energy loss from nonideal engines, is summoned to play an indispensable role in processes of self-organization. "We are tempted to go so far as to say that once the conditions for self-organization are satisfied, life becomes as predictable as . . . a falling stone."[18] Life's existence—perhaps; life's sundry forms—hardly. That is another matter altogether. Unpredictability is an essential feature of all creativity, including the creativity of organic evolution. "Organisms are, to a large extent, self-contained units that, so far as they survive, succeed in escaping, counteracting, or transmuting extrinsic causal determiners. As Hegel said, 'whatever has life does not allow the cause to reach its effect, that is, cancels it as cause. . . .'"[19]

Partly because our life span is so brief on the scale of geologic time, we find it hard to comprehend how life's sundry forms—the hummingbird, the lobster, and the composer—could have been produced from a primeval soup. The continuity of that slow historical process has been so well masked that any hint of it is a source of astonishment. We are astonished at evidence of the conservatism with which our internal environment is preserved, not only throughout the active life of the individual, but throughout life's nearly four-billion-year history. The proportion of salts in human blood resembles that of seawater, but not seawater as it is now, rather as it is calculated to have been much earlier in the history of our planet, when life made its first appearance on land. At that time, the seas had not yet acquired their present high salinity. The formulation of such connections between past and present is still astonishing, if no longer blasphemous. Even the jaded molecular biologist cannot suppress surprise at evidence for close relatives of human oncogenes (genes implicated in the selective growth of cancer cells) and human ubiquitin (a protein implicated in the selective degradation of other proteins) in yeast, or of human heat-shock proteins in both yeast and bacteria. We are dazzled by even a dim light shed on the long course of evolutionary history.

We are also taken aback at the illogic of that course. The evidence from bacteria suggests that particular small molecules and proteins that we now call hormones preexisted their hormonal function, preexisted even the existence of cellular specialization. Hormones were not designed; they were simply handy and presumably not already committed to other incompatible vital functions. Natural selection does not work as would an engineer, despite the envy engineers may feel for its accomplishments. The actual design, to use François Jacob's already famous expression, is the design of a tinkerer. There is no right way to produce a given structure, there are many ways. This is true even when it comes to producing something as complex as an eye with a lens. Jacob uses this example in his second Danz lecture,[20] noting the similarity in form of the octopus eye and the human eye, despite a major difference in their modes of evolution. An equally striking example comes from the monumental study, by Sydney Brenner and his colleagues, of the development of the tiny nematode worm, *Caenorhabditis elegans*. The cell lineage of each of its 959 cells is known. Many of those cells are arranged in symmetrical structures; yet their assembly is piecemeal, from cells of different lineages. The processes that generate the striking symmetry of vital structures are, as likely as not, asymmetrical and unpredictable. Such is the illogic of life. "Anything that is produced by evolution is bound to be a bit of a mess."[21] This messiness derives from the diversity of the interactions among the component events. An appreciation of the historicity in both the development of the individual and the evolution of the species leads one eminent molecular biologist, Gunther Stent, to assert the impossibility of discovering a general theory of development or even of approaching the subject objectively. Stent writes "we cannot expect to discover a general theory (and especially not the 'program') of development, no more than historians any longer expect to discover, as some once did, a general theory of history."[22] The contemporary biologist must make peace with this impossibility even as he or she must make peace with the other limitations that life imposes.

Acknowledgments

I thank Raymond Devoret, Martin Gellert, Vickie Koogle, Leonard Maximon, Howard Nash, David M. Robinson, Robert Rohwer, Attila Szabo, and Adam Yarmolinsky for constructive criticisms and Julie Ratliff for typing the several revisions.

Notes

1. François Jacob, *The Possible and the Actual,* University of Washington Press, Seattle, 1982.

2. Ernst Mayr, *The Growth of Biological Thought: Diversity, Evolution, and Inheritance,* Harvard University Press, Belknap Press, Cambridge, Mass., 1982, p. 53.

3. Barry Commoner, *Science and Survival,* Viking Press, New York, 1963, p. 43.

4. C. U. M. Smith, *The Problem of Life: An Essay in the Origins of Biological Thought,* Wiley, New York, 1976, p. xvi.

5. Erwin Schrödinger, *What Is Life? The Physical Aspect of the Living Cell,* Macmillan, New York, 1946, p. 90.

6. From "Although, as from a Prison," in Rainer Maria Rilke, *Poems from the Book of Hours,* Babette Deutsch (trans.), New Directions, New York, 1941.

7. Claude Bernard, *La Science expérimentale,* Baillière et fils, Paris, 1878, p. 52.

8. Georges T. Guilbaud, *What Is Cybernetics?,* Valerie MacKay (trans.), Heinemann, London, 1959, p. 35.

9. W. Ross Ashby, *Design for a Brain,* Riley, New York, 1952, p. 197.

10. Sewell Wright (1967), quoted in Mayr, *Growth of Biological Thought,* p. 57.

11. Edmund T. Whittaker, *From Euclid to Eddington: A Study of Conceptions of the External World,* University Press, Cambridge, 1949, pp. 58-60.

12. Francis H. C. Crick, "On Protein Synthesis," in *The Biological Replication of Macromolecules, Symp. Soc. Exper. Biol.,* 12: 138-63 (1958), see p. 153.

13. Max Delbrück, "Aristotle-totle-totle," in Jacques Monod and Ernest Borek (eds.), *Of Microbes and Life,* Columbia University Press, New York, 1971, p. 55. See also "Afterward: Aristotle and DNA," in Jeremy Campbell, *Grammatical Man: Information, Entropy, Language, and Life,* Simon and Schuster, New York, 1982, pp. 266-73.

14. Darwin's break with his predecessors was not as decisive as my formulation of Darwin's contribution implies it to have been. For example, writing about the evolution of our progenitors, Darwin suggested that "natural selection would probably have been greatly aided by the inherited effects of the increased or diminished use of the different parts of the body" (*The Descent of Man and Selection in Relation to Sex,* Appleton, New York, 1876, p. 35). Contemporary evolutionists do not take this possibility seriously.

15. Walter Benjamin, "The Storyteller: Reflections on the Works of Nikolai Leskov," in *Illuminations,* Harry Zohn (trans.), Harcourt, Brace & World, New York, 1968, pp. 90–91.

16. Norbert Wiener, *Cybernetics, or Control and Communication in the Animal and the Machine,* M.I.T. Press, Cambridge, Mass., 1948.

17. Milan Kundera, *The Unbearable Lightness of Being,* Michael Henry Hein (trans.), Harper & Row, New York, 1984, p. 4.

18. Ilya Prigogine and Isabelle Stengers, *Order Out of Chaos: Man's New Dialogue with Nature,* Bantam, New York, 1984, p. 176.

19. Mario Bunge, *Causality: The Place of the Causal Principle in Modern Science,* Harvard University Press, Cambridge, Mass., 1959, pp. 179–80.

20. Jacob, *The Possible and the Actual.*

21. Sydney Brenner, quoted in Roger Lewin, "Why Is Development So Illogical?" *Science,* 224: 1327–29 (1984).

22. Gunther Stent, "Thinking in One Dimension: The Impact of Molecular Biology on Development," *Cell,* 40: 1–2 (1985).

IMPOSSIBILITY IN MEDICINE

Intellectuals are always fascinated by the impossible.

Fernand Braudel, *On History*

The concept of impossibility plays a dual role in medical progress. One source of medical progress is the acknowledgment of impossibility, the differentiating of the truly impossible products of magical and wishful thinking from the pragmatically approachable realities of human physiology. However, a second source of fundamental progress lies in the systematic denial of the impossible and in frontal assault on obvious impossibilities. Quinine treatment of malaria and vaccination for smallpox are only two examples among many of highly efficacious treatments which, at the time of their introduction, had been impressively demonstrated to be both practically and theoretically impossible. For the physician, the denial of impossibility produces much of the heroism, excitement, and role identity as healer that characterize the applied science of medicine. Yet this attitude also creates conceptual and sometimes clinical problems. This chapter describes examples of some of these difficulties.

First, we illustrate the difficulty of proving a medical impossibility by reviewing the ancient but still unresolved question about whether human beings can live forever. Next, we use the example of the complex human brain to show how the denial of impossibility can lead to oversimplification and erroneous conceptual shortcuts. Finally, we critically review the development of the artificial heart as a potential example of the sacrifice of systematic analysis of the possible to a heroic assault on the impossible. Risk-benefit analysis provides a statistical approach to the task of making a practical decision about whether a procedure is too "impossible" to be usefully attempted. It is this kind of complex negotiation about what to define as impossible that is helpful in medical decision making, rather than the absolute theoretical concept of impossibility discussed elsewhere in this book.

The Impossibility of Living Forever

It is impossible to live forever. That seemingly obvious pronouncement has not necessarily permeated popular consciousness. One unspoken message of the current fitness boom is that if only we do the right thing—perform the right exercises, eat the right foods— then we will live longer, maybe forever. Actually, the idea of a finite life span, with some theoretical absolute maximum life expectancy, may be relatively recent. The "three score and ten" years mentioned as the good life in the Bible must be balanced by the nine-hundred-plus years of Methuselah. In many primitive cultures, death at any age is seen to result from malevolent forces; it is never "natural." In primitive human populations, just as in most populations of wild animals, the existence of a finite life span is not obvious from an examination of actual survival. In these groups survival curves tend toward the exponential (curve A in the figure on page 46). If the curve is exponential, the probability of death in the next year is the same whether the individual is 1 year old or 110. With an exponential survival curve, it is theoretically possible to live forever; the curve never reaches zero. In contrast, in populations like ours, with stable nutritional resources and effective public health measures (childhood vaccinations, adequate plumbing, etc.), most people survive into old age and then all of them die over a relatively short period. The midpoint of this fall in the survival curve is called average life expectancy. Barring an untoward event, most people can expect to survive to that average life expectancy, give or take a few years.

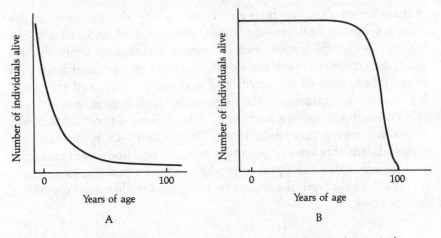

Two theoretical survival curves. Curve A shows an extreme example, survival in a society where death is mostly determined by external forces such as starvation, infection, war, or predation. The curve is exponential: it implies that your chance of dying during the next year is always the same whether you are one or a hundred years of age. Curve B is an extreme example of survival in a developed society with adequate nutrition and public health measures. The great majority of people survive into old age, when they begin to die rapidly. Although curve A gives you a poor average life expectancy, it also holds out the promise of immortality, because it never reaches 0. If you are lucky, you can survive to a thousand on curve A; no way on curve B.

In the modern world we are on curve B in the figure, and a glance shows that we cannot expect to live forever. We have a finite life span. This does not mean, however, that this particular finite life span is the one we are stuck with. In other words, there are no absolute arguments against the possibility of shifting the whole survival curve to the right, so that people would live on average into their one hundred twenties instead of their seventies. Many people are not immediately enchanted with the concept of living until 130 or so. Perhaps it is because they envision being in a wheelchair in a dark corridor of a nursing home for the last 50 years of their life. In actuality, if it turns out that human life span can be extended, then we know from animal experiments (described below) that vigor will be proportionately extended; that is, if we normally live to 130, then 110-year-olds will look, feel and act like today's 65-year-olds.

Is there any evidence that human life span can be extended? Yes, but it is all indirect. It would appear that we should dismiss the tales of 160-year-olds in the Caucasus or Peru as a combination of wishful thinking and local entrepreneurial spirit. Data from experimental animals is more encouraging. For example, if you starve a mouse, it will live longer. In fact, starvation is the best described and most successful way of increasing the life span of experimental animals. It deserves a detailed look. In the 1930s McCay and his colleagues reported that mice that were placed on a semistarvation diet between 3 and 12 months of age and subsequently allowed to eat as much as they wanted (ad libitum) lived an average of 48 months, as compared to an average of 32 months for control mice, which ate as much as they wanted throughout life. This 50 percent increase in life span translates in human terms to an additional 37 or so years, with an average life expectancy of 112 rather than 75. Further experiments by McCay and an increasing number of other investigators have allowed this phenomenon of life extension through starvation to be more fully characterized. It turns out that what is important is caloric restriction. It does not matter whether the dietary component being restricted is protein, fat, or carbohydrate, as long as total caloric intake is sharply reduced. And we are not talking about a "slimming diet." These mice are not slim; they are starving. In most experiments they receive 60 to 70 percent of calories needed to maintain normal growth. If growing animals are placed on this diet they become runts—long-lived runts, however. In the initial experiments some of the animals died during the period of semistarvation. Most such deaths have been eliminated, however, as researchers have supplemented the calorie-restricted diet with essential nutrients (vitamins and minerals) and have tried to protect animals on the diet from infections.

Mice are not the only species that live longer after starvation. Similar results have been seen with rats, rabbits, guinea pigs, gerbils, flies, and fish. Also, it is not necessary to starve the animals during their youth. In a series of experiments comparing the effects of starvation at different ages, rats fed ad libitum for the first 12 months and then restricted for 12 months also had a substantial life extension, although somewhat less than rats for whom this sequence was reversed.

Another interesting aspect of the starved animals is that even when they get old, they remain physiologically young. Generally, the function of many organ systems in the body tends to decrease with age. The kidney does not filter the blood as well; the stomach does not secrete as much acid; white blood cells do not divide or resist certain infections as well. But in animals that have been starved, all these organs function as well in old animals as in young. The white blood cells of a 36-month-old mouse that has been starved during the first twelve months of life work as well as white blood cells of young animals. When the tissues of these animals are examined under a microscope, they do not "look" old. Thus, starvation is not just allowing very old animals to continue surviving; it is keeping them young.

Is any of this relevant to humans? It is hard to say. Starving humans tend to die; they are prey to infections and other fatal diseases. It is not possible to keep humans in controlled, germ-free conditions, as we can do for rodents. There is some indirect evidence that individuals who survive a period of starvation have a markedly reduced mortality from certain diseases. For example, deaths from heart disease in Denmark fell considerably in the years after the famine at the end of the Second World War. Some populations gradually lose weight throughout adult life, for example, the Tukinsenta of New Guinea and the Masai of East Africa. In contrast, Western men and women on average show a steady weight gain during adulthood. Those populations that lose weight with age have almost no heart disease, the number one killer in the West. On the other hand, such populations do not produce very long-lived individuals, because other causes of death become more important. Indeed, even in Western developed countries, it has been calculated that totally eliminating heart disease as a cause of death would add only four years to the average life span. Cure of all cancers would add another two years. In fact, it is hard to envision how preventing or curing specific diseases will have a dramatic effect on human life span, though it will, of course, greatly reduce premature mortality. If starvation in humans has the same effect as it has in experimental animals, then it will not extend life by eliminating diseases; rather, it will do so by retarding the aging process itself, by keeping us young.

If the data in humans that caloric restriction prolongs life is weak, the data for the converse—that caloric excess shortens life—is even weaker. Obesity per se is not an independent risk factor for increased mortality. Overweight people have a greater chance of having diabetes and high blood pressure, both of which are associated with decreased life expectancy. But by itself, obesity does not constitute an increased risk.

Starvation is not the only path to life extension. Other putative means of postponing death have evolved from theoretical concepts about the etiology of the aging process. For example, one theory attributes aging to the gradual accumulation of damage from free radicals which are generated in many metabolic processes. Oxygen radicals, such as O_2^-, are quite toxic. Indeed, generation of these compounds is a mechanism whereby white blood cells kill ingested bacteria. These oxygen radicals can and probably do damage the lipid membranes of cells. The free-radical theory of aging proposes this mechanism as *the* cause of aging and offers daily ingestion of antioxidants as the ideal way to prevent the process. There have been a number of studies in which animals fed high doses of an antioxidant, such as vitamin E, lived longer than the control group of animals not fed the antioxidant. In none of these studies was the prolongation of life as great as in the studies of dietary restriction. In most of the studies with antioxidants, the treated animals lost weight, which raises the possibility that the life extention in the antioxidant group was secondary to decreased caloric intake rather than to a specific antioxidant effect.

One proposed method of life extension that has achieved some popularity in the United States is procaine administration. For the past three decades, this local anesthetic has been promoted both as a means of slowing the aging process and as a treatment for various diseases. It is most commonly marketed as "Gerovital H3." There is very little evidence one way or the other in experimental animals or humans as to the efficacy of procaine. The problems of verifying claims of efficacy for this and other "nonestablishment" therapies generate a medical impossibility in their own right and are discussed below.

What does all this have to do with the idea of impossibility in medicine? Consider your own responses as you read this section. Perhaps initially you felt it was flippant to question the impossibility of living forever, or even of substantially prolonging the human life span. However, you may have found yourself warming to the question as the experimental data were reviewed. This is what happens repeatedly to physicians, why it is so difficult for us to take the sensible course and simply renounce the impossible in order to concentrate on more practical issues.

Impossible to Prove

Some things in medicine are impossible to prove. Here we enter the realm of practical rather than theoretical impossibility. For example, what if taking 10 grams of vitamin C per day increases your life expectancy, on average, by five years, or what if it cuts down your chance of getting cancer by 25 percent? There are many people in the United States who believe something like that. The problem is, even if they are right, it may be impossible to prove. Here the impossibility stems from the nature of the experiment necessary to adequately test the claims. The supposed beneficial effects are sufficiently subtle that a long-term trial using a large number of people would be required to demonstrate them. A 25 percent reduction in cancer or a five-year addition in life expectancy may not seem "subtle." Such effects would have major impact on the public health. Nevertheless, a large, long-term trial would still be necessary to prove the point. For example, if we placed 100 individuals on vitamin C and 100 other individuals of comparable age, gender, occupation, health, smoking habits, race, and socioeconomic status on a placebo pill, and followed these groups for ten years, we might expect about 10 cancers in the control group receiving placebo. Even if vitamin C did reduce cancer, there is no way we would find it in this trial. If the vitamin C group had 7 or 8 cancers, that would not be statistically different from the 10 in the control group. Even if vitamin C did indeed reduce cancer by 25 percent, there still might be 10 or 12 cancers in the vitamin C group, simply because of normal random variation. We would need closer to 1000 people in each group, followed for ten years, before we could intelligently decide whether vitamin C reduces cancer. And that is only if we postulate that high-dose vitamin C reduces cancer by 25 percent. What if it reduces cancer by 5 percent? If true, that would still have a major impact on the public health, but it would take a trial involving many thousands of people to prove.

One might object that just because something takes a lot of work does not make it impossible. That is true, but we mention just one example, that of high-dose vitamin C. The trouble is, there are thousands of potential cancer-prevention regimes out there, from silenium to procaine to vitamin C to zinc to bran to low cholesterol to high cholesterol to fish oil, with many in between. In addition, some nonestablishment therapies have an impressive resiliency. If discredited as a treatment for one disease, they soon return as a potential treatment for another. An example is Laetrile, which was tested and disproven as an arthritis cure several years before it became a popular treatment for cancer. It is practically impossible to test all these possible treatments for all their possible indications. Another way of stating this thesis is that it is impossible to be certain whether any one of those "unproven" treatments helps people, hurts people, or has no effect.

"Impossibility to prove" is an important concept in medicine. It goes far in explaining why most physicians are so uncomfortable with, even hostile to, various alternative therapies. These therapies simply open up too many possibilities to think about. The practice of medicine is difficult enough as it is, without introducing the endless possibilities of alternative treatments. It is expecting too much of a physician to ask him to be competent at all the diagnostic and therapeutic modalities of establishment medicine and at the same time to have an "open mind" about any new nonestablishment therapies. In any field, especially in a field as diverse as medicine, one must often narrow one's focus in order to make progress. Thus, in medicine, impossible to prove becomes impossible to contemplate.

The Impossible Brain

It is impossible to comprehend the brain. Despite many assertions to the contrary, the brain is not "like a computer." Yes, the brain has many electrical connections, just like a computer. But at each point in a computer only a binary decision can be made—yes or no, on or off, 0 or 1. Each point in the brain, each brain cell, contains all the genetic information necessary to reproduce the entire organism. A brain cell is not a switch. It has a memory; it can be subtle. Each brain cell is like a computer. The brain is like a hundred billion computers all connected together. It is impossible to understand because it is too complex. As Emerson Pugh wrote, "If the human brain was so simple that we could understand it, we would be so simple that we couldn't." Such a concept may be repugnant to scientists. Science admonishes us not to give up too soon, not to call something unknowable merely because we have not yet figured it out. On the other hand, refusal to acknowledge the impossibility of understanding the brain contributes to one of the greatest conceptual anachronisms of the modern era—that of mind-body dualism.

While it is easy to trace the development of the concept of mind-body dualism, it is somewhat more difficult to understand why the last century of brain research has not led to the demise of that concept. The concept of a mind or a self separate from the body surfaced in Greek thought in the fifth century B.C., was further refined in the Christian concept of the soul, and was set in stone by Descartes, who divided all nature into the realm of the mind and the realm of matter. Thus, each individual is composed of, on the one hand, a "self" (or a "soul," or a "mind") and, on the other, a body.

Our graphic arts and literature, as well as our cosmology, take this view. It is perhaps impossible to think about *ourselves* without at least implicitly employing mind-body dualism.

Brain research has shown with increasing clarity that mind-body dualism is an artificial and fundamentally incorrect construct. There is no "mind" apart from the "body." The "mind" or the consciousness of self is a product of a functioning central nervous system, which is part of the body. All thought can be potentially reduced to organic events, changes in ion channels in nerve axons, release of neurotransmitters at nerve endings, release of neurohormones, triggering of feedback circuits, and so forth. Thus, were we to start anew today to develop a philosophy of selfhood, we would not need to call up a mind separate from the body. We cannot totally explain how the electrochemical reactions in the brain result in a concept of self, because the brain is too complicated; it is impossible to understand. But we no longer need go beyond the brain in order to explain selfhood. Mind-body dualism, a major part of western thought over the past several centuries, has become scientifically obsolete. This concept is not so easy to get rid of, however, as so many of the other philosophical constructs developed during these centuries reflect its influence.

How does the refusal to accept the impossibility of understanding the brain contribute to the continuance of mind-body dualism? Consider an argument between two individuals:

> First person: "There is no mind separate from the body. Your mind is simply nerve cells in your brain communicating with each other by means of electrical impulse."
> Second person: "That does not make sense to me. How can my appreciation of a sunset, how can *War and Peace,* how can love and sorrow and beauty and jealousy and creativity all be reduced to a series of electrical impulses?"
> First person: ". . . ."

The first person's initial statement is correct, but he is confused by the second person's assessment. We cannot explain *how* a series of electrical impulses in a brain results in a concept of self, because the brain is far too complex for us to understand. But that does not mean that the "mind" is separate from the body; it means that the part of the body responsible for the mind, the central nervous system, is poorly understood because it is so enormously powerful.

The ideological havoc wreaked by our culture's acceptance of mind-body dualism has perhaps had its most serious consequences in the field of medicine. Medicine deals with diseases. If the mind and body are conceptually separate, then we anticipate that there must exist diseases of the mind separate from diseases of the body. Diseases of the body are viewed on the whole as solid, organic, and respectable. We have no problem believing they can be inherited (like diabetes), caused by viruses (like hepatitis), or cured (like pneumonia). People with diseases of the body incur little blame. Susan Sontag, in *Illness as Metaphor,* has noted a disturbing tendency in the medical profession to generate guilt among cancer patients similar to the guilt and shame felt by tuberculosis patients several years ago, but these tendencies constitute an exception. On the whole, "organic" illnesses of the body are viewed as a misfortune over which the victim has little control. Not so for "mental" illnesses. These diseases of the mind become diseases of the "self." We (our "selves") can distance ourselves from our "bodily" illnesses: "my leg is broken" or "my heart is failing." But, because of mind-body dualism, our mind *is* our self. "My mind is sick" is not differentiated psychologically from "I am sick." We cannot distance ourselves, take a detached view of our minds: we *are* our minds. When a disease affects brain function, the afflicted person and those around him feel that the "self" must be somehow in control of the disorder of "self." "Pull your *self* together" we might say to the patient with brain dysfunction (although we would hardly say this to a person with heart or liver or lung dysfunction). Linguistically, we can refer to that individual as "a schizophrenic" or "a manic depressive." It is as if their disease is the same as themselves. We cannot call someone "a broken leg" or "a heart attack." We recognize that there is something of those individuals apart from their illness. With mental illness we are more likely to misperceive the person and the disease as one. Within this misperception, it is hard to envisage that a mental illness can be "cured." Bones can be set; damaged liver tissue can be repaired. But a "mind" is a "self"—it is harder to conceptualize how such an entity can heal. We are more likely to misperceive that the afflicted individual has "finally decided to behave" or undergone a religious conversion than to understand that brain cells and chemistry have repaired themselves. There is even an implication that to tamper with the mind might be such an intolerable assault on the very existence of the self that it should not be permitted, even if the tampering could result in cure. This attitude still produces legal and judicial barriers to treatments for the brain that would never be permitted to impede treatments for the heart, liver, or peripheral nerves. As we learn more about specific chemical and membrane changes associated with each "mental" disease, it becomes easier for us to approach the "mentally" ill in the same way as we approach the "physically" ill: both have physical illness; the symptoms of both represent organic changes in the body; and both should be amenable to therapy aimed at repairing those organic changes.

We are beginning to realize that the distinction between "mental" and "physical" diseases is misleading, that thought is a bodily process, that the brain is part of the body. Another aspect of this new synthesis is our understanding that the brain, through the peripheral nervous system and through the release of neurohormones, directly influences every organ in the body. Thus, just as all "mental" illnesses are "bodily" or "physical" illnesses, all "physical" illnesses are "mental," in that the brain influences all bodily processes. This realization came first for the so-called psychosomatic diseases—diseases in which the body was genuinely and organically altered, but the "mind" was clearly playing a role in causing the disease. An example is peptic ulcer disease. We could not call an ulcer a "mental" disease, because we could see it. On the other hand, it was clear that high anxiety and stress ("mental" states) contributed to the disease. In a way, people with so-called psychosomatic diseases were stuck in the middle, with both a "bodily" and a "mental" disease. Thus, they were subjected to standard medical treatments for "bodily" illnesses and yet also held partially responsible for their illness because of its "mental" aspects.

Enthusiasts like Norman Cousins, who advocate positive mental attitudes as helpful in organic disease, rarely foresee that by merely noting this connection they may exile those viewed previously as simply organically ill into the more ambiguous category of psychosomatics. A classic example is that of Saint Theresa of Avila. In her late teens she was systematically evaluated and probably accurately diagnosed by sixteenth-century Spanish physicians as having malaria and consumption. Her condition worsened, and she barely survived a three-day seizure that left her weak and bedridden. Fever by itself can cause seizures, but this one was more likely due to tuberculous meningitis. In the absence of effective somatic remedies, Theresa elected to use her mind to help her body recover. In this she succeeded completely. For her pains she was dubbed, by no less a light than William James, the patron saint of hysteria. Because Theresa was able to cure herself, mind-body dualism would decree that she also must have willed herself to be ill.

The belief in a distinct set of psychosomatic illnesses is gradually being replaced by the more sophisticated realization that all illnesses are to some extent psychosomatic. This is most easily demonstrated in experimental animals. When rats are subjected to stresses such as loud noise or overcrowding, the incidence of all diseases increases. Not only do the rats develop ulcers and other classical "psychosomatic" conditions, they also have a marked increase in diabetes, in infections, and in all types of cancer. There is similar evidence in humans from population studies. George Vaillant's study of a cohort of Harvard College graduates over three decades showed that those with good "mental" health in college maintained good "physical" health during the follow-up period whereas those with poor "mental" health tended to develop a variety of serious and sometimes fatal diseases. Other epidemiologic studies have shown that major stresses, such as loss of a spouse or major change in social environment, are followed by increases in the incidence of all diseases, not just the so-called psychosomatic ones.

The results of stress can be passed from generation to generation. Stressing a rat in its infancy not only makes it more susceptible to stress-induced disease in adulthood, but also makes its progeny more susceptible to such disease in their adulthood.

Thus, we are gradually coming to appreciate the power of the brain over the rest of the body, but the remnants of mind-body dualism—the distinctions between "mental" and "bodily" illnesses and between psychosomatic and purely organic illnesses— continue to influence medical care.

Why has mind-body dualism hung on so long? Why must we continue to separate these concepts? Early workers tried to combat mind-body dualism by trivializing the brain, but they failed. Watson tried to convince us that our thought was not different from that of pigeons, both being explainable as a series of simple conditioned responses. Most sentient beings had difficulty identifying with this model. The philosophical knots of mind-body dualism have not been untied by minimizing the awesome potential of the human brain. The mind is no more the sum of a series of conditioned responses than the body is a mere series of simple chemical reactions. The body *is* a series of chemical reactions, but it is absurd to think that we can ever comprehend it in that way. The organism is too complex, redundant, and multidetermined to be explained by any simple, single mechanism.

If we can tame our arrogance enough to accept that the brain is impossible to understand, then "psychosomatic" becomes the appropriate descriptor for all diseases, no longer a term of subtle opprobrium, and, even more important, the demise of an erroneous concept may finally be at hand.

The Denial of Impossibility in Medicine

Twentieth-century medicine can be seen as a systematic denial of the impossible. Most of the miracles of the New Testament are now everyday therapies: curing lepers, giving sight to the blind, healing the lame, and even, occasionally raising the dead. It is important to appreciate this point. Miracles occur when the impossible happens. Few of the medical miracles in the Bible would be miracles anymore (the loaves and fishes would still qualify, but that comes under the category of nutrition, not medicine).

The modern denial of the impossible in medicine has been systematic. Whatever would cross the mind of a three-year-old or any other primitive, ignorant about the laws of possibility, is exactly what medicine has done. If a body part is cut off, why not just sew it back on? If a woman wants to be a man, why not just make her a beard and a penis? If a mother wants to know the gender of her unborn fetus, why not simply take a biopsy of it or a picture? You say smallpox is a serious disease? Let us simply eliminate it from the face of the earth. The remarkable thing about these simple frontal assaults on impossibility is that so many of them work, given enough time, intelligence, and money.

One very simple yet very effective principle for twentieth-century medicine has been: if something is worn out, then replace it. This principle started with kidneys—first, with the development of artificial kidneys, then with transplants of real ones. Now it has spread to transplants of livers and lungs and hearts. The latest step, of course, is the artificial heart.

This has got to stop somewhere. Perhaps it has already gone too far. Of course, had enough people listened to that argument thirty years ago, then artificial dialysis and kidney transplantations would not be the almost routine yet life-saving procedures that they are today. The first kidney transplanted was taken from a cadaver and attached to the recipient's right forearm—an impossible thing to do. The initial assaults on other medical impossibilities were equally absurd. The arguments about why such highly experimental procedures could never offer tangible help to patients with failing kidneys could fill volumes. And yet kidney transplantation eventually did succeed, mostly because of the plodding attempt after attempt to replace what was not working, to treat humans as if we were used cars, to do the impossible.

Perhaps the denial of the impossible has reached its ultimate expression in the artificial heart program. The heart, as every first-year medical student knows, is a pump, but a rather miraculous pump, in that it puts out three ounces of blood 60 to 90 times a minute, or 40 million times per year, without ever resting. There are many reasons why artificial hearts are impossible. Blood tends to stick to artificial surfaces and form clots. Medicines that prevent this cause bleeding in vital organs such as the brain. Just pushing the blood around the circulation is not good enough. The pump has to mimic the pulsatile action of the heart; in other words, there has to be both a systole (brief period of pumping) and diastole (rest period between pumping), or organs such as the kidney and liver fail. Infections tend to form on the foreign surfaces of an artificial heart and, once formed, are impossible to eradicate without totally removing the infected material. This is no trivial problem. When we brush our teeth, or squeeze a pimple, or have a hard bowel movement, millions of bacteria are released into the bloodstream, only to be quickly coated by our antibodies and ingested by our white blood cells. Antibodies and white blood cells do not work when the bacteria are sticking to an artificial surface. With an artificial heart, brushing one's teeth becomes a risky business. And of course the artificial heart must not fail. If it stops, the recipient is dead. Even if it just stops for a little while, and only requires a few minor adjustments to function perfectly again, the recipient remains dead.

The question is, should we draw the line somewhere and say "No, we are sorry, but this really *is* impossible and we do not want anyone messing with it"? Should we, for example, tell people to stop tinkering around with artificial hearts? This type of medieval thinking is anathema to Western scientific thought. It violates our code of progress. Lewis Thomas, for one, would surely blanch at the idea of limiting scientific investigation and experimentation in any way. Raising the possibility of such a limitation recalls the Inquisition, the trial of Galileo, or book burning. But let us return to the question, Should we draw the line somewhere? Should we, as a society, tell the artificial heart people to stop, or, should we at least not unquestioningly support, both financially and emotionally, such programs? We will not go into the arguments against drawing the line, because they are part of our cultural fabric. We not only know them; we live them. Instead, we will focus on the arguments in favor of drawing the line, of deciding as a society that some things in medicine are better off impossible. And to make this discussion manageable, we will focus on the artificial heart program.

There is something almost Aztecan about the artificial heart program. In many ways it resembles a national sacrifice to the god of technology. Civilizations that practice human sacrifice often approach it in a stereotypical fashion. A sacrificial victim is picked. This individual serves as a representative and an offering from all the members of society. In the days before the sacrifice, the victim is honored and feted. The victim dies in a large public ceremony. The Aztecs plucked out the victim's heart and held it aloft for the waiting masses to see.

Television allows our society to fully participate in the human sacrifice of the artificial heart program. We watch the victims suffer and we witness their death. And through their suffering and death they become national heroes. Admittedly, the reports of the suffering are filtered through "hospital spokespersons"; thus, for most people the horrible reality is not visible but imagined. When we hear that the latest recipient has a "clouded sensorium" and "left-sided weakness," it perhaps takes some practical medical experience to picture the reality—a man lying in bed not knowing where he is or why he is there, unable to move his left arm, and with needles sticking in both arms and tubes into his chest and, possibly, a hole in his throat into which another tube is inserted.

Is it right to sacrifice these people so that the artificial heart might someday actually work? The proponents of the program say that the recipients were about to die anyway; so life with the artificial heart, however horrible it is, has to be weighed against certain death without it. That is absurd, perhaps the single most absurd aspect of the artificial heart program (and the heart transplant program, for that matter), because it is impossible to tell with precision when someone is going to die of heart failure.

Artificial hearts and heart transplants are very different from all other artificial or transplanted organ programs. With a kidney or a liver, we are adding something (a dialysis machine, a transplanted kidney) to a very sick patient who very well may die if nothing is done. The operation itself entails some risk, as does any operation; but, except for the stress of the operative procedure, the patient is better or at least no worse off after the procedure than before. In most cases, the patient still has his own liver or kidneys, bad as they may be; he still has a chance to make it on his own if the transplant fails.

Artificial hearts and heart transplants represent a whole new ball game. The surgeon has to decide and then convince the patient that "my heart (whether artificial or from a transplant donor) is better than your heart." That is, the decision is to *remove* one heart and put in another. This is a big decision to make. Do we really want this decision made by someone who collects $50,000 for performing the operation? One interesting aspect of the publicity surrounding the artificial heart program is that we all get to hear the surgeon, the recipient, and the recipient's family; so we get a very good idea of the way they think. It is clear that everyone connected with that program (and, by extension, everyone connected with heart transplant programs) actually believes that the recipient has "only two weeks to live without the artificial heart." We have absolutely no way of predicting how long someone with heart failure will live. Even in the most severe type of shock after a massive heart attack, at least one out of six patients recover.

Heart surgeons should be forced to read Boswell's *Life of Johnson*. In the last five years of his life, Dr. Johnson experienced several severe episodes of heart failure. For weeks on end he would remain in bed, hardly able to breathe. Then he would get better. Modern medicine is so used to intervening that we have forgotten the natural history of many serious illnesses. People sometimes get better. We do not know how or why, but we do not know how or why many illnesses occur to begin with. If Samuel Johnson had received a 1980's vintage artificial heart at age 70, he would never have lived to be 75.

The fundamental impossibility of medicine is the impossibility of ever knowing for sure what is going to happen to a given individual, whether they will live or die, stay healthy or become ill. Medicine is a profession, not a science. Practitioners of medicine sometimes play the odds, sometimes go on hunches, but we are never sure. Just as we are ready to turn off the respirator after a patient has been in a deep coma for over a month, we will be reminded of a case where a similar patient made a recovery after three months in coma. It is important to remember the real lesson of the Karen Ann Quinlan case. The argument was whether or not to turn off the respirator and allow this woman who had been in a deep coma for months to die. The point is, everyone on both sides of the argument, all the experts, assumed that she would die when the respirator was turned off. They were wrong. The respirator was disconnected, and she lived on in coma for many years. We simply cannot predict with certainty what will happen to any given patient.

A major task in the process of becoming a physician is to accept the impossibility of ever being sure, to become comfortable with the state of chronic uncertainty that characterizes the practice of medicine. This impossibility is difficult for nonphysicians (and some physicians) to accept. Patients are always asking "How long do I have?" The only honest answer is "I don't know."

The artificial heart program is, at the time of this writing, confined to one center, but the heart transplant program is spreading fast, fueled by the decision of medical care insurers to pay for the procedure. A private hospital in Albuquerque, New Mexico just announced a heart transplant program. In an interview with the local paper, the heart surgeon said he would have to do a minimum of 12 transplants per year or continuation of the program could not be justified. What if it is mid-October and only 8 transplants have been done that year, and you are lying in bed with heart failure? Are the criteria for replacing your heart going to be as rigorous as they were last January?

And what about the cost? In this nuclear age, scientists occasionally have had to ask the question, "Is this new fact good or bad for my civilization?" rather than simply, "Is this new fact really a fact?" We are not now nor should we ever be entirely comfortable with this new question, but it is often there. Would it have been better if fission and fusion were declared impossible? Once again, a medieval thought, but not without attraction to a society dominated by fear of nuclear extinction. In medicine, the question of whether a new discovery is "good" is coming up increasingly often. The artificial heart is again a prime example.

Presumably, after a certain number of deaths and strokes and other terrible complications, the artificial heart will no longer be impossible. It may someday evolve into a true life-saving procedure. Can we afford it? We are now spending 11 percent of our gross national product on medical care, a percentage far higher than in other Western countries. Much of this expense comes from modern medical miracles—doing the impossible. Depending on one's bias, an argument can be made either way as to whether a greater expense devoted to medical care is recouped in the greater productivity of a healthier society. Once the artificial heart becomes generally available, it will no longer be possible to ask if we can afford it. Physicians will be faced with individual patients with failing hearts and with, they are convinced, only a few days to live. The artificial heart or a transplant then becomes the only possible solution. Economic issues are irrelevant when deciding on the health care of an individual, especially if the costs are not directly assumed by the individual. In medicine, the critical decision *not* to do something often has to be made early or it can never be made. For example, it is impossible for most physicians to pull out a feeding tube from a comatose patient. Many of us simply cannot emotionally accept the responsibility for a positive action (pulling out a tube) that directly results in the death of a patient by starvation. On the other hand, it is somehow easier to decide not to insert the feeding tube in the first place. It is, after all, an extraordinary measure, threading a tube through a comatose patient's nose, down the esophagus and into the stomach so that a special liquid diet can be administered. Most physicians would not feel that such a measure was morally necessary or appropriate for all patients in coma, particularly if the chance of recovery is nil. But many nursing homes are full of such patients because the tube was put down without much thought, and the decision to pull out the tube is somehow on a different ethical level than the decision not to put it in. Analogous decisions are made with the development of medical technologies. Once they are available, it becomes almost impossible not to use them. The decision has to be made at the development stage—should they be left as impossible?

Can we afford the artificial heart emotionally? Can we as a society afford to participate in the systematic sacrifice of victims while the artificial heart is being perfected? Will not there be some deadening effect from this national concordance that the ends justify the means? Certainly, the victims have given informed consent. Can someone who has been told he has two weeks to live give informed consent? Some of the Aztec victims were volunteers, too.

The answers are not clear, at least not to us. As we stated earlier, such attitudes as we express here, had they been prevalent in the preceding decades, could well have prevented the development of modern medicine, and it would take a real misanthrope to deny the benefits of modern medical technology. But this is a book on impossibility. Impossibility is relative, and what we see as impossible is constantly changing. Every contribution in this book gives evidence for that change. There is a grey zone between the possible and the impossible. It is just as possible to take something from that grey area and declare it impossible as to declare it possible. We as a society can decide that something is impossible and will stay impossible; we declare it impossible by consensus. This does not toll the death knell of civilization; it happens all the time. For example, many concepts regarding racial differences have been declared by consensus impossible to explore, because the consequences of that exploration might be destructive to our society. Concepts and hypotheses in medicine may soon be judged similarly hazardous and, by some rule of expedience and common sense yet to be articulated, may be relegated to the realm of the impossible.

THE IMPOSSIBLE
IN MEDICINE

M edicine, someone has said, is the art of making adequate decisions based on inadequate evidence, which is another way of saying that medicine is, at its core, inexact. Certainty, the organizing ideal toward which medicine strives at both the clinical and basic scientific level, is generally beyond the clinician's grasp, and, in at least an absolute sense, beyond that of the basic biomedical scientist as well. It is, in effect, impossible to achieve.

Proceeding from the idea that certainty is fundamentally unattainable in clinical medicine, we can see that the systems that have evolved in diagnostic reasoning, in workup and management tactics, and in therapeutics are all techniques for managing (i.e., reducing or minimizing) uncertainty.

The natural sciences in medicine are likewise ultimately bound by uncertainty. The theories of pure science are explanations of observed phenomena that satisfy the observations, do not clash with related explanations of related phenomena, and have predictive value. The strong inferences that can be drawn from such formulations permit new experiments to be designed, modifications of theories to be offered, and explanations of natural phenomena to be refined. Nevertheless, scientific theories retain a core of tentativity that permits the possibility of revision or extension. The analogies to clinical medicine are rich. The present essay will concern itself with the clinical issues.

If certainty is impossible and uncertainty the rule, clinical medicine can be seen as based on systems of predictions or probabilities. The domains of diagnostic reasoning, clinical tactics, and therapeutic management may be considered as expressions of processes that start with maximal uncertainty and, through systematic reductionistic reasoning, reduce that uncertainty to a minimum. Uncertainty, in this paradigm, may be considered to approach the zero level but never to reach it.

Based as it is on systems of probabilities, clinical medicine strives to deal effectively with the fact that derangements of physiological processes and alterations of anatomical arrangements can for the most part be appreciated only inferentially.[1] This can be understood further by examining the diagnostic process.

The diagnosis "pneumonia" is based on clusters of data (chills, fever, cough, rales heard over the affected lung segment, abnormalities in the white blood cell count and in x-rays of the chest) rather than on direct observation of inflammation of the lung as one would see it under the microscope. Likewise, the diagnostic term "congestive heart failure" connotes a mix of symptoms (shortness of breath), signs (enlargement of the heart, gallop rhythm, rales in the lungs, enlargement of the liver, swelling of the feet), and physiological aberrations (elevation of certain intravascular pressures) rather than reflecting direct evidence at the level of the heart muscle itself (i.e., that it is "failing," performing its hydraulic functions inadequately because of abnormalities in contractility). Clusters of data such as these, arranged so as to permit diagnostic formulations to be made, amount, in effect, to clinical syllogisms. These syllogisms, however, are rarely rigorous, because most signs, symptoms, and laboratory data are not disease specific but represent samplings of the rather limited repertoire of reactions to injury, recognizable by clinical techniques, which are possessed by each organ or organ system. Thus, chills, fever, rales, pleuritic chest pain, and cough are not specific to pneumonia, but may be features of a large number of disorders.

In attempting to understand the problem in a diagnostic sense, the clinician must estimate the frequency with which the phenomena observed in his patient are produced by various diseases, when grouped as they are in the particular patient at the point in the course of the disease which appears to obtain. He must also estimate the degree to which such initial estimates must be modified by the absence of characteristics that *might* be present in the disorders under consideration but are not. And he must estimate how often the observations in the particular patient do *not* appear in the courses of the various disorders that may appear initially to enter the list of diagnostic possibilities. The patient's presenting syndrome and the clinical behavior of a number of candidate disorders are in this way examined for "fit."

Further complexity is introduced by the fact that even those clinical features of a disease that are found to be present are not equally important as diagnostic evidence and hence must be assigned weights in order to be valued appropriately. In the patient who presents with cough, bloody sputum, and fever, for example, shaking chills or a markedly elevated white blood cell count would be viewed as strong evidence suggesting pneumonia or lung abscess; headache, muscle pains, and loss of appetite would carry less weight, because of the frequency with which they appear in a variety of other acute illnesses. The ability to weight clinical phenomena reliably is a key element in the armamentarium of the diagnostician. Like the rest of the process, it is based on knowledge of the behavior of diseases, extended and enriched by the clinical experience of the physician. In fact, it is one of the key contributions of experience to expertise.

On the basis of estimates such as these and the interplay among them, an array of diagnostic possibilities and a rank ordering of their likelihoods can usually be constructed. Other clinical features that might refine the diagnostic probabilities can then be sought through the testing procedures of the diagnostic workup and through observation of the course of the disease until uncertainty concerning the identity of the underlying process has been minimized to the extent possible. During the management of the disease the physician is likely to repeat this process, to a greater or lesser degree, as new clinical facts appear, derived from the natural course of the disease, responses to therapeutic maneuvers, epidemiologic data, or other sources.

Additional uncertainties are introduced when more than one disease is present. This situation is becoming increasingly common, as the population ages and as improved treatment allows more diseases to be managed over long periods. Complexities are added not only by the need to assign clinical data to the various disorders present, but also by the need to evaluate the degree, if any, to which simultaneously occurring diseases are mutually affecting clinical presentation, course, or therapeutic responsiveness.

Other factors may also add complexity to the diagnostic process. For example, difficulty in obtaining a clear clinical history (due to language barrier, mental dullness, or other factors), prior therapy, or nonexistence of confirmatory diagnostic tests for a particular disease may all prevent the acquisition of crucial data and force the diagnostic process to a halt at a greater level of uncertainty than would otherwise obtain.

Diagnostic uncertainty has its roots in incomplete knowledge not only of the disorders of biological processes that underlie, but also of the array of diseases that may express themselves. Thus, "new" diseases continue to be identified and their clinical features and courses described. In recent years, for example, Lyme disease, acquired immunodeficiency syndrome (AIDS), Legionnaires' disease, and lactase deficiency (a diarrheal disorder due to deficiency of an intestinal enzyme) have all been newly identified. The amount of diagnostic confusion caused by thus far undescribed disorders can only be guessed at but is doubtless substantial.

Another factor leading to diagnostic uncertainty relates to the limitations generally present in test procedures. Every diagnostic test is characterized by some degree of inherent error, as are all the other data-gathering procedures used, including the medical history and the physical examination. In the case of diagnostic tests, a variety of measures have come into use as a result of efforts to quantify their reliability and usefulness. These measures include *sensitivity* (the proportion of those with the disease who have a positive test), *specificity* (the proportion of those without the disease who have a negative test), *predictive values* (the proportion of positive tests that are true positives and the proportion of negative tests that are true negatives), and estimates of the pre- and posttest probabilities of the presence of the disease. Some idea of clinically acceptable ranges may be gleaned from the fact that, for the chest x-ray, sensitivity ranges from 58 to 75 percent and specificity from 97 to 98.7 percent, in studies of a variety of disorders.[2]

The tentativeness inherent in the clinical transaction can thus be seen to be not only pervasive, but dominant; that is, it shapes and drives the entire process, and the diagnostic process in turn operates so as to deal with it. The clinician must be satisfied with explanations that satisfy to a reasonable degree the data he has; absolute proof is not commonly available.

Nonetheless, clinicians are able to function, and for the most part fairly effectively, by approaching and managing clinical data in a probabilistic, reductionist manner. Data are assembled from the medical history, the physical examination, various ancillary tests and procedures, and observation of the course of the disease. The data are accumulated, sorted, and placed, in the mind of the physician, into various patterns or combinations. Sometimes, recognition of a characteristic pattern may narrow the diagnostic possibilities fairly promptly to one or two leading candidate disorders. Under other circumstances the pattern that emerges may be considerably less specific and permit only broad categorical diagnostic estimates to be made, such as infection, or malignancy, or metabolic disorder. In such a case, considerably more clinically relevant information may be required before patterns suggesting specific diagnostic probabilities emerge. With enough data a probability of considerable likelihood can usually be selected—one that best explains the facts assembled. At this point the clinician considers that, with a reasonable degree of confidence, the disorder has been identified, and a therapeutic plan can be constructed.

Arranging clinical data in meaningful clusters in a search for patterns suggestive of particular disorders and pattern recognition itself are complex processes based on knowledge of variations within the normal range and of the behavior of diseases. Since the knowledge base of medicine is in a constant state of flux—involving expansion, revision, and the discarding of disproven or outmoded concepts or techniques—the facility with which the clinician carries on his activities depends on familiarity with the state of his field. It depends also, as noted above, on clinical experience, which enhances knowledge of variability in disease manifestations and permits realistic weights to be assigned to clinical data.

In outlining the diagnostic process in this fashion, my intention is to offer it as a paradigm of clinical activity. Similar trains of reductionist logic as a technique for minimizing uncertainty apply also to the design of the technologic diagnostic workup itself, the reasoning that leads to therapeutic decisions, and to estimates of prognosis. In all these fundamental clinical activities, as the outcome of these systems, techniques and processes, confidence is often possible, even precision (of method), but certainty is not.

The uncertainties and approximations of the clinical process result in a number of tensions in the management of illness and disease.[3]

To a considerable extent, clinical uncertainty stems from ignorance concerning basic disease mechanisms at the cellular or molecular level. Clinical activity achieves increased precision in relation to the detail of its information base. For example, appreciation of specific enzyme activity and the ability to identify reduction or absence of that activity in galactosemia, or glucose 6-phosphate dehydrogenase deficiency, allows the physician to recognize and prevent or at least manage the resultant disease with greatly enhanced clarity and effectiveness. In this manner, clinical medicine and basic and clinical research are intimately connected. The aggregate uncertainty of the entire field is reduced at the rate and to the extent that such research, oriented around clinical problems, is successfully pursued.

A second tension is generated by the central fact that clinical medicine is concerned with *human* illness and disease. This fact imposes constraints on the application of the technology, including time constraints. There is often pressure to take therapeutic steps despite residual diagnostic uncertainties. The wry comment cited at the beginning of this essay, concerning adequate decisions based on inadequate information, reflects in part the clinician's urgent need to act in his patient's behalf. Thus, the degree of uncertainty that must be accepted is a function of both the adequacy of the relevant knowledge base and the derivative technology, and also of the urgency of the clinical situation. The core nature of medicine—the nexus of the bioscience base and human need—is illuminated by this quandary.

That uncertainties must be accepted in clinical care has important implications elsewhere in the medical enterprise. In teaching, for example, the tentativity of clinical decisions must be identified and explored. Paradoxically, the uncertainties of clinical care, as well as those of physiological and biochemical theory, become more apparent as the knowledge base of the student increases. Faculty must be meticulous in identifying the knowledge gaps that pervade medicine, in explaining the scientific method, and in transmitting techniques of critical, quantitative thinking for application to research issues and to clinical problem solving. Clarity in framing the questions and intellectual rigor in approaching them are the key tools in managing medical uncertainty. Teaching these needs and techniques is a formidable task; learning them is an ongoing requirement for the physician, a requirement to which he is introduced during formal medical education and which he must continue to meet throughout his professionally active life. Intellectual maturity in medicine is measured by the degree to which the uncertainty of clinical decision making is managed through isolating the relevant questions and applying sequential, adaptive logic to resolve them to the extent possible, and by the effectiveness of this process, as measured in clinical terms. Medical education itself has in fact been characterized as training for uncertainty.[4]

At the level of clinical care, recent developments in technology have raised new and painful kinds of uncertainty, which the physician must confront. New life-support systems of ventilatory, cardiovascular, and metabolic support have, in many cases, made even the diagnosis of death a tentative one. Initiation or termination of such treatments often requires complex judgments. Decisions embrace difficult quality-of-life questions, the views of the patient and his family, prognostic estimates, and cost considerations. They impose especially difficult kinds of uncertainty on the physician both because of the inadequacy of the relevant data base, especially in relation to prognostication, and because such questions have strong ethical overtones that defy ready solution. These issues underline the complex interplay among technical decisions, social forces, and the human factors that dominate clinical care. A new clinical/ethical literature has arisen in response to the dilemmas produced by recent technological developments,[5] and the courts have also begun to address these dilemmas. The physician must synthesize and coordinate all the factors operating in any given case so as to act in terms of the patient's welfare. Nonetheless, the decision as to which is being prolonged—living or dying—is often a difficult one, calling for wisdom and compassion of a high order.

In recent years there has been gathering a growing public awareness of both the complexity and the uncertainty intrinsic to clinical medicine. The effects of personal and family experience with major illness, hospitalization, and critical and terminal care, and of widespread interaction with a health system that has become increasingly technology intensive, have been reinforced by mass media attention to medical care. Thus, the public debate surrounding the swine-flu immunization program of a few years ago, and the appearance of cases of Guillain-Barré syndrome among vaccine recipients, focused attention in a particularly graphic way on medical uncertainty, not only at the clinical level, but also at the level of public health policy. The fact that the Guillain-Barré cases clearly represented an unexpected, stochastic event, even to top-level medical scientists and planners, shocked many and appeared to shake public confidence.

Newspaper and television coverage of implantation of mechanical hearts in several patients has produced a perhaps unprecedented degree of public immersion in dramatic technological innovation. Organ transplantation programs, oncogene research, dialysis for end-stage kidney disease, publication of laboratory precautions imposed by the National Institutes of Health upon those doing recombinant DNA research and of concerns regarding the possible escape into the environment of "new" microorganisms developed through recombinant techniques, and extensive media coverage of the questions involved in terminal care—all have served to further heighten public awareness not only of the increased capacities and widening science base of modern medicine, but also of the uncertainties they have brought with them. In part as a result of this expanded public sophistication, medical care itself has become much more horizontal, with the physician assuming a less authoritative, *ex cathedra* stance, and the patient and his family accepting—in fact, requiring—more responsibility in clinical decisions.

Thus, the concerns of the individual patient reflect a broader concern throughout a society that has become increasingly informed about medical matters and that, in the process, has become uncomfortably aware of some of the limitations inherent in medicine, in bioscience, and, as Renée Fox has pointed out, in the probabilistic nature of medical logic and medical thinking about uncertainty, benefit, and risk.[6] Plainly, our society has yet to come fully to terms with these new realizations, and it must digest them along with broader social, political, and global uncertainties that appear to be contributing to, if not generating, a rather pervasive unease. At the same time some understanding of these uncertainties must result in a maturing of attitudes among the constituencies of medicine, especially the patient population, toward the nature of the clinical enterprise and, one hopes, some increased sympathy for its incompleteness and its strivings.

The impossibility of certainty in medicine has shaped systems of clinical care, education, and biomedical research as we know them, and has in this way been extraordinarily productive. Medicine functions not only despite the intrinsic uncertainties that characterize it, but, in a profound sense, because of them. The same may perhaps be said of much of human enterprise; medicine is thus not unique in this regard.

What of the future? What kinds of developments might emerge from our present base of uncertainty? Clearly, continued efforts to validate more firmly the concepts, processes, and procedures of medicine must be the central response. Research and technological innovation are fueled by curiosity and personal drive, by institutional agendas and by benevolence, but they are driven by uncertainty, by the palpable incompleteness of the intellectual and procedural basis of medicine, and by the pervasive sense of pressure generated by that deficit. The mutability of fact and theory have become axiomatic in medicine in the years since biomedical research began to demonstrate its power; paradoxically, change has become the only constant in medicine. Thus, the idea of progress is central as we assault the roots of our uncertainty; the process of building on the insights of the past is based on confidence in progress as the ultimate necessity. Nisbet has said, "the idea of progress holds that mankind has advanced in the past—from some aboriginal condition of primitiveness, barbarism, or even nullity—is now advancing, and will continue to advance through the foreseeable future." He notes two related but distinguishable concepts of progress: first, that of a "slow, gradual and cumulative improvement in *knowledge*," and second, a concept of progress centering "upon man's moral or spiritual condition on earth, his happiness, his freedom from torments of nature and society, and above all his serenity or tranquility."[7] These two concepts, it can be argued, meet in the idea of *medical* progress, in the uncertainty-driven effort to know and thereby to achieve medicine's ambition—that of joining knowledge and insight, compassion and techniques, in the service of human needs.

Notes

1. A. R. Feinstein, *Clinical Judgment*, Williams and Wilkins, Baltimore, 1967, pp. 72–88.

2. M. F. Roizen, in "Routine Preoperative Examination," in R. D. Miller (ed.), *Anesthesia*, Churchill Livingstone, New York, 1981.

3. The distinction between disease and illness is essentially the following: "disease" refers to biological aberration in structure and/or function at any level from the organ system down to the molecular, whereas "illness" is a subjective set of discomforts, fears, and psychosocial dislocations. Thus, disease is an objective phenomenon, but illness has strong subjective connotations, consisting of all that we mean when we say we are sick, including all the symptoms, concerns, and implications of that state.

4. R. Fox, "Training for Uncertainty," in R. K. Merton, G. G. Reader, and P. L. Kendall (eds.), *The Student Physician*, Harvard University Press, Cambridge, Mass., 1957, p. 207.

5. A. R. Jonsen, M. Siegler, and W. J. Winslade, *Clinical Ethics*, Macmillan, New York, 1982.

6. R. Fox, "The Evolution of Medical Uncertainty," *Milbank Memorial Fund Quarterly/Health and Society*, 58: 1 (1980).

7. R. Nisbet, *History of the Idea of Progress*, Basic Books, New York, 1980, pp. 4, 5.

IMPOSSIBILITIES IN CHEMISTRY: THEIR RISE, NATURE, AND SOME GREAT FALLS

This essay examines a number of chemistry impossibilities, illustrates them with examples, and seeks to catalog them.

Some impossibilities in chemistry stem directly from experimental findings. Such impossibilities remain in force as long as the supporting facts are valid—perhaps forever. Others rest on definitions, which once accepted are logically impregnable. Yet others may be only temporary impossibilities, although how long it may take before they become possible cannot be known. For such impossibilities, the optimists would change "Thou canst not" to "Thou canst, but it will take a little while."

Fundamentally, chemistry is an inductive science, spiced with insights and leaps of intuition. If a generalization develops, it will stand or fall depending on its interpretive and predictive power and on the support it receives from experiment. Some statements of the impossible are so inextricably enmeshed in a web of supporting experiments as to be regarded as inviolable. On the basis of such generalizations, trusted and at times stately deductive edifices have been erected. But, even here, there always remains a twinge of reservation.

Will tomorrow bring new data that will be readily accommodated by the established belief, or will a new fact be like David's stone—small, but big enough to bring down mighty Goliath?

Indeed, there are impossibilities in chemistry that were accepted at one time as truths but that have been either significantly changed or toppled and abandoned. Prohibitions once regarded as gospel have become nothing more than interesting paragraphs in the history of chemistry. Several examples of such erstwhile impossibilities are also included here.

The degree of faith in different impossibilities varies widely, ranging from weak reliance to hard-core, total acceptance. However, little attempt is made to draw a sharp line between impossibilities that might soften and yield and those whose overthrow would be in the realm of science fiction.

We start with three special kinds of impossibilities.

Factual, Time-Dependent, and Logical Impossibilities

Some impossibilities in chemistry are tantamount to statements of fact. To assert the opposite would be a flat contradiction of verifiable truth.

The following examples will illustrate this category.

- To warm an open block of copper and observe that its volume becomes smaller is impossible.

- When pure ice melts under ordinary pressures, its temperature cannot be anything but 32°F (0°C).

- If water leaks into the gasoline tank of a lawnmower left out in the rain, the water will sink to the bottom of the tank and the gasoline will layer out on top. To find the water above the gasoline is impossible.

- It is impossible to avoid some uncertainty in any measurement. Even counting items one at a time is subject to error.

- A candle cannot burn for long in a small airtight space.

- The presence of any element in pure water other than hydrogen and oxygen is excluded.

- If two gases are placed in contact, they will soon intermingle. It is not possible that they remain apart.

Thousands of statements of this type may be found in chemistry libraries. Such peremptory declarations summarize the results of repeated experience. Most involve what can be termed "properties." The last example, dealing with the mixing of gases, is not only a summary statement of experimental findings, but also the result of a rigorous probability analysis, which shows that although there is a chance that the gases will fail to mix, the probability is so minute as to be essentially zero. The reliability of this class of impossibility is high.

Another kind of chemistry impossibility is the "not yet" variety, which refers to recognized goals that have as yet not been reached. In many cases, there will be a body of scientific opinion holding that the barrier between the goal and its realization is not insurmountable. For these, an optimistic note is in the air, a feeling that the impossible is but temporary.

Let us consider some illustrations:

- Converting graphite (a form of carbon) to megacarat, gem-quality diamond is impossible.

- Neither chemotherapy nor molecular biology will develop a cure for cancer.

- Generating energy in a controlled, practical way from a terrestrial nuclear fusion process will never be accomplished.

- A nonmetallic plastic that in ordinary usage is able to conduct electricity as easily as copper will never be developed.

- No totally safe place for the long-term storage of harmful chemical wastes will ever be found.

- Given the complexity of the chemistry and physics of the brain, it is impossible to develop an artificial intelligence with superior wide-ranging capability.

- An equivalent or a better substitute for chromium in the manufacture of stainless steel is not known and will never be found.

- Finding a liquid that under ordinary conditions will smoothly dissolve platinum, Teflon, and gasoline is out of the question.

Confidence in the future of these different impossibilities will vary widely. In all likelihood chemists would turn in a spectrum of opinions. Most might show decreasing optimism as the list is read from top to bottom. Nonetheless, any of these impossibilities could emerge as possible tomorrow; they are all time dependent.

A third variety of impossibility is absolute, since violation of such impossibilities would involve a logical contradiction.

- If a solid is regarded as an object that holds its shape in or out of its container, then wine poured at the dinner table cannot be characterized as a solid.

- It is impossible to study chemistry without considering matter and energy.

- If hydrochloric acid is classed as "dilute" if it contains no more than 10 percent acid, then it is impossible to consider 20 percent hydrochloric acid as dilute.

These examples are based on definitions, and once a definition is accepted, there is no way to refute it. Although included here somewhat lightheartedly, these examples do serve to comfort; they have the rare virtue of total truth.

Trusted Impossibilities

Some impossibility generalizations in chemistry are so firmly established as to be regarded as unassailable truths—as scientific scripture not subject to question. While these "laws" are still dependent on experimental results, they are so solidly grounded that the burden of validation is shifted from the generalization to the fact. That is, if a fresh piece of information clashes with the law, the new datum is suspect rather than the generalization it disagrees with. There would be a strong presumption that the new result is in error.

But what if the new datum is confirmed as correct? What if checking, double-checking, and rechecking always give the same result? In this case, the old "truth" finds itself authentically contradicted; the established law becomes threatened by a stubborn fact. The aftermath of such a development could be far from tranquil. One school of chemists clings to the old law; they choose to disregard or reject the disturbing datum, relegating it to the category of "anomalous exception." Other chemists, admitting the difficulty in accommodating the new result in the old law, seek to revise the law or, if this proves unsatisfactory, are driven to discard it altogether and search for a better one. Such change is turbulent and painful. Chemists feel lost without old faithful, their security blanket. They are cast adrift on an uncharted sea of facts with no means of finding their way. Decades of thinking and thousands of interpretations must be critically reviewed and reevaluated.

But then, as Thomas Kuhn has pointed out, sooner or later a new paradigmatic law emerges, consistent with *all* data and presumably more comprehensive than its predecessor. The interregnum is stressful, but eventually order prevails again.

Later in this chapter there are accounts of several such revolutionary changes. But for now let us focus on the rocklike reliables, standing proud and showing no signs of erosion.

Four such impossibility generalizations have been selected for review. They deal, respectively, with the discontinuity of energy, the persistence of matter, the immortality of energy, and last but not least, with a very special property of energy.

• • •

Around 1900, Max Planck, Albert Einstein, and Niels Bohr, all subsequent Nobel prize winners, advanced the striking idea that energy in radiation (ultraviolet, visible, etc.) is not continuous but comes in discrete units. Energy as a continuous stream is impossible; it is more like a line of speeding bullets from a machine gun. Radiant energy can be transferred, but only in integral numbers of these unit packages, or quanta.

Further, the energy content in matter cannot increase or decrease smoothly but only in steps. Matter acts to absorb energy by raising its energy state from an assigned lower energy slot to a preexisting higher energy slot. In the absorption of radiant energy by a molecule (or an atom), only when there is a match between the package of radiant energy delivered and the difference in fixed energy levels in the molecule can the energy be transferred. If the radiation quantum presented is too small or too big, the radiant energy will be rejected; absorption of energy will not be possible.[1]

Conversely, when a molecule gives up some of its energy in the form of radiant energy, the parcel of radiant energy that leaves must correspond in size to the decrease in the energy content of the molecule as it falls from a fixed higher energy state to a fixed lower energy state.

Considering the wealth of observations successfully interpreted and predicted on the basis of these discontinuity principles, scientists generally regard the principles not so much as man-made but rather as nature's law. Any interpretation or any new theory that violates this gospel is ruled out as ipso facto impossible. Nevertheless, the discontinuity principles draw their validation from facts, and consequently, the impact of new evidence cannot be lost sight of. Perhaps, one day, even the theories of Planck, Einstein, and Bohr will have to be supplanted.

Two other trustworthy sweeping generalizations have long been accepted as cornerstones in science. These are the two conservation laws—the law of conservation of mass and the law of conservation of energy. The laws have served science, especially chemistry, faithfully for many years and, with but one very significant modification (see p. 84), still do. As long as the nature of the experiment permits this modification to be disregarded—a proviso that is satisfied more often than not—it is impossible to realize a process that fails to conform to the conservation laws. Violating the laws is not possible.

The mass conservation law states that matter can be transformed in many ways but, no matter what the change, the amount of matter—the mass—remains the same. A corollary is that it is impossible to produce matter de novo or to reduce matter to nothing. Matter can be manipulated, but the total amount of matter in the universe is fixed. The following exemplify the kinds of changes governed by the original mass law:

- ice melting to water
- glass smashed to smithereens
- a diamond transported from the bottom of the ocean to the surface of the moon
- hydrogen and oxygen combining to form water
- sugar fermenting to alcohol and carbon dioxide
- salt before and after it dissolves in water
- gasoline burning with oxygen to form water and carbon dioxide

In each case, careful mass measurements before and after the change would show no difference. There is so much trust in the mass conservation law that an experimental result of this type that does not conform is automatically treated as false and rejected. Prospective studies that seek to circumvent the law would be regarded as unsound.

An equivalent statement of the law emerged when Dalton postulated that matter was composed of atoms (see p. 85) and that atoms were unchangeable entities, the same yesterday, today, and forever.

• • •

So far as the law of conservation of energy is concerned, nineteenth-century natural scientists realized that there must be something in the universe, which was called energy, that could be manipulated and that could take on different guises. They identified the several manifestations of energy, examined their properties, and studied their interconversions. The principle emerged, summarized by the energy conservation law (ca. 1850), that although energy forms can be changed, all have the same common denominator, so that the total amount of energy existing before and after any energy manipulation must be the same.

The following examples illustrate the kinds of everyday, familiar transformations governed by this conservation law.

- mechanical work (e.g., friction) producing heat energy
- electrical energy generating heat and light energy
- the conversion of the stored chemical energy in ingested food to movement
- the utilization of the stored energy in a burning log to produce heat, which is directed to making steam from water and thereby storing the energy in steam; the subsequent utilization of this energy to drive an engine (mechanical energy), which in turn raises a heavy load to the top of a hill (stored energy)
- solar energy absorbed by plants and converted in part to heat and in part to plant materials full of stored energy

Many more examples can be given; all would conform to the law of conservation of energy. For all changes of this kind, it is impossible to create or annihilate energy; the total supply of energy in the universe is fixed.

An alternative statement of the energy law is given by the first law of thermodynamics, a respected principle in chemistry. In essence it states that nature does not allow energy to be produced from nothing. (We can note in passing that the energy conservation law serves as a basis for considering perpetual motion machines as fantasy. You can't build a machine that puts out more energy than is required to run the machine.)

The two original conservation laws have served well in systematizing, interpreting, and guiding many kinds of experiments. We shall see later how the two laws were blended, but if for the time being we hold this in abeyance and deal with everyday chemistry phenomena, then it is true that no observation has ever been made that disproves the generalizations. Breaking these laws appears to be impossible.

• • •

In concluding this short survey of reliable possibilities and impossibilities in chemistry, we turn to an aspect of thermodynamics, a branch of science dealing with energy, its conversion, and especially its utilization. Of the three or four principles serving as the foundation for thermodynamics, we shall be concerned with one in particular, the second law of thermodynamics. This law bears on the conversion of thermal energy to other kinds of energy. Since thermal energy is involved to a major or minor extent in so many processes (possibly all), the second law may lay claim to an exceedingly wide jurisdiction. It was developed originally as the result of a rigorous analysis of the steam engine, in which the thermal energy of hot steam is converted to mechanical energy. The second law says that this kind of directed energy utilization cannot be accomplished with 100 percent efficiency. Unfailingly, a portion of the heat employed (or developed during the process, e.g., by friction) will persist as heat and so be diverted from the desired conversion.

The second law defines a theoretical efficiency, which is the maximum fraction of starting thermal energy that can be captured for useful work. Exceeding this limit is impossible; some of the energy will always remain as heat instead of undergoing the complete desired conversion. If energy were toothpaste, the first law would say that you can't get more toothpaste out of a tube than was in the tube to start with. The second law goes further and would say that you shouldn't expect to squeeze *all* the toothpaste out; some will always stay in the tube. A perceptive chemist puts it this way: If the first law of thermodynamics says, "You can't win," the second law says, "You can't even break even."

Even worse, the theoretical maximum efficiency itself can never be reached. Practical energy-conversion devices strive to approach the maximum but they never get there. An important aspect of the work of energy engineers is to bring the actual efficiency as close as possible to the theoretical maximum.

The following illustrations should help the reader appreciate this kind of second law impossibility.

Gasoline Utilization.   Second law estimates, based on routine operation, show that it is impossible to harvest much more than two-thirds of the stored chemical energy in gasoline for the purpose of moving an automobile. The actual realized efficiency could be considerably smaller—on the order of 20 to 30 percent. Most of the chemical stored energy in the gasoline and oxygen is wasted as heat.

Humpty Dumpty.   A cyclic process—one in which all material changes as well as all energy conversions are reversed, so that there is a return to the initial state—is impossible. The second law precludes total restoration of any change. Every step would involve some kind of directed energy utilization, so inevitably there would be an energy diversion. The final stage in the restoration would find more "low-grade" heat energy present in the universe than there was before the change. There is no way to get around this energy leakage.

Mother Goose must have had the second law in mind when she wrote:

> *Humpty Dumpty sat on a wall,*
> *Humpty Dumpty had a great fall;*
> *All the king's horses and all the king's men*
> *Couldn't put Humpty back together again.*

A Firecracker Restored.   When a firecracker explodes, its stored chemical energy is thrown off as heat, light, sound, and motion. To reconstruct the original firecracker, together with a totally unchanged environment, is not possible. The environment would always be left warmer as the result of the sidetracked, wasted heat energy. The alert second law would not allow complete reversal of the process. You can't deexplode a firecracker.

Perpetual Motion.   As discussed, the first law of thermodynamics precludes any kind of perpetual motion machine that performs in a cycle of operations and that manufactures energy out of thin air.

The second law of thermodynamics excludes a perpetual motion machine with a more modest goal, that of producing only enough energy to keep itself running. Where heat energy is the starting point, inevitably some of the energy would persist as heat. If the input energy is different from heat, some heat will be developed as each step in the cycle is passed. Sooner or later these parcels of heat will warm the machine as well as the surroundings. This constitutes a drain in the energy required to maintain the operation; eventually the machine will run down.

New kinds of perpetual motion machines of this type appear at intervals. Science, with the backing of the second law, regards all such inventions with deserved skepticism.

Butter Recreated. Swallowing a pat of butter starts it on a long metabolic journey, during which it is changed to many derived substances. Eventually, oxygen enters the picture, and the final products leave as carbon dioxide and water. At various places along this chain of events, the original stored chemical energy in the butter is transformed to other forms of energy—mechanical, electrical, chemical, and heat. The second law makes it impossible to regenerate the butter from the carbon dioxide and water and to restore everything in the environment to the state it was in originally. This is another Humpty Dumpty situation. Much more energy would be required for the reconstruction than could be harvested from the metabolism, with the extra energy ending up by warming the environment.

Since, in one way or another, so many changes involve transforming thermal energy to nonthermal energy, there is no end to the number of relevant examples that can be cited. All will be under the control of the second law. The great faith placed in this law is well deserved. Perhaps the second law impossibilities will last forever.

Paradigms Lost

At different periods, various impossibility generalizations reigned supreme, serving chemistry and the other sciences as guiding truths, or in Thomas Kuhn's terminology, as paradigms. Then, reliable experimental results emerged that could not be reconciled with the prevailing wisdom. The paradigm found itself challenged by facts, and then by more facts or by a fresh theory. Gradually—sometimes with much sound and fury—the old generalization would fall into disrepute, lose its adherents, and be abandoned in favor of something new and better.

What follows are accounts of five fallen "truths," once regarded as sacrosanct but now remembered as lessons in humility. Specifically, we shall look at a remarkable substance called phlogiston, at the weakening and death of Vital Force, at how the conservation laws had to be modified, how Dalton's immutable atoms became mutable, and how inert gases showed signs of life.

Phlogiston, or What Happens in Burning?

An early theory of burning proposed that anything that burns must contain an entity called phlogiston. Burning was explained as the release of phlogiston from the combustible material to the air. Air is essential, since it had to provide a home for the released phlogiston. There is a limit to the phlogiston transfer, since a given volume of air can absorb only so much phlogiston. When the air becomes saturated, no additional amounts of phlogiston can leave the combustible and the burning must stop. Burning also stops when the combustible is emptied of all its phlogiston. So went the theory.

Phlogiston was a queer substance, hard to pin down. Nobody had ever isolated it and experimentally determined its properties. At times it showed a *negative* weight: the residue left after burning weighed *more* than the material before burning. This was true, for example, when magnesium burned. Sometimes phlogiston showed a positive weight: When, for example, wood burned, the ash weighed *less* than the starting material. And since so little residue was left when alcohol, kerosene, or high-grade coal burned, these obviously different materials were concluded to be pure or nearly pure phlogiston. Some imaginative, even mysterious, properties had to be ascribed to phlogiston.

Antoine Lavoisier, on the basis of elegant experimentation, was led to propose a different theory of burning, one that required a constituent of air—later shown to be oxygen—for combustion. The crux of the new theory was that burning occurs by a combination of the fuel with atmospheric oxygen. Since the weight of oxygen is always added, the weight of the combustion products, including the evolved gases, will always be greater than the weight of the starting fuel.

Lavoisier's interpretation was more reasonable and straightforward than that of the phlogistonists. Phlogiston, always clumsy, became suspect, and eventually fell into scientific disrepute. The phlogiston possibilities and impossibilities, suitably reinterpreted, were neatly taken over by the new ideas.

Interestingly, the phlogiston theory *is* self-consistent. But reliance on phlogiston leads to awkward explanations. Scientific empiricism and pragmatism eventually made it inviting to declare loyalty to the new paradigm and difficult, even embarrassing, to cling to the old.

Death of Vital Force

In the eighteenth century natural philosophers held that it was impossible to produce substances in the laboratory identical with those isolated from animals or plants. No material made by any living system could be synthesized by combining inanimate chemicals in a lifeless container. What made the artificial synthesis of such life-products impossible was the absence of a "Vital Force," an enabling factor present in living but not inanimate objects. Any material isolated from a living source, and therefore put together with the help of the Vital Force, was called organic, that is, derived from a living organ.

So long as no organic substance was prepared in the laboratory, the vitalism theory stood unchallenged. But one day in 1828, Frederick Wöhler realized the impossible. Starting with two materials he could legitimately consider nonorganic, and utilizing only routine laboratory equipment, he produced urea, a substance hitherto known only as an organic product. Other examples followed. Vital Force, with its explicit statement of the impossible, was on the way to being discarded, crowded out by brute facts. Today, of course, anything from fermentation alcohol to mold penicillin—and so *very* much more—can be synthesized from lifeless chemicals in glass equipment. Vitalism is of historical interest only.

Einstein and the Conservation Laws

The conservation laws of energy and of mass stood for many years as unshakeable pillars of chemistry. Both laws were confirmed many times; both successfully guided experiment and theory. They appeared unassailable.

It was Albert Einstein who, in the early years of this century, had the temerity to tamper with the laws. Einstein postulated that the realms of energy and of matter were not sealed off from each other. Energy could be generated from matter, and matter from energy. His equivalence relation places the proposal on a quantitative basis—

$$E = mc^2$$

or

$$\text{Energy} = \text{mass} \times \text{speed of light} \times \text{speed of light}$$

Einstein reformulated the two laws by combining them into one; that is, the summed amount of matter *plus* energy in the universe is fixed. There *can* be an increase in the energy form, but only at the expense of some matter, which disappears. There *can* be an increase in the amount of matter in the universe, but then there would be less energy. In fact, whatever essential difference there might be between matter and energy becomes fuzzy and blurred. According to Einstein, matter and energy are simply alternate ways of describing the same entity.

Einstein's postulate was fully substantiated when the era of nuclear changes arrived. Matter-to-energy conversion is now accepted as the mechanism for the vast, continuous outpouring of energy from the stars. It is also the basis for the controlled production of energy in nuclear power plants, for the uncontrolled release of kinetic and radiant energy in atomic explosions, and for the annihilation process, whereby matter and antimatter come together and vanish in a burst of energy.

Practically speaking, the separate conservation laws are still useful. In everyday, nonnuclear transformations of matter, not enough energy is involved to significantly alter the amount of matter in the universe. In accordance with Einstein's equation, there is change, but it is too small to be concerned with. And in routine energy manipulations, such trivial amounts of matter are obliterated or created as to leave the balance on the energy side of the ledger essentially undisturbed. Thus, for most purposes, the impossibilities dictated by the separate conservation laws stand unchanged.

Today, the old conservation laws are taught as such, but the Einstein caveat always accompanies the presentation. Like the Dalton atom, discussed in the next section, the two conservation laws are far from being euthanasia cases; rather, they are like two great corporations that have come under the same management.

Dalton's Immutable Atoms Became Mutable

In the early 1800s, John Dalton, building on the work and ideas of many, advanced his notion of the nature of ultimate matter, the atom. Dalton asserted that atoms are indivisible, that they constitute the smallest possible piece of any element and therefore of any material. He maintained that atoms of different kinds of matter are different but that all atoms of the same element are identical in every respect. Moreover, although an atom may be inserted here and removed there, it will never lose its identity, regardless of the form or combination in which it appears. Atoms cannot be created or destroyed; they were born before time, they are immutable, and they live to eternity.[2]

The Daltonian atom proved useful for interpretation as well as prediction. It lasted with but little modification for almost a century. During this time it brought a new degree of order to chemical theory and practice. Violating Dalton's dicta did nothing but introduce confusion and, in fact, became a scientific high crime.

As useful as Dalton's model was, it began to show tiny and then bigger cracks. Eventually, all of his impossibilities became possible and his rigid prohibitions had to be relaxed.

First, in 1897, came the discovery that atoms could be induced to extrude electrons, which were shown by J. J. Thomson to be particles of matter, far lighter than any atom and electrically negatively charged. Thus it became necessary to abandon Dalton's indivisibility postulate. The conclusion was forced that atoms were composite and could be broken apart. They must contain at least two species of matter, one of which is the electron.

Another step in the direction of revealing a structured atom was taken by Ernest Rutherford in the early 1900s. Rutherford's experiments led him to propose a nucleated atom, in which a very tiny, heavy, positively charged center (the nucleus) is surrounded by a voluminous swarm of lightweight electrons. His model is still accepted as correct.

Almost concurrently, Henri Becquerel and then (preeminently) Marie and Pierre Curie reported their work on radioactivity. They found that the elements uranium, polonium, and radium give off penetrating rays, one variety of which was later shown to be electrically charged atoms of the element helium. Then another hitherto undiscovered element was found among the products from radium. The new element was named "radon." An incomplete summary statement could now be given as:

radium	gives rise to	helium	plus	radon
(element variety A)		(element variety B)		(element variety C)

But this process describes the transformation of one element, radium, into two different elements, helium and radon, a transformation that Dalton held was impossible.

Follow-up investigations showed that this was by no means a unique example. Some elements, such as the original three, disintegrate spontaneously into different elements. Later it was shown that with the proper tools and techniques, practically any element can be transformed into one or more different atoms. Another of Dalton's postulates—the persistence of atomic types—had to be abandoned.[3]

Dalton's model of the atom suffered yet another blow at the hands of F. W. Aston, who developed a method for measuring the masses of individual atoms. Aston discovered that the element neon is composed of atoms that do *not* all have the same mass, a finding in direct conflict with Dalton's postulate of total similarity. Later work showed that naturally occurring samples of all elements are made up of atoms with two or more different masses.

In short, the Dalton picture of the atom had been shredded:

- Atoms, instead of being blobs, show features and parts. Atomic dissection has not ended even today. High-energy physicists are still uncovering new, ever more intricate details.

- Atoms are *not* eternal and indestructible. They can be torn apart, and they can be transformed into other kinds of atoms.

- Atoms of a given element are *not* all identical in every respect.

Through the years, new techniques and new facts emerged, requiring modification in Dalton's original description. As each impossibility was shown to be possible, the change was incorporated in an improved model. Interestingly, the old model has not been discarded—it has enough truth in it to survive. So long as the original model is not pushed outside the boundaries of Dalton's set of facts, it remains valid. Within these limits, Dalton's impossibilities, taken with a scientific grain of salt, are as useful today as they were in the nineteenth century.

Inert Gases Show Signs of Life

In 1894, William Ramsay and Lord Rayleigh announced the discovery of a new gas in the atmosphere. They called the gas "argon." Occurring in low concentrations, it had escaped detection for many years. Shortly thereafter another new gas, helium, was discovered. Study of solar light had already produced evidence for the presence of this very same gas in the sun. Continued research uncovered other new gases—krypton, neon, xenon, and lastly, radon.

These gases, newcomers to the known forms of matter, have characteristics suggesting that they are all close relatives, belonging to the same family of elements. For example, all were found to be atomically antisocial in the extreme, refusing to link with *any* form of matter. The members of this new family were known variously as rare gases, noble gases, or inert gases. The behavior of inert gases led to the generalization that they are inherently unable to bind to other atoms. This generalization, at first based on experiments but soon provided with theoretical underpinnings, was presented as chemical truth to several generations of chemistry students.

Then, in 1962, Neil Bartlett, a Canadian chemist, succeeded in building a compound in which xenon was joined with platinum and fluorine. An inert gas had been captured in a compound. Soon other combinations appeared. Now there is a small but respectable corner of chemistry dealing with chemical combinations of the noble gases. Yesterday's "impossible" lasted only until the right experiment was performed.

The "noble" gases have bent a little; "inert" gas is now a misnomer.

Coda

This chapter has surveyed impossibilities in chemistry, identifying, organizing, and presenting the various kinds and the several degrees of impossibilities. Even cursory reflection will show that a common thread running through most of the varieties is the dominance of verifiable fact. Although liberally laced with theories, chemistry remains basically an inductive science, in which the highest court of appeal for prohibitions and permissions is experiment.

Notes

1. The aforementioned incremental increase in energy involves elevating electrons from lower to higher energy level. The energy supplied comes from radiation quanta carrying energy parcels

smaller than that required to eject the electron altogether; that is, the process pertains to *nonionizing* radiation. Where an electron is actually expelled and finds itself far from its home base, the energy slots available to it fall so close together as effectively to constitute a continuum. This situation has some analogy in metallic conductors as well as in semiconductors, where there are so many available energy levels coming so close together that they blend into a band. The result is that a range of virtually continuous energy values can be accepted by the solid instead of only discrete energy quanta.

2. Interestingly, this permanence proviso is consistent with and serves well in interpreting the mass law (see p. 78).

3. Centuries before, alchemists had searched for the "philosophers' stone," which was supposed to serve as a kind of magic wand by which cheap elemental metals, such as iron, could be turned into elemental gold. The alchemists failed to find what they were seeking. But now, with these transmutations of elements, they nodded and smiled in their graves—perhaps their dream was possible after all.

LIMITS AND INADEQUACIES IN ARTIFICIAL INTELLIGENCE

The electronic computer, as currently used, is a useful and powerful tool, but it is certainly no match for a human mind. A computer can solve a great variety of problems, but only if a human has given it a program—that is, a painstaking, step-by-step description of what it should do. It cannot parallel the richness of the human mind: the mind's understanding of the world around it, its creative power, and its capacity for learning. On the other hand, we understand computers and programs much better than we understand brains and minds. Computation theory is precise, exact, and well defined; psychology, though older and much more studied, tends to be vague, intuitive, and imprecise.

Artificial intelligence (AI) is an attempt to bring computer science and psychology closer together, based on the presumption that thinking is in some ways similar to computation. AI researchers have three objectives. First, we want to build computers and programs with humanlike mental capacities. Second, we wish to discover a precise theory of the human mind and to state it in computational terms. Finally, we wish to create a mathematical theory of intelligence, knowledge, and reasoning in general, of which both the intelligent computer and the human mind will be particular instances. These objectives may be called *technological, psychological,* and *theoretical,* respectively.

Clearly, these objectives are tremendously ambitious. Even if we ignore the supreme feats of the human mind, the accomplishments of Einstein or Bach or Shakespeare, and restrict our attention to the most mundane human activities, we face extremely difficult problems. Tasks like recognizing a scene, taking part in a conversation, handling food with utensils, or planning the activities of a day, all done almost effortlessly by any normal adult human, do not easily lend themselves to the kind of analysis used in developing computer programs. Progress in AI has accordingly been slow. No existing programs can do any of the tasks mentioned above except in very limited ways and this situation is not expected to change in the near future.

In fact, a number of thinkers—most notably, Hubert Dreyfus, John Searle, and Joseph Weizenbaum[1]—have argued that these objectives are impossible and that AI is intrinsically a hopeless activity. The gap between the neurophysiology of the brain and the semiconductor physics of the computer, it is argued, necessarily involves an equal gap between cognition and computation; there is no useful level of abstraction that describes both. Consciousness cannot be attributed to a machine that merely juggles symbols or electric potentials. The "successes" of AI to date are essentially superficial and misleading. "The brain is like a computer" is just an updated version of "the brain is like a telephone switchboard" and is destined for the same oblivion as a uselessly simplistic analogy. Other thinkers have argued that, on the contrary, computers potentially possess all the qualities of human minds and that it is literally accurate to speak of computers thinking, perceiving, or feeling.

But these arguments that AI is necessarily possible or impossible do not, in fact, affect the day-to-day work of the AI researcher. Such arguments are external to his[2] framework of thought, in the way that solipsistic doubt of the existence of the physical universe is external to the work of a physicist. They do not present him with anything constructive that he can incorporate into his theories or with any particulars that he can avoid. If the arguments against AI are correct, the only proper response is to go into some other line of work. If the arguments for it are correct, the only difference it makes is that he can sleep more comfortably.

My own feeling is that the a priori arguments on either side are irrelevant and unhelpful. These arguments generally address the "big question," "Can a computer think?", and its variants, "Can a computer feel real pain?" "Can a computer be conscious?" "Are mental acts the same as computations?" Careful study of such questions mainly reveals that one's ideas of thinking, pain, consciousness, and mental acts are rather vague. (Daniel Dennett has some interesting discussions of these issues.[3]) The real questions are "How similar to a human mind can we make our computer programs?" and "How useful are computational theories in providing languages for psychological theories?" These questions can only be answered by actual research, by trying to build the programs and develop the theories. If ultimately we fail to produce any very powerful programs or theories, we will probably be justified in saying that computers do not think. If we do succeed in producing complete programs and theories, our success will change what we mean when we speak of "thinking." For the forseeable future, though, we will be dealing with gradually improving partial successes—with theories and programs that account for or simulate a small but steadily growing part of human cognition. As long as this state obtains, the question "Is AI possible?" is unanswerable and probably pointless.

Impossibilities Within AI

The impossibilities that do concern AI are more limited. They are statements of inadequacy; they assert that a particular technique of carrying out a task cannot be made to work. You might think that you could write a program to translate from German to English simply by building in a German–English dictionary and rules for changing German sentence structure to English sentence structure. It cannot be done. As we will discuss below, the problem of ambiguous word meanings becomes overwhelming. You might think that you could build a program that would recognize known objects by matching the patterns of light and dark that it sees against those it remembers. This cannot be done; the patterns vary much too much under different conditions of viewing and lighting. You might think that you could build a chess-playing program that decided on a move by exploring all its possible consequences and seeing if it led to victory. You can write such a program, but the sun will have burnt out long before your program gives you any answer.

Impossibility statements like these do not apply merely to one particular kind of program or machine. Rather, they are built into the nature of the tasks themselves or into the nature of computation as a whole. It is an intrinsic fact about the nature of language and its variations that translation cannot be word for word. It is intrinsic to the game of chess that not all consequences of a chess move can be foreseen explicitly in reasonable time. These statements are part of the underlying theory of AI. We believe that they have the same scope of truth as mathematical statements; that they will hold necessarily for human minds, electronic computers, or any other intelligent system.

Impossibility statements do not emerge easily from the natural course of AI research. How does an AI researcher go about his job? First, he picks some particular task he wants his program to do—for instance, to recognize airplanes in aerial photographs, or to translate newspaper articles about the stock market, or to play GO and gradually improve with practice. Next, he thinks about the problem, and comes up with a technique that, he claims, will solve it. This is a statement of theory; it relates a certain kind of computation to a certain kind of problem. The researcher now moves on to the technological stage by implementing the technique in a computer program and running the program. If the program succeeds in carrying out the task, then he may have found a truth about possibility (though we will suggest some limitations on this below) but he certainly has not found out anything about impossibility. If the program fails, then has he proven that his technique is inadequate? Not at all. The program may have failed for any number of reasons. The program is almost always a much more complex and specific structure than the technique that it tests. Perhaps the researcher has a good underlying theory but has chosen a poor way to implement it as a program. Or, there may be large parts of the program that do not reflect on the theory at all but are purely ad hoc, and the flaw may lie in these. Finally, his program may simply be clogged with bugs of varying depths and significance; experimental AI programs tend to be large and to be written very quickly. Even with very careful analysis of the behavior of the program, it may be difficult to determine where the fault lies.

The failure of a single program therefore does not prove any impossibility result; at most it suggests one. In this respect it is very much like an unsuccessful experiment in natural science; one does not at first know whether the problem is in the theory or simply in the execution. Several different kinds of evidence are usually needed for real certainty that a technique is unworkable. We must in general have a history of program failures, an explanation of these failures in terms of the inadequacy of the technique, and, most important, a repertoire of disparate and important examples that can be shown by argument to be beyond the reach of the technique.

Somewhat surprisingly, a similar analysis is needed to determine that a technique *does* work. The mere fact that a program uses a technique and works does not prove that the technique is any good. The first problem is that AI programs almost never achieve an absolute and unequivocal success. They work for a few examples or a small class of examples. Thus, as we will explain below, getting a mechanical translation program to work on a large corpus of text involves "programming in" an enormous amount of knowledge about the world; and it is not currently known how to make this kind of knowledge available to a computer. So, if you have a good idea about how to do machine translation, you pick a very small class of texts about one particular subject—the stock market, say—and you program in the knowledge your program will need about that subject in a more or less ad hoc manner. However, if and when your program works, you cannot conclude that your translation technique is good in general. It may be that your technique is only good for stock market stories and that entirely different methods are needed for stories about Winnie-the-Pooh. Similar problems arise in practically every AI domain.

A second problem is that, just as the failure of a program cannot necessarily be attributed to the underlying technique, so also the success of a program. A program, particularly one that only works on a very small class of examples, may work by virtue of everything else it contains. The technique being tested may be irrelevant or even a hindrance to the program.

Acceptance of a technique, therefore, requires more or less the same conditions as rejection: a history of several successful programs that used it, a corpus of example where the technique can clearly be seen to work, and an argument that this range of examples is fairly general. Psychological evidence can also be very powerful in the acceptance of a theory. If it can be shown that people use a certain technique to solve a problem, then that is good evidence that the problem can be solved that way.

In short, theoretical knowledge in AI deals with the adequacy or inadequacy of different techniques as applied to different problems.

Problems are characterized by a corpus of important, typical examples. The most important evidence for or against a technique is simply an argument that it should or shouldn't work on examples of these types. Other kinds of evidence are also factored in: the experimental results of actual programs that use the techniques; psychological knowledge, formal and informal; and the mathematical constraints of computation theory.

A Classic Inadequate Theory

The best-known demonstration of an inadequate AI theory was the result of early attempts at machine translation. In the late 1950s and early 1960s a great deal of effort was put into creating programs that translated scientific texts. The idea was the one mentioned above: a program that translated from German to English could be built using an automated German–English dictionary, rules about the morphology of words, and rules about how to change German sentence structure to English sentence structure. For example, to translate the sentence "Ich leibe dich nicht," the program would use the dictionary entries "Ich = I (nominative)," "liebe = love (present)," "dich = you (accusative)," and "nicht = not," along with the rule that the German structure "<Subject Verb Object Negation>" becomes in English "<Subject Form-of-*do* Negation Verb Object>," to produce the translation "I do not love you." Idioms that could not be translated word for word could be saved in a special idiom dictionary; for instance, "Ich heisse" could be stored as a phrase meaning "My name is."

Major research projects on machine translation were initiated at a half-dozen universities starting in about 1956. A 1964 review by Bar-Hillel, however, found that none of these programs gave translations that were in any degree useful.[4] The programs were all being swamped by the same problem—that of removing ambiguities. They had no method of determining the most likely meaning of a word and therefore repeatedly resorted to the expedient of printing out all possible meanings, leading to wholly illegible text. The following translation from Russian was typical. Words combined by slashes represent different possible translations.

Biological experiments conducted on various/different cosmic
aircraft, astrophysical researches of the cosmic space and flights of

Soviet and American astronauts with the sufficient/rather persua-
siveness showed/indicated/pointed that momentary/transitory/
short orbital flights of lower/below than radiation belts/regions/
flanges of earth/land/soil in the absence of the raised/increased/
heightened sun/sunny/solar activity with respect to radiation
are/appear/arrive report safe/not-dangerous/secure.[5]

Bar-Hillel concluded that this research, proceeding in its current direction, could not hope to solve the problems confronting it. Ambiguities can be removed only by a program that understands the
meaning of the text. Bar-Hillel gave as an example the word "pen"
as used in the sentences "The ink was in the pen" versus "The box
was in the pen." To decide which meaning of "pen" is involved, one
needs to know something about ink, boxes, writing implements, and
cages. In fact, such problems arise all over the place in language
translation. Only vast knowledge of the world permits unambiguous
translation of words and syntax.

But the implications of these examples go far beyond either the
particular research programs or the particular problem. The basic
principle involved is that computers cannot deal with natural-language text, except at the most trivial level (printing it out, say), without some understanding of what it means. This applies equally to
translation, paraphrase, indexing, answering questions, carrying out
commands, generating responses, and so on. This conclusion has
been central to almost all subsequent work on natural-language
processing.

Not every impossibility result, of course, requires ten years of research and twenty million dollars of government money to uncover.
But the story illustrates the general pattern: a theory is proposed, it
is tried out, examples are found which cannot be made to work, and
an explanation is given of why these examples are necessarily beyond the range of the theory.

How AI Theories Fail

An AI theory consists of a problem and a solution. The problem
specifies the kind of input the program gets and the kind of output
it should produce in doing a certain task. A solution specifies three
things: what the program knows before starting the problem; how it

represents what it knows; and what it actually does in solving the problem. We thus have five components to the theory, which means there are five ways in which the theory can be wrong. Theories can fail in two other ways, besides: the method proposed can be right in principle but run too slowly; or, the whole theory can work perfectly but not correspond to the way in which human beings happen to think.

Some of these kinds of failures do not lead to interesting impossibility results. If a problem is wrongly stated or a theory is psychologically invalid, that is generally just an error, not a symptom of some larger impossibility. Impossibility statements in AI have the form, "Such-and-such a problem cannot be solved by any technique of such-and-such a kind because something is too weak or too slow." Either the background knowledge is too weak, or the representation is too weak, or the method is too weak, or the method is too slow.

Inadequate Mechanisms

Sometimes the technique proposed as a problem solution in an AI theory turns out to be radically too weak. A famous example was perceptron theory, a theory of visual perception proposed by Frank Rosenblatt in the late 1950s. Perceptrons consist of a large number of detectors, each of which looks for a particular feature in a small section of a visual field. A detector outputs "1" if it finds the feature and "0" if it doesn't. An overall computer uses these 1s and 0s to recognize objects. For each different object, the computer associates a characteristic set of weights associated with the different detectors and a threshold. The computer adds together all the weights of the detectors reporting "1." If the sum exceeds the threshold, the computer reports that the object has been seen.

The attraction of the theory was its simplicity, which made it amenable to mathematical treatment. Moreover, it was easy to see how such a computer could learn to recognize an object better; all that was needed was to adjust the weights in response to training. However, the whole theory collapsed in 1969, when Minsky and Papert determined that a perceptron machine was, in principle, incapable of detecting certain basic properties of an image.[6] For example, they showed that no perceptron machine can detect whether a region is connected (i.e., is one in which any two points can be joined by a curve lying entirely in the region). Since we believe that connectedness is an important property which we should be able to see, this rules out perceptrons as a theory of vision.

Another, more typical, example of inadequate mechanisms was the TALESPIN storytelling program.[7] To invent a story, TALESPIN would create a number of characters and place them in a situation with features determined either by a human user or at random. TALESPIN would then use simple physical and psychological rules to predict what the various characters would do and what would happen. Not surprisingly, this procedure led to rather humdrum stories, along the lines of "Joe Bear was hungry. He went to look for honey. He found some honey. He ate it. The End." Creating more interesting stories requires that the writer use his craft to aim the story toward some goal.

Too Slow

Sometimes AI theories are correct in principle but simply take much too long to be interesting. In particular, this tends to be true of programs that solve their problems by using "exhaustive search"—that is, by generating all possible solutions in sequence and then checking each one. Many AI problems are actually tractable this way, given enough time. One could write a vision program that worked by enumerating all possible scenes with all possible lightings, calculating the images that would be produced, and comparing them to the perceived image.[8] One could write a theorem-proving program that worked by enumerating all possible sequences of mathematical formulas until it stumbled on a proof of the desired theorem.[9] All one needs is patience—eons of it. But if you need an answer within, say, the expected lifetime of the sun, then you had better try another approach. It is, in fact, impossible using these methods to get an answer other than very, very slowly.

Insufficient Background Knowledge

Intelligent behavior must be based on a broad body of knowledge about the real world. One of the major developments in AI, psychology, and linguistics over the past thirty years has been the growing appreciation of the scope and importance of this principle. Very few cognitive activities can be performed autonomously. A theory of a cognitive task that does not consider the kinds of background knowledge needed is therefore destined for trouble.

A good example of such a failure was the attempt at machine translation, discussed above. Real translation must be based on some degree of understanding—that is, some amount of basic knowledge—about the subject matter of the text. (Some of this knowledge can, of course, be acquired from the text itself.) It is impossible to build a translation program that starts only with the knowledge of a dictionary and a grammar.

Another common example of such an error occurs in naive theories of learning from example. The problem of forming general rules from specific examples is of very great interest, since it is a basic mechanism, not only in personal learning, but also in the development of scientific theories. Naive theories of learning often assume that the learner starts with a tabula rasa so that one rule is as likely as any other. A system that starts without any bases of discrimination will make very slow progress, however. It will look for the simplest rule it can find that distinguishes the examples from the nonexamples, without any idea of what kind of distinction it is looking for. For example, if the program is asked to learn the difference between hawks and vultures from a series of photographs, it may start with rules like "Hawks are on odd-numbered photos; vultures are on even" or "Hawks have clouds in the photo; vultures do not" and concentrate on such irrelevancies for a long time before deciding to focus attention on the details of the birds. It is impossible to do this task effectively without preconceptions as to the useful categories.[10]

Inadequate Representation

We have seen that an intelligent computer needs a lot of knowledge. In order for a computer to be able to know anything, it must have some system for expressing its knowledge—some language in which it can express what it believes. Unfortunately, no existing language is suitable for this purpose. Computer languages such as FORTRAN or BASIC are good for talking about values and calculations, but they cannot express the facts of the real world. There is no way to say in FORTRAN that pigs can't fly. On the other hand, natural languages like French and English, which are good for talking about the real world, are too amorphous and ill defined to use in a computational system. The rules of a natural language are complex and ill defined, and the sentences are often vague and ambiguous. The notation for an AI system should ideally have a syntax as simple and a meaning as fixed as those of computer languages but a scope that includes every possible object of thought.

The issue here is different from the issue of providing adequate background knowledge, though it is somewhat related. There, the problem was to make sure that, at the start, the program knew enough to do its task. Here, the problem is to make sure that there is a coherent notation in which to express this knowledge. An encyclopedia may have all kinds of useful information in it, but if it is written in Aztec, it is of no use to an English speaker.

The invention of such a notation is, in my view, the most important problem in AI today. It is also a very difficult problem, and many AI theories have come to grief because their notations were too vague or too limited for the task at hand. For example, many programs have to reason about the causal relationships between quantities. An engineering program must know that raising the temperature of a liquid will usually raise its volume. An economics program must know that raising inflation tends to lower unemployment. One notation that is often employed asserts simply that one of the quantities has a positive or negative effect on the other. Temperature has a positive effect on volume; inflation has a negative effect on unemployment. This model is very easy to reason about, particularly if it is further assumed that the system of effects has no feedback. However, it is much too weak to model realistic situations. In reality, the effect of changing one variable on another may depend on the value of a third (turning up the thermostat will not change the temperature if the furnace is off) or on what other variables are held constant (adiabatic vs. isothermal expansion). Feedback is very frequently a factor that dictates the behavior of a system. Nor can the time element be ignored: the rate at which one variable affects another may influence the order and even the nature of the events that will occur.

Another typical notation problem is in describing actions. In early AI programs, an action was considered to be something that changed the state of the world.[11] At one state of the world, Kissinger is in Cairo. Then he executes the action "Fly to Jerusalem." The resulting state of the world is just like the starting state, except that Kissinger is now in Jerusalem. In the starting state, you have the ingredients for a stew; you execute the action "Make stew"; and the result is that the ingredients are gone and you have a stew. In this model, planning becomes a matter of stringing together actions to achieve the changes you want. To get to San Francisco, you first execute "Drive to airport," which brings you to the airport, then the action "Buy ticket," which puts you in possession of a ticket, then "Fly to San Francisco," which puts you in San Francisco.

This model is too weak to handle any problems outside a very limited range. There is no way to talk about actions that take time, simultaneous actions, interrupted actions, or changes to the world not caused by actions. There would be no way in such a system for Kissinger to plan to write a letter to Nixon while flying to Jerusalem, or for him to worry about being shot out of the sky. It is, in fact, impossible to design a program that understands about actions in general with such an impoverished notation for describing changes over time.

The Inadequacy of Deduction

The inadequacy principles that we have considered so far have limited scopes. Each refers to some fairly narrow class of techniques and problems. AI also uses principles of much broader range. These, in general, predate AI, deriving from philosophy or psychology, but AI uses and illuminates them in its own particular way. Of these principles, the most important and simplest is the following: no intelligent creature can always be right. Cognition, to be useful, must necessarily involve some guessing, some shortcuts, and therefore some chance of error.

To make this a little more precise, as well as more tendentious, let us define two technical terms. By "inference" we will mean any process that derives new beliefs from old beliefs—any process that allows a creature to think about what it knows and to decide on something new. By "deduction" we will mean an inference process that never errs; whenever it starts with true premises, it arrives at true conclusions. Our principle may now be stated aphoristically: Deduction is inadequate for inference.

The significance of this principle is not just that we must give up any science-fiction fantasies of building a computer with all the right answers. At the moment, the principle represents a major limitation on our ability to do AI, because deduction is the only kind of inference that is really well understood. The abstract study of deduction was begun by Aristotle and has been pursued in great depth by the logicians of this century (Russell, Tarski, Church, etc.). In particular, research into the foundations of mathematics was very valuable here, since it turns out that deduction *is* adequate for mathematics—in fact, in some views, mathematics is identical with deduction. As a result of all this work, we now possess an extensive and precise theory of deduction. We can characterize a correct deduction, we can write programs that do deductions, and we know something about the limits on the speed with which computers can perform very complex deductions. All this is lacking for nondeductive inferences. We cannot characterize any other kind of inference in detail.[12]

What does AI bring to this principle that deduction is inadequate for inference? For one thing, we can make use of the categories of failure discussed earlier to determine *why* deduction may be inadequate in a given case.

1. Deduction may be the wrong mechanism for a given problem; the type of the inference may be intrinsically nondeductive. For example, as has been discussed by philosophers for centuries, *induction* or *generalization*—the process of going from individual instances to a general rule—is not deductive inference. There is no deduction from "All the swans I have ever seen are white" to "All swans are white."

2. There may not be enough data to support deduction. AI programs must often make educated guesses to fill in a chain of inferences. For instance, a language program that reads the sentence "Sidney picked up *Newsweek*" will infer that Sidney proceeded to read it. However, this is only a guess; Sidney may have picked it up to swat a fly, or he may be interrupted.

3. There may not be enough time to do the problem deductively. There is a deductive way to play chess; enumerate all possible games and see which plays lead to victory. This method takes too long. More importantly, there is good reason to believe that *any* deductive method of playing chess—that is, any method that guarantees winning—will take too long. (This has actually been proven with regard to some other games, such as GO.)

4. There are cases where, though a deductive solution to a problem exists, people apparently use some other kind of method. For example, Kahneman and Tversky have shown that people's judgments of likelihoods violate the basic axioms of probability.[13] In one of their experiments, undergraduate subjects were presented with the following personality sketch: "Linda is 31 years old, sin-

gle, outspoken, and very bright. As a student she was deeply concerned with issues of discrimination and social justice and also participated in antinuclear demonstrations." The subjects were then asked which of the following statements was more likely: (*a*) Linda is a bank teller or (*b*) Linda is a bank teller who is active in the feminist movement. The vast majority—86 percent—judged the second statement more likely, despite the fact that this violates the basic rule that a more general state (being a bank teller) is never less likely than a more specific state (being a feminist bank teller). (Perhaps more surprisingly, 43 percent of the psychology graduate students who were given the same question made the same mistake.)

AI also brings a new focus to the issue of nondeductive inference. Philosophers who have looked at nondeductive inference have been largely, though by no means exclusively, concerned with the problem of justifying such inferences. This problem is of no direct importance to AI. Rather, the key issues raised in AI are the following: First, how are nondeductive inferences characterized and how are they performed? Second, given that you will sometimes make mistakes, how can you recover from them? One approach to the second problem has been to study so-called nonmonotonic logics, logics in which facts which were previously believed may be found to be false. This approach has produced some interesting theories but all such logics developed so far suffer from very substantial weaknesses.

The inadequacy of deduction—the impossibility of resting intelligence on a purely deductive basis—is thus both an obstacle and a starting point. We must recognize this limitation and chart out its scope, its causes, and its significance in order to proceed beyond it.

The Significance of Inadequacy Statements

The word "impossible" is grim and forbidding. The word "inadequate" is even worse; it is a wimpy, mealy-mouthed word, redolent of failure, impotence, chickenheartedness, and giving up. In intellectual parlance, it goes with drastic inconclusiveness. "The data are inadequate to suggest a theory." "The evidence is inadequate to support the conclusion." "The techniques are inadequate to obtain reliable measurements." These typical usages are pure and simple confessions of failure with nothing positive in them. In most areas of research, discovering inadequacies is at best the clearing of dead-wood; sometimes useful, never exciting or inspiring.

In AI, likewise, discoveries of inadequacies are generally unsought and undesired. (Minsky's and Papert's work on the limitations of perceptrons is unusual in this way.) Research is generally aimed at discovering solutions that are adequate; an inadequacy is discovered when a project fails. How, then, can I claim that these inadequacy statements form an important part of our knowledge of AI? And what precisely is their role within AI?

In the first place, a good understanding of the limiting factors on AI theories will be very helpful in developing theories. Almost ten years ago, Drew McDermott wrote, "AI as a field is starving for a few carefully documented failures."[14] This is still largely true—partly because of people's reluctance to examine their own work for flaws, but more because of a lack of techniques and theory for evaluating AI work. A good understanding of inadequacy statements in general will very much enhance our ability to analyze a new theory and to find where it has to be improved.

For example, the categories of inadequacy enumerated earlier can be roughly associated with techniques for improving a theory. If your representation is inadequate, you had better go back and reconceptualize the domain, this time thinking about a broader range of examples. If your background information is inadequate, then you must consider what kinds of information are necessary and how they can be incorporated into your theory. If your mechanism is inadequate, you might look for a flaw in the assumptions and constraints that underlie it, or you might look for some way in which you are underusing your data. If your algorithm runs too slowly, you should look for shortcuts, approximations that will speed it up at a tolerable cost in accuracy.

These are very rough guidelines for very general categories. As our understanding of inadequacy statements increases, we may be able to make these rules more precise and helpful.

Inadequacy statements can also be useful in explaining anomalies of human cognition. A number of cognitive scientists have proposed theories that relate particular kinds of error made by people to the limitations of particular computational techniques. These arguments are especially cogent if it can be shown that all computational techniques to solve a given problem suffer from the same limitation. For example, it is often possible to relate optical illusions to requirements of vision systems in general and to argue that any system that does vision in general will have to make guesses that leave it open to being fooled by deceptive pictures. To explain why humans solve some problems, such as probability judgments, using techniques which are clearly less than optimal, it is hypothesized that these techniques have in fact been developed for use in a broad context, where they are effective.

Finally, inadequacy statements are of intrinsic interest throughout computer science. Computer science is concerned both with the possibilities and with the limitations of computation. Determining what problems are incomputable or intractable is just as important as finding new algorithms. In physics, the inadequacy of the theory of epicycles is of purely historical interest, as a failure of ancient astronomers, whereas the impossibility of detecting absolute motion—the inadequacy of detectors to determine absolute motion—is an important physical fact. The inadequacies in AI and computer science are more like the latter; they serve to constrain the world. Thus, that natural language cannot be translated word for word and that no program can play perfect chess are fundamental to understanding these domains—more fundamental, perhaps, than the productions of a working translation or chess program. Computer scientists often say that you do not really understand how to do something until you can program a computer to do it. Even that is not enough; you also have to know what programs will not do it.

Envoi: The Great Possibility

More important, more obsessively fascinating to the AI researcher than all these inadequacy results is the fact that we know our problems are solvable. While we create and study our AI programs—slow, fragile, terribly limited solutions to particular problems—we confront one overwhelming reality: the human mind. Not only does the mind address problems of astonishing range and computational difficulty, but it has extraordinary capacities to focus efforts on those problems that are most important, to come up with adequate solutions when time or data are inadequate to support complete solutions, and to learn over time and thus continually improve its performance. Furthermore, the mind has many features that we are totally at a loss to characterize computationally: consciousness, dreams, emotions, judgments of value. We take these for granted in every human mind, but they are entirely extraordinary. When we consider this mighty original, we AI researchers feel like barbarians building thatch huts in the shadow of the Parthenon.

The speed of the human mind is almost as astonishing to the student of AI as its power, particularly when he considers the slowness of the underlying machinery. AI is used to very slow programs running on very fast electronic computers. The "cycle time" for an electronic computer—the time it takes to perform a basic operation, such as an addition or a comparison—ranges between one one-hundred-millionth and one-millionth of a second. An AI program to do a relatively simple vision task might take ten minutes—that is, several billion machine cycles. By contrast, the cycle time for a neuron—the time for it to fire and recover—is about two one-thousandths of a second; and humans can do simple visual recognition tasks in about two-tenths of a second; that is, in about one hundred machine cycles. One hundred machine cycles! Our programs are still clearing their throats at that point.

The brain does have one great hardware advantage over the computer. Conventional computers do only one thing at a time. Even if they are serving more than one user, they manage this by very rapidly shifting their attention from one to the other. Recently, newer machines have been built which have the capacity to carry out 2 or 8 or 128 operations in parallel. By contrast, each of the hundreds of billions of neurons in the brain can act simultaneously. By distributing the problem over the neurons, the brain can carry out many separate operations in the hundred cycles available to it.

But this merely moves the brain's feat from the domain of the impossible to that of the almost unbelievable. We do not know very much about how to solve problems on highly parallel systems. We do know that though with some problems you can make full use of parallelism, so that having a billion separate elements gives you a speedup of one billion, there are other problems where parallelism buys you nothing. For the latter, a system with a billion parallel elements works no faster than a system with one; each step of the calculation has to be carried out in sequence. In general, one can only make full use of parallelism if the algorithm has particular simplicities in its structure; it must involve many independent calculations. AI algorithms in general are rather complex and do not obviously lend themselves to parallelism. (The only important expectations so far in AI are the first stages of visual processing, which involves applying operators to every point in a visual field, and the playing of certain kinds of games, where different board positions may be considered in parallel.) In short, we know that the brain's use of parallel operators makes its tremendous speed possible; but we do not understand how it possibly can.

To fill this gap, there is, presently, at all levels of computer science, a great deal of research into developing parallel machines and programs that will use their parallelism effectively. When this domain is better understood, another type of inadequacy will become important: an AI program will be inadequate if it cannot be effectively parallelized.[15] As our researches progress, other kinds of impossibilities and inadequacies will undoubtedly emerge to help us describe the subtle relation between computation and intelligence.

Acknowledgments

I thank Dr. Michael Katz for his careful criticism and many suggestions. Philip Davis, Sanjaya Addanki, and Leora Morgenstern also gave me valuable help.

Notes

1. See, for example, Hubert L. Dreyfus, *What Computers Can't Do: The Limits of Artificial Intelligence*, Harper & Row, 1979; John R. Searle, "Minds, Brains, and Programs," in John Haugeland (ed.), *Mind Design: Philosophy, Psychology, Artificial Intelligence*, MIT Press, 1981; Joseph Weizenbaum, *Computer Power and Human Reason: From Judgement to Calculation*, Freeman, 1976.

2. For "his," "he," "him," read "his or her," "he or she," "him or her" throughout.

3. Daniel Dennett, *Brainstorms: Philosophical Essays on Mind and Psychology*, Bradford Books, 1978.

4. Yehoshua Bar-Hillel, "The Present Status of Automatic Translation of Language," in F. L. Alt (ed.), *Advances in Computers*, Academic Press, 1964.

5. From John R. Pierce, "Language and Machine: Computers in Translation and Linguistics," *Publication 1416*, National Academy of Sciences/National Research Council, 1966; cited in Eugene Charniak and Drew McDermott, *Introduction to Artificial Intelligence*, Addison-Wesley, 1985.

6. Marvin Minsky and Seymour Papert, *Perceptrons: An Introduction to Computational Geometry*, MIT Press, 1969.

7. Roger Schank and Christopher Riesbeck, *Inside Computer Understanding: Five Programs Plus Miniatures*, Lawrence Erlbaum, 1981.

8. There would still remain the problem of using contextual information to resolve ambiguities.

9. The reader may be reminded of the scheme for writing Shakespeare by hitching a lot of monkeys to typewriters. The problem there is that we do not know how to write a program that can read a play and determine whether it is of Shakespearean quality.

10. It may be argued that, as a species, we started with a collective tabula rasa with respect to forming scientific theories about the universe. In the first place, I imagine that some categories are built into us, having evolved as useful mental constructs. In the second place, even if we ignore these, we must consider that mankind had a million years or so to determine the useful categories and teach them via the structure of language.

11. Alan Newell and Herbert Simon, "GPS: A Program That Simulates Human Thought," in Edward Feigenbaum and Julian Feldman (eds.), *Computers and Thought*, McGraw-Hill, 1963.

12. I do not wish to give the impression that AI has settled all problems with deductive inference; however, the range of problems is considerably narrower. The major problem here is to focus the deduction process so that "important" facts will be inferred.

13. Daniel Kahneman and Amos Tversky, "On the Study of Statistical Intuition," *Cognition*, 11: 123–41 (1982).

14. Drew V. McDermott, "Artificial Intelligence Meets Natural Stupidity," SIGART Newsletter No. 57, April 1976; reprinted in John Haugeland (ed.), *Mind Design: Philosophy, Psychology, Artificial Intelligence*, MIT Press, 1981.

15. This criterion is already a consideration in evaluating theories of early vision. The most notable example is Berthold Horn's theory of deriving shape from shading, which has been challenged as having no efficient parallel implementation. (David Marr, *Vision,* Freeman, 1982.)

The submarine of Alexander the Great. Miniature from *The Romance of Alexander,* c. 1300, Bibliotheque Royale de Belgique, Brussels.

THE IMPOSSIBLE IN TECHNOLOGY: WHEN THE EXPERT SAYS NO

One ought not to desire the impossible.

Leonardo da Vinci

T he pursuit of science is sometimes justified to the practical minded on the grounds that it enables us to distinguish what is technically possible from what is not. In the early days of modern science, this justification was certainly valid. Thus Leonardo da Vinci, who was both an eminently practical man and a technological visionary, was one of the first to recognize the practical value of a basic understanding of nature. Like his intellectual successors from Galileo and Bacon onward, he wanted to discover natural principles (*ragioni*) in order to arrive at rules of practice (*regole*).[1] Asking himself what the use of his investigations is, he replies that the rules "enable you to discern the true from the false, and thus to set before yourselves only things possible.... They prevent inventors and investigators from promising themselves and others things that are impossible."[2]

Three centuries later Sadi Carnot justified his work on thermodynamics on similar grounds: the second law (which states, in essence, that heat will never spontaneously flow uphill) imposes a limit on the efficiency of an engine beyond which it is impossible to go. Even in this century basic results have had a profound effect on technology. An example is Claude Shannon's theorem relating the bandwidth of a communications channel (the range of frequencies that it can transmit) to its information-carrying capacity. (The implications of this theorem are the subject of an entertaining and informative article by Aaron Wyner.)[3]

However, today when a technologist says that something is impossible he rarely means that it is contrary to the known laws of nature. Usually it can be assumed that the laws relevant to the problem in hand are sufficiently well understood that no one would think of making a proposal that contradicted them. I say "usually," because counterexamples do exist; for instance, I once knew a building engineer who designed a plumbing system that required water to run uphill. And, as Park remarks in his chapter ("When Nature Says No"), people do go on inventing perpetual motion machines. Only recently a great deal of publicity and some funding was attracted by the "inventor" of a car engine whose claimed efficiency greatly exceeded that permitted by the law of conservation of energy. However, such cases belong to the pathology of technology, not to its normal functioning.

What, then, do we mean when we use the word "impossible" in a technological context? Implicit in the word are unstated qualifications: "within the limits of current technology," "now and for the foreseeable future," or "unless some totally unforeseen development occurs." Nontechnical considerations also enter; for example, "we can make such and such, but it will be impossible to market." Fundamental limits are indeed discussed; we will consider later, as an example of such limits, possible upper bounds to the rate at which information can be processed. However, as we shall see from this example, such discussions either are limited to a particular technology or else are conducted at an extremely abstract level. In the latter case, the limits arrived at are so far beyond those of current practice as to be meaningless to the technologist. All he can do when presented with statements like "quantum gravitational effects . . . perhaps give rise to a bound 10^{42} operations per second . . . to the speed of information processors,"[4] which is a factor of 10^{32} faster than present capabilities, is to smile politely and turn to more mundane matters.

If, then, "impossibility" in technology is a relative concept, our reasons for using the word must be quite different from those considered in some of the other chapters. When something is said to be technologically impossible, this is the expression of a judgment, not a statement of fact. What are the grounds for this judgment, and why should we believe it? What are the qualifications of the speaker? Experts who can deliver such pronouncements with confidence and accuracy are in great demand, since obviously no one wants to sink a lot of money into a venture that will turn out to be impossible. However, experts are human and therefore not always right. In this chapter we are going to look at some recent cases where acknowledged experts pronounced some technological idea to be impossible, only to be almost immediately proven wrong. By analyzing such erroneous judgments, we may cast some light on what is meant by the possible and the impossible in technology.

Occasionally a proposal is declared impossible on the grounds that it is contrary to the laws of nature. One example, mentioned on p. 178, is the *New York Times*'s criticism of Goddard's rocketry on the grounds that it contradicted Newton's laws. Another example occurred during the prosecution of Lee De Forest, inventor of the first successful amplifying vacuum tube, for federal mail fraud. (He was eventually acquitted, although two of his shadier business associates went to jail.) He had told potential investors that the human voice would before long be transmitted across the Atlantic. According to the prosecutor, this statement was "absurd and deliberately misleading." De Forest's prediction was in fact fulfilled in within three years.[5]

A recent example is the alleged self-destructive potential of the "strained layer superlattice," which will be discussed later. As already mentioned, however, such declarations of physical impossibility are now rare, and for good reason: they are almost always incorrect.

In this chapter we will begin by looking briefly at the concept of a fundamental limit in technology, using as an example the current status of such limits in computing. We will find that these limits are not so fundamental as they seem at first sight and that we should look elsewhere if we are to understand what a technologist means by "impossible."

We then turn to the main theme of this chapter, which is the variety of ways in which one can be wrong about what is possible and what is not in technology. We will first consider two cases of clear-cut scientific misconception. Some technical detail is necessary to explain these fully, however, these sections can be skipped without affecting one's understanding of the rest of the chapter. The first example, the semiconductor laser, is one in which I was personally involved as one of the nay-saying "experts." The error here was of a type fairly common in the field of solid state science: a failure to recognize which properties of the materials involved are relevant and which incidental. The second example is the strained layer superlattice already mentioned—an instructive if rather unusual case where the experts got their basic physics wrong.

In these two cases, the errors were purely technical and had little effect on technological progress. Much more serious consequences ensue when the experts are in managerial positions. Their judgments of possibility and impossibility lead to decisions that affect the work of large numbers of people and that are difficult to reverse if they turn out to be incorrect. As an example, we will consider the failure of Bell Labs to take the lead in developing large-scale integrated circuits, in spite of having invented the basic technology. A technical judgment of impossibility, initially correct but rapidly made obsolete by events, became a managerial policy decision whose inflexibility led to disaster.

In technology, judgments of marketability are as important as purely technical ones. We discuss briefly the success of the telephone and the failure of the Picturephone. In both cases the outcome in the marketplace turned out to be contrary to the expectations of the professional experts.

Finally, in the summing up, we look for a common factor in these cautionary tales and find it in arrogance. To judge accurately whether a given technological proposal is impossible, one must be ready to approach the facts with humility and with an open mind. This is hard if one considers oneself, and is considered by others, to be *the* expert on a subject.

Of course hindsight is always 20/20, and the telling of these case histories does not necessarily imply criticism of the subjects. On the whole the "experts" discussed below fully deserve the designation and have many successful predictions to their credit. That is what makes their failures interesting.

"Fundamental" Limits to Information-Processing Rates

The medieval mapmaker, when he drew the sign "hic sunt leones," really meant "I'm sorry, I haven't been there, how could I possibly know?" Computer scientists tend to have a similar reaction to the many mysteries that physics holds for them. . . . Almost anyone can put together a few physical constants and a little dimensional analysis, and come up with good-sounding names for lurking monsters: $E = kT$, the "thermodynamical barrier to computation," or $E = h/t$, the "quantum barrier," or $E = mc^2$, the "relativistic barrier"... but *somebody* must go out and look.[6]

The advent of large-scale integrated circuits has made possible an enormous increase in the speed and complexity of electronic circuitry, particularly in computers.[7] Does nature place any fundamental limits on the capabilities of such systems, beyond which it is impossible to go by any means whatsoever? It is certainly true that any given technology has such limits. For example, optical lithography, which is currently used to make silicon integrated circuits, cannot reproduce features much smaller than the wavelength of the light used. But this is not the issue. The question we are asking is, are there limits inherent to the computation process itself, independent of the particular technology? It seems that the answer is probably no; at least, as remarked in the introduction, any fundamental limits are so far beyond our present capabilities as to be entirely academic. This is not a universally accepted view,[8] and in this section I will try to explain the nature of the dispute.

The basic building block of every computer is the logic "gate." A gate, at its simplest, is a device with two possible output states, usually a low- and a high-voltage state, conventionally called "0" and "1." The output is determined by one or more inputs, each of which in turn must also be "0" or "1." For instance, an AND gate (illustrated schematically in part A of the figure on page 116) has two inputs, and its output is "0" unless both its inputs are "1." In a computer the outputs of some gates are applied to the inputs of others to create a logical network.

Memory cells and communication channels can be regarded as special-purpose gates, in which the output is logically identical to the input but at a different time or place.

After the input voltages have been applied to a gate, there will always be a delay before the output reaches its proper value. This delay limits the speed with which the gate can be opened and closed, and thus determines the ultimate performance of the computer. The delay will be a function not only of the device itself but also of the acceptable error rate (i.e., the probability that the gate will appear to be closed when it should be open or vice versa). It can be shortened by applying a higher voltage; however, the energy dissi-

A
AND gate

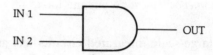

B
Fredkin gate

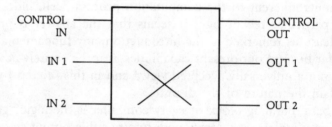

(A) Conventional representation of an AND logical gate: the output is "0" unless both inputs are "1s." (B) The Fredkin (reversible) gate. If the control line is at "1," the information on input lines 1 and 2 is interchanged at the output; it is left unchanged if the control line is at "0."

pated during the switching process then goes up, and there is always a limit to the rate at which energy can be removed from the system. Gates have to be placed very close together in order to minimize transmission delays, but cooling systems, however sophisticated, can only cope with a limited power density.

Consequently, discussions of fundamental limits concentrate on the energy dissipated per switching operation, commonly called the "power-delay product" E_d. Such discussions usually consider a simple system with two possible states as a model for the logic gate. It is found that both thermodynamics and quantum mechanics put lower limits on the power-delay product necessary to achieve a given error rate.

At "low" speeds (less than 10^{10} switching operations per second; this is still somewhat faster than the fastest system currently in use) the thermodynamic limit rules. This limit is a consequence of the thermal fluctuations that are always present in a circuit. Fluctuations in the output voltage will lead to errors. In order to keep the error rate below a given value p, the power-delay product, E_d, must exceed the average fluctuation in energy by a factor of order of the natural logarithm of $1/p$. This average fluctuation is proportional to the absolute temperature and is commonly called kT. For a computer with a million gates, making 10^{10} operations per second, to run error free at room temperature for three years we need an error rate less than 10^{-24}; the minimum value of E_d is then $55\ kT$ or 2×10^{-19} joule, a little more than an elecron-volt (the energy of an electron at a potential of 1 volt). It is thermodynamically impossible to achieve the desired error rate if the power-delay product is less than this value.

This "absolute" minimum power-delay product is very much less than the minimum practical value using current technology, which is of order $10^7\ kT$. The reasons for the difference are many, but they are all connected with size. (Nature, working on a smaller scale than we do, does much better: DNA replicates its information with an error rate of a few parts in 10^4, at a cost of about $100\ kT$ per bit, within a factor of 10 of the thermodynamic limit). At present the minimum size of the individual features in a controllable circuit element is somewhat less than a micron (10^{-4} centimeter). This is determined by the wavelength of light (used in the optical lithographic process by which the circuit is patterned onto the surface of the chip), by the precision of the etching process that translates the pattern into actual circuit structure, and by the necessity to avoid "crosstalk" (unwanted coupling of one part of the circuit to another). Since each circuit element has many features, it typically has to be 10 microns or more across. A given size of device has a certain capacitance, that is, it requires a certain quantity of electrical charge to build up the voltage necessary to operate it. The same is true of the interconnections that join the different components on the chip. In a switching operation, some or all of this charge must be removed, and energy is dissipated. In order to approach the thermodynamic limit, new devices—possessing dimensions on an atomic scale and operating with the charge on a single electron—will be required. X-ray lithography is now being developed and, if it turns out to be practical, will reduce the size limit considerably, since x-rays have much shorter wavelengths than visible light. Improved circuit design may overcome the crosstalk problem. However, it will probably be a long time before the atomic scale is reached in a practical logic device.

In communication channels (to which the same limits, mutatis mutandis, also apply) the detection of small quantities of energy is quite normal: single photons with energies of order 1 electron-volt are detected routinely in research applications. With the development of "quantum-counting" semiconductor diodes, which amplify the electrical impulse generated by a single photon up to the level where it can be used to drive a logic gate, practical communication systems detecting single photons at rates of 10^9 photons per second or higher will soon be available. Is it really impossible to go much further?

> If we know where the damping (dissipation) comes from, . . . this is also the source of the fluctuations.[9]

We need to look a little more carefully at the source of those thermodynamic fluctuations. Imagine a physical system with a limited number of mechanical or electrical degrees of freedom ("moving parts"), which are totally isolated from the "heat bath." ("Heat bath" is shorthand for the multitudinous thermal degrees of freedom of the environment. It includes the internal vibrations of crystals and the random motion of gas molecules. We need to know nothing about it except its statistical properties.) An actual example of such an isolated system is a ring made from a superconductor, in which the current will continue to circulate, forever as far as we know, as long as the ring is kept cold enough. Such a system has no fluctuations. Now let us "open a window" to the heat bath. Energy will leak out through the window and be irretrievably ("irreversibly" in the thermodynamicist's jargon) lost; thus we have introduced dissipation. The energy of the heat bath fluctuates, and the fluctuations will leak back to our system through the window. Fluctuations and dissipation are inextricably linked.

Why do we have to have dissipation during computation? Take the basic logical operation AND. Since it only puts out a "1" when both inputs say "1," its truth table is:

IN 1	IN 2	OUT
0	0	0
0	1	0
1	0	0
1	1	1

The input specifies the output, but the output is compatible with more than one combination of inputs, so that the process is irreversible. Irreversibility implies (on average) dissipation; for example, in the second and third lines of the truth table for AND we start with a "1," represented by some stored energy, and end with a "0," represented by none. So long as our basic building blocks are gates of this irreversible type (an OR gate is no better, nor are NOR and NAND) we will have dissipation and the associated fluctuations. Thermodynamics, then, places a limit beyond which it is impossible to go.

But do we *have* to have irreversible building blocks? There exist on paper, and even in a crude form in practice, logic devices that are in principle reversible and nondissipative. One such device is called the Fredkin gate. Part B of the figure on page 116 shows how it differs from a conventional gate. It has three inputs and three outputs. Instead of giving the same output for several different combinations of inputs, it merely switches the information on the input lines IN 1 and IN 2 from one output line to another, according to the state of the control line. A logical network made up of Fredkin gates can do anything a conventional network can do, but it generates a lot of garbage (output that is not needed for the computation). Dissipation of this garbage inside the computer would negate the advantage of the Fredkin gate. However, in principle it is possible to design a computer in which the amount of garbage generated does not exceed the amount of input. The garbage can then be removed from the computer by a number of lines equal to the number of input lines, and the energy associated with it dissipated harmlessly outside.

No one has ever built a computer along these lines, and it would have to operate infinitely slowly to be truly reversible. However, the existence of the Fredkin gate shows that there is no *fundamental* reason why one should not be able to improve on the thermodynamic limit. It is a limit of our present technology but not of any conceivable one.

What about quantum effects? At high speed and low temperature we might expect quantum-mechanical limits to come into play. The details are complex, but the basic physics is simple enough. The uncertainty principle of quantum mechanics states that it is impossible to measure the energy of a state with a precision better than h/t, where h is Planck's constant and t is the time taken to make the measurement. For $t = 10^{-10}$ seconds, this imprecision is of order 10^{-23} joule. The energy needed to obtain a given error rate increases proportionally to the speed.

This is all very convincing, but, as Landauer has said, "anyone can write $E = h/t$ on a napkin and persuade you over lunch that it imposes a fundamental limit on the power-delay product. The trouble begins when people publish their napkins."[10]

Laudauer's point is twofold: the time t in the uncertainty relation is the time taken to make a measurement, and there is no fundamental reason to identify it with the switching time; furthermore, uncertainty does not necessarily imply dissipation. The question of what constitutes a measurement in quantum mechanics still arouses intense and acrimonious debate among philosophers of science. It is usually skirted by practicing physicists, who use quantum mechanics but don't pretend to understand it. The most useful answer to this question in the present context, and the one most physicists would give if subpoenaed, is that a "measurement" occurs when something irreversible happens, for example, the exposure of a grain in a photographic emulsion. This definition has the great advantage (or disadvantage, for the idealistically inclined) of leaving mind out of it: the quantum mechanical "observer" can be any device that records the result of an experiment irreversibly. So we come back to the same question of reversibility.

The principles of a reversible quantum-mechanical computer have been sketched out by Feynman.[11] Its performance is not limited either by quantum mechanics or by thermodynamics. Unless the particular technology by which the computer will be realized is specified, no level of performance can be ruled out as "impossible."

The Semiconductor Laser

The helium-neon laser, because of the visibility of the light it produces, its safety, reliability, and low cost, is the workhorse of the teaching laboratory, of the surveyor, and of the check-out counter. It is what most people think of when they hear the word "laser," unless, bemused by fantasies of star wars and death rays, they think of vast X-ray lasers driven by nuclear explosions. However, the most profound technological impact has come from the semiconductor laser. This tiny laser, which consists of a strip a few microns thick on a chip less than a millimeter across, is the heart of the compact disk record player, of the laser printer, and, most important of all, of the fiber optic transmission systems that are revolutionizing long-distance communications.

The idea that stimulated emission (i.e., laser action) might be possible in a semiconductor diode goes back to a suggestion of John von Neumann in 1953, five years before Schawlow and Townes proposed a laser using atomic transitions. The latter proposal led to a frenzy of activity, which culminated in the ruby laser in 1960 and the helium-neon laser in 1961. Von Neumann's idea, on the other hand, fell on stony ground, as did Pierre Aigrain's independent proposal of 1958. As late as June 1962, most people who thought they understood the subject considered a semiconductor laser to be impossible.[12] Yet, by the fall of that same year, groups at IBM, General Electric, and Lincoln Lab had, almost simultaneously, made working lasers out of the semiconducting compound gallium arsenide.

To understand why laser action in a semiconductor had generally been regarded as impossible, consider the conditions that must be satisfied for stimulated emission to occur. The active medium (solid, liquid, or gas) must be highly excited by some external source of energy, so that some of its excited states are more heavily populated than states lower in energy. This condition is called "inversion." Inversion cannot be achieved if the energy being pumped in is continually being converted to heat. Lasing is only possible in an optically efficient material, that is, one which reemits as light the energy it absorbs, rather than dissipating it as heat. When inversion is achieved, light that is normally absorbed will instead be amplified. This amplification ("gain") must be large enough to overcome the losses in the laser; to keep these losses down, the medium must be of good optical quality. Losses at the ends can be overcome by making the laser long enough. Thus we have the following requirements for a laser material; it must be optically efficient; it must be available in large pieces, of good optical quality; and its internal losses must be low. Semiconductors seemed to fail on every count.

I was one of those who pooh-poohed the semiconductor laser, and I will take a little time to explain what was in the minds of skeptics like me. At that time I was in a laser group working on materials like ruby, and before that I had worked on gallium arsenide. Like most semiconductor physicists at the time, I regarded it as a rather messy material.

By 1962 there had already been fifteen years of work on the semiconducting elements germanium and silicon by people whom we would now call materials scientists. This work had led to the routine growth of single crystals whose purity and crystal perfection were many orders of magnitude better than those of any other solid known. To the semiconductor physicist, these elemental semi-conductors were the ideal toward which all other materials should strive.

At the other end of the solid state pecking order were the phosphors. These seemed to us to be witches' brews of doubtful structure and unknown composition. Their vast and empirical literature was reminiscent of nineteenth-century zoology—with lots of facts unrelated by principles, and nothing that a solid state physicist would recognize as understanding. Phosphors contained mysterious impurities and defects, which went by such titles as "activators" and "sensitizers," names that seemed to smack more of the medieval "hypotheses," so despised by Isaac Newton, than of scientific theory. "Hypotheses non fingimus" we said proudly and left these lowly concoctions to the chemists until such time as phosphors could be produced in perfect, pure, single crystal form.

Whatever their faults, semiconducting phosphors such as zinc sulfide have one great virtue. When stimulated with almost any source of energy, they are very efficient sources of light. Silicon and germanium, on the other hand, for all their conspicuous purity, are seriously deficient in this respect. In 1957 Richard Haynes of Bell Labs succeeded in extracting infrared light from them, but the intensity was small and the effort great. Their low efficiency contrasted with that of the known laser materials: quite ordinary synthetic ruby, for example, reemits almost 100 percent of the light it absorbs.

Crystals of gallium arsenide were grown by techniques analogous to those used for silicon and they resembled it: black, shiny, solid ingots, which could be cut and polished along accurately known crystallographic directions. They looked very different from the phosphor powders used to coat the insides of fluorescent lights and TV tubes. On the other hand, these gallium arsenide crystals were very difficult to grow, and they were decidedly imperfect and impure compared with germanium and silicon. To expect gallium arsenide to be a better light emitter seemed absurd. We regarded it as a junior aspirant to semiconductor sainthood and quite failed to notice that it had one property in common with those despised phosphors and that that property was vital.

Gallium arsenide resembles zinc sulfide and almost all other semiconducting phosphors in that its energy gap is "direct"; that of silicon and germanium, on the other hand, is "indirect." What this means is the following. Semiconductors are held together by chemical bonds joining the constituent atoms. Electrons can be removed from a bond, leaving "holes" behind, by shining light on the material, by bombarding it with high-energy electrons, or simply by making it very hot. The minimum energy needed to create an electron and a hole is the "energy gap." The electron and hole behave as separate particles, free to wander through the crystal; when an electron meets a hole and drops into it, light is emitted, a process called radiative recombination.

If the energy gap is direct, the two particles have wave functions of the same predominant wavelength. They stay in phase as they move and can recombine easily. If the gap is indirect, on the other hand, the wavelengths are different. The relative phase changes from point to point, and recombination cannot occur. As a very crude analogy, one might liken the two particles to a couple trying to kiss while dancing. In the direct case, the dance is a waltz; the couple moves as one and can easily get into a clinch. In the indirect case the dancers are jitterbuggers, who stay close together but perpetually change their relative positions, so they can only snatch an occasional peck.

Some impurity atoms can compel the electron and hole to stay in one place, so that they recombine. However, in most cases this process makes the impurity atom and its surroundings vibrate violently, so that the energy released by the recombination is given up to internal vibrations of the crystal, that is, as heat, rather than as light. Such recombination is referred to as "nonradiative." A vibration of the crystal lattice (a "phonon") can modify the wave functions slightly and permit radiative recombination even in an indirect gap semiconductor; however, this is a very weak process. It is the inability of this "phonon-assisted" radiative recombination to compete with the nonradiative processes due to impurities that makes indirect gap semiconductors such inefficient emitters of light. In direct gap materials, such as gallium arsenide, radiative recombination is fast enough to compete on level terms, and the radiative efficiency is high.

Besides the expectation of low radiative efficiency, based on experience with germanium and silicon, there were other reasons to believe that the semiconductor laser was impossible. All lasers up to that time had to be very long in order to give sufficient optical gain (amplification of light) to overcome the losses at the ends. Such a size was not practical for semiconductors, where only small crystals were available. Also, semiconductors were known to absorb light strongly; this seemed to imply that loss would always exceed gain.

Once the significance of the direct gap was grasped (first by William Dumke of IBM), all these objections fell away. The strong absorption was realized to be an advantage, since it automatically implies high gain if inversion could be achieved. The gain is so large in direct gap material that the length of the light path through the semiconductor crystal need be only a fraction of a millimeter. The problem turned out to be, not how to make the crystal large enough, but how to keep so small a crystal cool when so much energy was being pumped into it.

As for the fundamental problem of all lasers, how to achieve inversion, the technology for this already existed. The p-n junction, which is a structure made from a semiconductor by selectively "doping" it with impurities, is the heart of semiconducting diodes and of most transistors. The impurities are chosen to introduce electrons into the material on one side of the junction (the negative, or "n," side) and holes into that on the other (the positive, or "p," side). When a voltage is applied, electrons are pushed ("injected") from the n to the p side. If enough are injected, more electrons are available to make downward transitions, emitting light, than make upward, absorptive, transitions. Light is amplified, instead of being absorbed, and lasing is achieved.

At the GE Laboratory, the "impossible" gallium arsenide p-n junction laser was made to work only two months after the project started.[13] This must be one of the shortest time spans from conception to execution in the history of technology.

The "Self-Destructive" Strained Layer Superlattice

In the past fifteen years various techniques have been developed by which solids can be built up atom by atom, the composition of each layer of atoms being under the control of the crystal grower. It has become possible artificially to create solids that do not exist in nature and to tailor them to achieve some particular purpose. Such "custom-made" materials promise to be of great value in lasers and detectors for optical communications and in many other applications for which nature has failed to provide us with exactly the material needed.

One such artificial structure is the so-called superlattice, which consists of alternating layers of two different materials, each layer being a few atoms thick and atomically flat. Superlattices made from two different semiconductors have already found interesting applications in lasers and in high-speed transistors. Until recently they suffered from a severe limitation: the two materials had to be "lattice-matched," that is, they had to have the same atomic spacing. If the spacings differed, dislocations (regions where the local atomic arrangement deviates from the ordered arrangement of a perfect crystal) would develop at the interfaces between the two materials. Since dislocations are death to electrons and holes, essential to the operation of lasers and transistors, it was believed that devices could only be made from lattice-matched materials. Such a match is extremely rare. If it were not for the unexpected kindness of nature in providing us with an almost exact lattice match between gallium arsenide, aluminum arsenide, and alloys of the two, it is unlikely that the superlattice business would ever have got off the ground.

It came to be realized in the late 1970s that this limitation was not absolute. If the layers are sufficiently thin, they stretch or shrink elastically to take up the lattice mismatch, and no dislocations need form. Crystal growers have produced superlattices out of materials whose interatomic spacings differ by several percent, without an appreciable number of dislocations being formed. Page 126 shows an actual picture, taken with an electron microscope, of the atoms at an interface in a superlattice. In spite of the $1\frac{1}{2}$ percent mismatch in the interatomic spacings of the two materials when unstrained, the planes on which the atoms lie run right through the interface without any change in spacing. The right-hand picture shows what happens when the lattice mismatch is 3 percent: this mismatch is too large to be taken up by strain, so that dislocations now form during growth. "Stacking faults" (regions where the registry of successive atomic planes is upset) associated with the dislocations show up clearly in this picture.

In spite of the successful creation of dislocation-free strained layer superlattices as in the left-hand picture, skeptics still held that such structures must be inherently unstable. It would be impossible to construct reliable devices, they argued, because the structures contained a "built-in self-destruct mechanism." The basic point of the criticism is that strain requires energy; the layers are stretched or compressed like springs, and if this strain were relieved, the stored energy would be released. Such a transition to a lower energy state might be expected to occur if, for example, the device were kept hot for a long time.

This criticism is incorrect and is in fact an example of failure to apply the appropriate natural law: the law that stable equilibrium is reached in the lowest energy configuration. If strain were the only

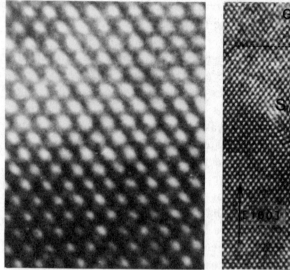

Left: An electron micrograph showing the individual atoms in a small region of a strained layer superlattice, magnified about 16 million times. The superlattice is a multiple sandwich consisting of alternate layers of silicon and of a 40 percent germanium–60 percent silicon alloy. A section about 100 atoms thick has been cut at right angles to the layers. We are looking down on the section so that each bright spot represents a column of about 100 atoms. In the alloy, the column contains both silicon and germanium atoms, and the spot is brighter because the germanium atom has more electrons in it than silicon does. An interface separating the pure silicon from the alloy runs horizontally across the picture and shows up as an abrupt change from "large" atoms (germanium-silicon) to "small" ones (silicon). The planes of atoms run right through the interface as if it were not there. This picture and the one following were taken by Robert Hull, and the superlattices were grown by John Bean, both of A.T.&T. Bell Labs. Reproduced by permission.

Right: The same as shown above left but with a 75 percent germanium–25 percent silicon alloy. The magnification here is less: about 5 million. The position of the interface is indicated by the dashed line. The mismatch of the atomic spacings is twice as large as in the micrograph on the left, and dislocations form to relieve the strain. S_1 and S_2 are pairs of dislocations running parallel to the interface. The dislocations in each pair are connected by a stacking fault, which is a region where the registry of the successive planes of atoms is upset. The stacking faults can be seen most clearly by tilting the page and looking diagonally along the lines of atoms. Reproduced by permission.

source of stored energy, the skeptics would have been right; strained superlattices could then only be grown dislocation-free under nonequilibrium conditions and would indeed be unstable. However, it also takes energy to create a dislocation. In equilibrium the superlattice will grow, with strain and without dislocations, so long as the energy due to the strain is less than the energy required to create the dislocations. Since the strain energy increases with the thickness of the layer, while the number of dislocations needed to relieve the strain does not, layers can only be grown dislocation-free up to a certain thickness. This "critical" thickness depends on such material parameters as the lattice mismatch and the elasticity. For the materials commonly used it turns out to be of the order of a hundred angstroms (an angstrom is 10^{-8} centimeter, and typical atomic spacings are a few angstroms), which is quite large enough to be useful.

This story is unusual in that it is rare for "experts" to get their basic physics so badly wrong. The misconception is of the same type (though more subtle) as that of the *New York Times* editorial writer who argued from Newton's third law that rocket propulsion was impossible outside the atmosphere.

Large-Scale Integration: When Management Says No

> For some time now, electronic man has known in principle how to extend his visual, tactile and mental abilities through the digital transmission and processing of all kinds of information. However, all these functions suffer from what has been called "the tyranny of numbers." Such systems, because of their complex digital nature, require ... tens of thousands of electron devices. ... Each element must be made, tested, packed, shipped, unpacked, retested, and interconnected one at a time to produce a whole system. ... The tyranny of large systems sets up a numbers barrier to future advances if we must rely on individual discrete components for producing large systems.
>
> *J. A. Morton, Vice President for Device Development, Bell Labs, 1958–71*[14]

The replacement of the vacuum tube by the transistor in the 1950s led to a dramatic increase in the reliability, and decrease in the size and cost, of electronic equipment. However, people soon discovered that beyond a certain point it was impossible to take advantage of these improvements to increase the complexity (and therefore the capabilities) of the circuitry. Efforts to do so were blocked by the "interconnection problem." An engineer could design a computer requiring perhaps two hundred thousand components, whose size and cost would be reasonable. However, the cost of assembly and of wiring up all the interconnections, as well as of correcting the errors inevitable in this process, was so great as to make the price almost prohibitive. Only the military or a large central computer installation could afford it.

It was particularly frustrating that, in Robert Noyce's words, "Here we were in a factory making all these transistors in a perfect array on a single wafer. Then we cut them apart in tiny pieces, and had to hire thousands of women with tweezers to pick them up and try to wire them together. The answer was, of course, don't cut them apart in the first place—but nobody realized that then."[15]

• • •

The next logical step after the transistor is to make electrical equipment in a solid block, with no connecting wires. The block may consist of insulating, conducting, rectifying and amplifying materials, the electrical functions being connected directly by cutting out areas of the various layers.

G. W. A. *Dummer, Head Components Testing Group,*
Royal Radar Establishment, 1952[16]

The Physics Division of the Royal Radar Establishment (RRE), where I was a research fellow in the late 1950s, considered itself to be the best solid state laboratory in Europe. We took a lofty attitude to the rest of RRE and held in particular contempt the Components Testing Group of G. W. A. Dummer. To end up in the "Dumpire" was the worst fate that we could imagine; banishment to it was threatened as the ultimate deterrent when we were careless with the division's irreplaceable stock of helium or committed some equally heinous offense. Although it later came to be realized that "Dummer carried inspiration around on his back like pollen," at the time his integrated circuit idea received no support. The head and creator of the Physics Division dismissed the integrated circuit idea as moonshine and even refused to allow the silicon crystals grown by the division to be diverted to this "impossible" project.

Across the Atlantic, Bell Labs did not just consider itself the best in the world, it knew. Bell Labs' arrogance was (and still is) proverbial among outsiders. At conferences the Bell contingent was regarded with fear and resentment tinged with awe. By 1960, Bell Labs had made all the major advances in semiconductor technology that could make Dummer's dream of a circuit on a solid block a reality. The first working integrated circuit, a four-transistor ring oscillator, was made at Bell in 1957 by Art D'Asaro. Yet, when the first large-scale integrated circuits (kilobyte memories and microprocessors) became available in the early 1970s, no Bell Labs design was among them.

Why was this? The answer lies, in part, in decisions as to what was technologically possible made by the management of device development at Bell Labs in the mid-1960s. Much of the story, in particular the details of how the managerial decisions were in fact arrived at, is not yet available. What I give here is a simplified and possibly inaccurate version, arrived at by comparing the published views of the managers with the actual experience of some of the technical staff involved. Many other factors, such as government regulation, internal politics, and the untimely death in 1971 of the principal strategist (J. A. Morton), undoubtedly affected the outcome; these I will ignore, since they are not germane to the theme of this chapter.

The story turns on the question of *yield*—the fraction of the devices made that actually work. When many integrated circuits are made on a piece of silicon, a certain number will be faulty, because of defects in the material and in processing. The larger the device, the more likely it is to have such a defect within its area, so that the yield goes down as the circuits get bigger. Furthermore, larger and more complex circuits need more processing steps, and the probability of failure increases with each step added. Beyond a certain size, the yield will drop so low that it is essentially impossible to make the device at all. With the defect densities available in the early 1960s, Bell Labs calculated that this size limit was less than one hundred transistors per device. This was not nearly enough for the complicated digital circuits that were needed if the integrated circuit was to have a major impact. Large-scale integration was decided to be "impossible."

It seemed, however, that there was a solution at hand. Bell Labs had developed a technique by which small devices could be placed contiguous to each other like tiles on a bathroom wall. Electrical connections were made by cantilevered "beam leads," which mortised one circuit to its neighbors, and were bonded together automatically. It therefore seemed unnecessary to try to make large integrated circuits as single devices. Quite small ones could be made and tested separately, and the survivors of the tests could then be assembled into circuits of the size and complexity required by the application. The resources of Bell Labs were committed to this "Beam Lead Technology," and all other possible approaches were abandoned.

• • •

You only arrive at the invention when somebody develops a method that everyone else has decided is obviously wrong.

Jack Kilby

As time went on, it gradually became apparent that the premises on which this decision was based were no longer valid. Bell Labs had ceased materials research on silicon in 1962, but the quality of the silicon available commercially continued to improve. It was found that the defects in a crystal tend to cluster together, so that, as device size was increased, yield dropped off much more slowly than the calculations predicted. Improvements in lithographic technique permitted a device of given complexity to be made in a smaller area, reducing the risk of finding a defect within it. Changes in circuit design made circuits less sensitive to defects intrinsic to the silicon, while improvements in processing reduced the risk of introducing defects during manufacture. News filtered through from Silicon Valley in California that out there large-scale integration was being made to work.

Beam lead technology, on the other hand, turned out to have serious and unforeseen problems, which necessitated ever-increasing complexity in the production process. The technical staff working in the laboratory began to realize that they were developing a technology that would be obsolete by the time it was ready to market. It was not too late to change direction, but the decision to do so was never made. Why not?

There is a basic incompatibility of the inventor and the large corporation. Large corporations have well-developed planning mechanisms which need to know at the beginning of a new project how much it will cost, how long it will take and above all, what it's going to do. None of these answers may be apparent to the inventor.

Jack Kilby

The problem is always in the details.

Bob Ryder, Bell Labs[17]

Communication up and down the chain of command in a large laboratory is so cumbersome that it is surprising that a correct decision ever gets made at all. Suppose, for example, that the board wants to know how a certain project is progressing. The word is passed down to the manager of the project. He calls together his subordinates who supervise its various aspects, and they in turn discuss what is to be said with their technical staff, the ones who are actually doing the work. The supervisors put their respective stories together, carefully constructing them to make their groups look good. There must be no inkling of the time wasted pursuing red herrings, of the unexpected problems that arose in conjunction with the technique chosen, or of the possibility of other approaches that might have been more successful. Above all, it must never be admitted that other groups might have obtained comparable or better results.

As the presentation makes its way up through the hierarchy, cosmetic is applied at each level and all contact with the laboratory bench is lost. Everything is rearranged, more expensive viewgraphs are prepared (the cost of graphics for a single talk in a management presentation can exceed $10,000), and only when every level of management is satisfied is the final production presented to its intended audience.

Even if the true story reaches management, it may not be believed. "There's none so deaf as those that won't hear." Large laboratories, particularly if they have been acknowledged leaders in a field for a long time, are extremely susceptible to the "NIH" ("not invented here") syndrome. They are reluctant to admit, even to themselves, that any other organization can do what they have declared to be impossible. It seems inconceivable that they should be beaten by (in their eyes) upstart fly-by-night outfits like the firms in Silicon Valley. The result is that management decisions, once made, acquire their own momentum and are unlikely to be modified in the light of new facts.

The personal computer on which I am typing this cost $2000 and has a memory capacity equal to that of the million-dollar General Electric computer that Bell Labs installed as its sole central computing facility less than twenty years ago. The difference is almost entirely attributable to the application of the "impossible" large-scale integration.

Bell, Gray, and the Picturephone: Impossibility in the Marketplace

> The telephone . . . has no practical application . . . it is a mere scientific, though highly interesting, curiosity.
>
> *Telegrapher* (1869)

> No business man would have developed the telephone. It's got to be a maverick—some guy who's been working with the deaf and gets the crazy idea that you could actually send the human voice over the wire. A business man would have been out taking a market survey, and since it was a nonexistent product, he would have proved conclusively that the market for a telephone was zero.
>
> *Robert Noyce*

"It will be impossible to market." This has been said of practically every major invention. In the 1950s it was argued that the demand for computers would be saturated once the few machines then under construction were up and running. Even in the 1960s the new IBM 360 computer was described as a poor marketing idea, since one would be quite enough. Such skepticism extended even to the telephone, which seems now to be the most obviously marketable of the major technological advances of the last hundred years.

The story of the simultaneous invention of a workable telephone by Alexander Graham Bell and Elisha Gray, following the first formulation of the concept by Philipp Reis in Germany, has been admirably told by David Hounshell in a number of articles,[18] and I won't attempt to improve on his exposition. Hounshell seeks to explain the fact that, while Bell and Gray invented almost identical devices and even filed for patents on the same day, Bell's name is indelibly atttached to the telephone whereas Gray's is forgotten. The subtitle of one of Hounshell's articles, "On the disadvantages of being an expert," sums up the moral of his tale.

Bell and Gray came to the problem of the electrical transmission of speech from very different starting points. Bell was a teacher of the deaf who learnt his physics from Helmholtz's "On the Sensations of Tone." As an inventor he was an amateur. However, as professor of vocal physiology at Boston University he was accepted as a professional colleague by such eminent physicists as John Tyndall and Joseph Henry. Gray, on the other hand, was a professional inventor, originally an engineer with Western Union. He had a long line of important inventions to his credit. He shared Thomas Edison's contempt for "the bulge-headed fraternity of the savanic world" and, like him, measured everything "by the size of a silver dollar." Gray's main concern was to increase the capacity of telegraph lines, as was Bell's at first. The idea that came to them both independently, and set them working on parallel lines, was that one could transmit many different signals on a single telegraph line by using different frequencies, each modulated independently. This procedure is now called "multiplexing."

Both Gray and Bell soon realized that the same principle could be used to transmit speech, and they came up with similar solutions to the problem of making a transmitter and receiver. Bell, the amateur, at once recognized the potential; he wrote to his father, "The whole thing is mine, and I am sure of fortune and success." Gray, on the other hand, concentrated on the multiplexed telegraph and considered "the talking telegraph" as a beautiful scientific toy. "While this is very interesting scientifically it has no commercial value," he wrote, "I don't want to spend my time and money for that which will bring no return." Even after Bell's demonstration of the telephone at the Centennial Exposition in Philadelphia had generated widespread interest and publicity, Gray was writing that "Bell has talked so much and done so little." He regarded his own Octuplex, transmitting eight telegraph messages at once, as of far greater significance. Expert on the telegraph, he would not see beyond it. Bell, concerned with human communication, could.

• • •

Picturephone service . . . may turn out to be as big a jump in communications over the telephone as was the telephone over the postal and telegraph service.

J. A. Morton[19]

In the early 1960s the rapidly increasing capacity of electronics and of transmission systems enabled the telephone organizations of many countries to consider seriously the development of video service. (In the United States this was to be called the Picturephone.) A television screen was to replace the telephone set, and people would communicate face to face, instead of as disembodied voices. In Morton's words, it would "provide the kind of multidimensional feedback which is so essential in eyeball-to-eyeball problem solving."[20] A combination of the telephone and television, both enormously popular, had to be a winner.

Bell Labs mounted a large and technically very successful effort to develop the Picturephone. Of the many components that had to be developed, the silicon vidicon, a camera tube cheap and reliable enough to be placed in millions of homes and offices, stands out as a major triumph. The Picturephone was the centerpiece of the Bell exhibit at the 1964 World's Fair. However, when it was made available to the public, this technological marvel turned out to be impossible to market. Hardly anyone signed up for it, and those who did spent most of the time gazing at their own image, rather than watching their interlocutor. A mirror would have done the job. After a disastrous pilot run in Chicago the project was abandoned.

Summing Up

> The idea of it ["molecular electronics"] was, well, you lay down a layer of this and a layer of that and maybe it will serve some function. It was absolutely the wrong way to solve anything. It wasn't built up from understandable elements. It didn't start with fundamentals because they were rejecting all the fundamentals. It was pretty clearly destined for failure.
>
> *Robert Noyce*

"Molecular electronics" was a hypothetical solution to the numbers problem backed by the Air Force in the 1950s. The name was something of a misnomer, since molecules were not involved. The idea was to lay down a solid structure with circuit elements built into it on an atomic scale. As was pointed out in the discussion of "fundamental" limits to computation, such a structure will be necessary if these limits (which apply to the irreversible logic elements used in all existing computers) are to be reached. We also saw, in connection with the strained layer superlattice, that solids can now be built up atom by atom. These new techniques permit the fabrication of simple structures on an atomic scale, although we are still far from knowing how to make a useful device in this way. In the 1950s, Noyce was right to dismiss molecular electronics as technologically impossible.

As this story illustrates, at any particular time there is a right size for any given technological leap. Too large a leap will turn out to be impossible, either for technical or for marketing (i.e., human) reasons.

There seem to be no generally applicable and objective criteria of technological impossibility. We have seen that "fundamental" limits are not so fundamental and that in technology impossibility is a relative concept. It seems that we can't do without experts, but their pronouncements must be treated with caution. We have seen, in the case of the semiconductor laser, how unexpected physics can trip us up. The strained layer superlattice episode illustrates the dangers of glib application of the wrong physical law.

In those two cases we were considering experts with no organizational power. We went on to find that a different type of expert, the technical manager, was just as likely to make erroneous judgments of impossibility, with far more serious consequences. Finally, we looked at two cases where the experts were wrong, not in their technical judgment, but in their judgment of the market. They understood the product but not the people who would use it.

> First come I, my name is Jowett,
> There is no knowledge but I know it.
> I am the Master of this College
> And what I don't know isn't knowledge.

Balliol College song

While expert knowledge is necessary, it is not sufficient. It must be combined with open-mindedness. The one element common to all the stories that are told in this chapter, and to dozens that are not, is arrogance. It is usually present when a good proposal is dismissed as impossible or when resources are wasted on a bad one. Intellectual arrogance leads us to jump to conclusions on the basis of what we are already familiar with. It prevents us seeing the problem before us as it really is. We forget that the problem exists in its own right and that, much as it may resemble those already familiar to us, it has features of its own, which must be carefully studied before judgment can be made. The most insidious thought of all, when one is faced with a new idea, is "*I* didn't think of it, so it can't be right." This leads inevitably to "Of course, in fact I did think of it and rejected it on the following grounds." One's energy is thereafter entirely devoted to finding compelling arguments for the proposal's impossibility.

There is also what one might call "organizational" arrogance: the unspoken belief that one's own organization has a monopoly on truth and that details can be left to underlings. It is an occupational disease of managers and is particularly prevalent in large organizations. In combination with organizational inertia, it makes prompt response to new circumstances difficult. It is much easier to find excuses to dismiss disturbing information as unimportant or a new proposal as impossible than to respond to either on its merits. It is fatally easy to organize things in a way that ensures such information and such proposals never reach the decision makers at all.

> **technology** . . . a technical method of achieving a practical purpose; the totality of the means employed to provide objects necessary for human sustenance and comfort
>
> *Webster's Dictionary*

Every technological innovation must ultimately be applied to some human purpose. The thoughts, feelings, and prejudices of the potential users are far more relevant to the question "Can it be marketed?" than are the technical specifications, however impressive these may be. It is, of course, the recognition of this fact that has led to the prostitution of psychology in the service of the advertising industry and to the concomitant manipulation of people for profit. The contempt that most engineers and applied scientists feel for this seamy side of the marketing process is justified, but they still remember that technology is for people.

This is getting to be a sermon and I'd better stop.

Notes

1. Gernot Boehme, Wolfgang van den Daehle, and Wolfgang Krohn, "The Scientification of Technology," in W. Schaefer (ed.), *Finalization in Science,* D. Reidel, Dordrecht, 1983.

2. Leonardo da Vinci, *Notebooks,* E. McCurdy (trans.), Reynall Hitchcock, New York, 1938.

3. Aaron D. Wyner, "Fundamental Limits in Information Theory," *Proceedings of the Institute of Electrical and Electronic Engineers,* 69: 239–51 (1981).

4. David Deutsch, "Is There a Fundamental Limit to the Rate at Which Information Can Be Processed?" *Physical Review Letters*, 48: 286–88 (1982).

5. Lee De Forest, *Father of Radio: The Autobiography of Lee De Forest*, Wilcox and Fallet, Chicago, 1950.

6. Tom Toffoli, "Physics and Computation," *International Journal of Theoretical Physics*, 21: 165–75 (1982).

7. James D. Meindl, "Ultra-Large Scale Integration," *IEEE Transactions on Electron Devices*, ED-31: 1555–60 (1984).

8. See Robert W. Keyes, "Fundamental Limits in Digital Information Processing," *Proceedings of the Institute of Electrical and Electronic Engineers*, 69: 267–78 (1981); Charles H. Bennett, "The Thermodynamics of Computation: A Review," *International Journal of Theoretical Physics*, 21: 905–40 (1982).

9. Richard P. Feynman, Robert B. Leighton, and Matthew Sands, *The Feynman Lectures on Physics*, Vol. 1, Addison-Wesley, Reading, Mass., 1963.

10. Rolf Landauer, "Uncertainty Principle and Minimum Energy Dissipation in the Computer," *International Journal of Theoretical Physics*, 21: 283–97 (1982); "Fundamental Physical Limitations of the Computational Process," in "Computer Culture," *Annals of the New York Academy of Sciences*, 426: 161–70 (1983). The quote is from a talk given at the American Physical Society meeting in Dallas, March 1982.

11. Richard P. Feynman, *Quantum-Mechanical Computers*, paper given at the Conference on Lasers and Electro-Optics, Anaheim, Calif., June 19, 1984 (*CLEO Technical Digest*, 1984, paper Tu-AA2).

12. See Robert N. Hall, "Injection Lasers," *IEEE Transactions on Electron Devices*, ED-23: 700–704 (1976).

13. Ibid.

14. Quoted in Thomas R. Reid, *The Chip: How Two Americans Invented the Microchip and Launched a Revolution*, Simon & Schuster, New York, 1984.

15. All quotations from Robert Noyce and from Jack Kilby, co-inventors of the planar integrated circuit, are from Reid, *The Chip*.

16. Quoted in Ernest Braun and Stuart Macdonald, *Revolution in Miniature*, 2d ed., University Press, Cambridge, 1982.

17. R. M. Ryder, personal communication, 1985.

18. David Hounshell, "Elisha Gray and the Telephone; on the Disadvantages of Being an Expert," *Technology and Culture*, 16: 133–61 (1975); "Bell and Gray: Contrasts in Style, Politics and Etiquette," *Proceedings of the Institute of Electrical and Electronic Engineers*, 64: 1305–14 (1976); "Two Paths to the Telephone," *Scientific American*, 245: 156–63 (1981).

19. Jack A. Morton, *Organizing for Innovation: A Systems Approach to Technical Management*, McGraw-Hill, New York, 1971.

20. Ibid.

WHEN NATURE SAYS NO

I t is impossible to leap tall buildings at a single bound; a kite will not fly in a vacuum; you can't pull down a healthy tree with a little piece of string. Anything else? It is not possible to make a perpetual motion machine. These are four statements of impossibility, but the last is not as obvious as the others. I know this very well because though nobody ever sends me designs for a kite that will fly in a vacuum, I had a correspondence only a few years ago with someone who thought he knew how to procure perpetual motion. A perpetual motion machine is essentially a device to provide free electrical or mechanical power. I think such a machine cannot be made: it is impossible. I also think it is impossible to add two positive numbers so as to get a negative number, but that is a different kind of thing. Arithmetic is an activity for which we have made the rules. It is barely possible that there is an inconsistency in the rules that nobody has noticed, but if not, then these rules require that the sum of two positive numbers be a positive number and that is that. With machines it is different. We make the machine but we do not make the rules. There is nothing logically impossible, nothing self-contradictory, about a perpetual motion machine, but all the same, I don't think we shall see one. The idea conflicts with too much we know about how the world works—know in the sense of experience, not logic. The empirical kind of knowledge does not look very different from mathematical knowledge when it is written down—it is no less sharp and quantitative and exact; we simply know it in a different way. We could always be wrong, and I must write something later on about how likely this is.

No conclusion of any consequence follows from the physical impossibility of Superman's jump. It is too obviously impossible. Since this knowledge can be compressed into the single sentence "Don't even try," I propose to call it negative knowledge. On the other hand, the impossibility of perpetual motion machines leads to and follows from two very general and powerful laws of nature, the first and second laws of thermodynamics, to be described below. Knowledge of this kind I will call positive. Obviously it isn't always possible to distinguish between the two—knowledge that is negative for one person may be good news to another—but for the examples in this chapter the distinctions ought to be clear enough. The first few will be of negative knowledge, the kind that says No and closes the door. Afterward will come examples of knowledge that in closing one door opens a larger one leading to thoughts we might not otherwise have had.

Negative Knowledge

> The Space Captain looked around the control room. "Sit tight, everybody," he said. "We're going into overdrive." His hand moved a small lever. There was a slight, almost imperceptible shudder, and a purple light glowed on the control panel as the ship streaked toward Antares. Lieutenant a'Glurr delicately scratched an eyebrow with the tip of a polished and needle-sharp claw. "Captain," it mewed. . . .

In other stories you get to Antares by catching a spacewarp. Spacewarps and overdrives are strong medicine, but the reader must take his spoonful without asking what is in it (nobody ever says) or else the adventurers will not get very far out of the solar system—the distances are simply too vast for the speeds available and the duration of life. As every reader of science or its fictional offshoots knows, the speed of light is believed to be an upper limit on all speeds. This means that if our Galaxy is 80,000 light-years across, it will take a spaceship 80,000 years at the very least to go from one side to the other.

How do we know? Because relativity theory, which says so, is very firmly established by experiment. Particles are accelerated to great speeds in the laboratory. If anyone staged a race between a flash of light and an electron from the Stanford Linear Accelerator from the Earth to the Moon, the light would win, but by less than 3 inches. Raise the electron's energy still higher and its speed will increase marginally, but not enough for it to catch the flash of light. And if anything did go faster than light, relativity theory says that you could use that thing to send a message to Theodore Roosevelt—but that is another story, to be told when firelight flickers.

The relativity theory which kills the hope of superluminal speed offers a consolation: the slowing of a moving clock. If any kind of clock moves through space it slows down, relative to one that has not moved; the effect can be verified (and has been) when a clock that has traveled is checked against one that stayed home. If the clock's speed is very close to that of light it is slowed very much. Now look at a trip across the galaxy from the standpoint of the travelers. To them it appears that they arrive sooner at the other side and return home sooner. For them, if their speed is 99.99 percent of the speed of light, the whole trip will last only 2262 years, if that is any consolation, while for the people at home it will still have taken 160,000 years.

If it is not practical to try to cross the Galaxy let us try something more modest. Let us go to Alpha Centauri, the nearest star, only 4 light-years away, and let us go the whole way moving fast enough so that for us the time taken is 10 percent of 4 years, about 5 months. Never mind how to achieve the requisite speed; it can be shown[1] that at maximum efficiency this can be done provided that 95 percent of the rocket's mass is fuel, leaving 5 percent for the rocket itself, the crew, and appurtenances. The 5 percent is a theoretical upper limit. Any practicable rocket drive will allow much less than that.

If these figures seem extreme, consider what happens when Alpha Centauri comes in sight. The ship will turn around and fire its jet forward, consuming 95 percent of the remaining mass of the ship. Thus, when the astronauts get out on whatever surface they may find, the ship will have dwindled to 5 percent of 5 percent, or

0.0025 of its original mass. But later they will want to go home, and fuel consumption will again diminish the mass to 0.0025 of what it was leaving Alpha Centauri. Thus, when the ship finally docks on Earth, it will have a mass only 0.00000625 as great as it had at departure. If it originally weighed 10,000 tons, it will now weigh 125 pounds.... But why pursue the fantasy any further? No doubt humans will go to Mars, or even to the outer planets. Someday a rocket will take off for Alpha Centauri or some other nearby star, loaded with television equipment and returning many decades or a century later to report to the descendants of the engineers who sent it out. Someday we will know much much more about the Galaxy, and perhaps even living beings in it, than we do now; but no future development is likely to erase the epitaph that Sir Richard Woolley, once Astronomer Royal, carved on the tombstone of optimistic hopes many years ago: "Space travel is bilge."

Positive Knowledge

Simon Stevin was born in 1548 in Bruges. He was essentially self-taught, beginning as a bookkeeper and military engineer, but he entered the university when he was 35 and thereafter cultivated science. He was one of the first European admirers of Arabic numerals and the decimal system, and he argued for decimal coinage and decimal systems of weights and measure, both of which are at last almost universal. In 1605 he published a book on what might be called pure machinery, machinery in which the parts do not stick or bind but rather move without friction—magic machinery, governed not by practicality but, like the idealized rocket just mentioned, only by the principles of pure science.

One of Stevin's problems is to find the force that must be exerted to keep a ball resting against an inclined surface from moving down the surface. Page 143 shows his solution as illustrated on the title page of his book. The motto WONDER EN IS GHEEN WONDER says that the magic is not magic. As an example, let the triangle's longer leg be twice the shorter one. Thus the chain will have twice as many weights on the longer side as on the shorter one. But they must both pull downhill with equal force; otherwise, the whole chain would start to revolve around the triangle, one way or the other, and, as Stevin says, "this motion would have no end, which is absurd." Thus he derives the rule for the force necessary to keep the

ball in place: if the vertical distance between the top and bottom of the plane is kept constant, then the force varies inversely as the length of the plane—provided, of course, that a continually revolving loop of chain is absurd. It would be nice if not absurd. We could use it to drive a pencil sharpener year in, year out, free of charge or, on a larger scale, to light a city or power the world.

Stevin's conviction is that the world is a place where it is impossible to get energy for nothing, a principle that in the nineteenth century was generalized and refined and called variously "the conservation of energy" or "the first law of thermodynamics."

If you think about it, though, why bother to create energy? The world is full of it, all around us. The air and ground contain heat energy, which can be extracted by cooling them. Why not cool them and get the energy and use that? That is quite possible; an electric refrigerator is a device for removing heat energy from things and spilling it out into the room. But we must expend energy to accomplish this; so the heat produced isn't free. What we would like is for heat to flow spontaneously uphill, so to speak, from a cold region to a warm one; but there is a law of physics, verified a thousand times by actual test, that says this never happens. It is called "the second law of thermodynamics." Otherwise, we could heat our houses free, and heat engines could be made that would turn endlessly. Such a machine is called a perpetual motion machine of the second kind. It, too, is impossible.

So far, it may be hard to discern anything positive behind this cloud of No. But think for a while about the lengths to which one might go to circumvent it. Chemical reactions give off heat. There might be a chain of chemical reactions, ending up with the same substances it began with, a molecular analog of Simon Stevin's chain, that took heat from a cooler place to a warmer one. No. Something complicated and electric? No. Some combination of the above? No. Something involving living things in an environment controlled so that they do not subtly steal from the environment the commodity they are supposed to produce? Still no. In order to close off such possibilities, the first and second laws must encompass all nature, living and dead. Wherever man or nature sets up a process their writ must run, and that is their strength. These laws, which emerged slowly from the work of many scientists during the nineteenth century, are two of the most general scientific principles we have; they govern and control the entire universe, insofar as we understand it.

If heat always tends to flow downhill, this means that temperatures always tend to equalize—hot things will not always remain hot. Stars are hot. The Sun is running down. The energy of the universe is becoming continually less available; as time goes on, the stars will go out one by one; mankind will perish when its time comes; finally all light and warmth will cease. Further, if the universe is running down, it cannot be infinitely old or it would be much more nearly at a dead level of equilibrium than is the world we see around us. This was not what modern-minded people thought in the late nineteenth century. The observations and reasoning of geologists like James Hutton and Charles Lyell had laid to rest the six-thousand-year time scale of Biblical history and opened the prospect of infinity. In his *Theory of the Earth* (1795), Hutton had summed up his findings: "The result, therefore, of our present enquiry is, that we find no Vestige of a Beginning—no Prospect of an End." The late Victorians were faced with a definite if unfathomable beginning and a dragging but inevitable end. Nothing has happened in the last hundred years to change the picture much. We know how our own planet will come to an end: if it is not struck or sent flying by a passing star, it will be scorched a few billion years from now, when the Sun, entering the next phase of its existence, expands to become a red giant. Afterward it will get very cold. There are now several other reasons for believing that the universe is of finite age, but much of cosmological theory depends on ideas that originated only a little over a century ago in attempts to design more efficient sources of power.

Symmetry

Imagine a blank, square piece of paper. Turn it 90 degrees. It looks just the same; you can't tell that it has been rotated. The square has four symmetries of this kind, and more if you start turning it over. Symmetry in mathematics means that something has been changed but looks just the same as before. In physics it means that something has been changed but there is no way to tell by physical measurements that it has been changed. The kind of question people used to ask each other in the Middle Ages was, Why didn't God, in the Creation, put the center of the universe (the Earth) one foot to the right of where He did put it?—Why did He not start things off one day sooner? These questions get their point from the suspicion that it would not have made any detectable difference, that there is a symmetry. In that case, what reason could He have had, or was His act purely arbitrary? Does God perform acts for no particular reason? Asked for a one-sentence summary of the theory of relativity, Einstein replied "There are no milestones in the universe." Without a milestone it doesn't mean anything to imagine the universe a foot to the left of where it is. There would be no way to tell.

Relativity theory involves another point as well, which became important for the first time when Copernicus argued for the heliocentric system in *De Revolutionibus* (1543). To put the Sun instead of the Earth at the center of the universe, he had to show that there is no immediate way of telling whether the Sun travels around the Earth or vice versa. Copernicus quotes the *Aeneid*: "Forth from the harbor we sail; the land and the cities slip backward." He goes on: "For when a ship moves calmly along, sailors perceive its motion in terms of things outside, while the ship and everything in it seem to them to be standing still" (Book I, Chapter 8). If there were milestones in the universe, you could establish that one thing is moving and another is not; in their absence, it is impossible. Copernicus's postulate was stated again and very clearly in our own century, both by Einstein and by Henri Poincaré, a French mathematician who was thinking about the same questions as Einstein. In a lecture delivered in 1904 at the St. Louis Exposition, Poincaré named this postulate the principle of relativity, and the next year Einstein developed it in a paper entitled "On the Electrodynamics of Moving Bodies," which set forth what was later called the special theory of relativity.

The principle of relativity is far from trivial. On p. 178 is a statement from the *New York Times* proving that rocket travel to the Moon, or anywhere outside the Earth's atmosphere, is impossible. At about the same time the *London Graphic* published an article pointing out that the Earth and the Moon travel at speeds that would make it impossible to hit the Moon with a rocket aimed from the Earth. Obviously the writer imagined himself on the Sun. As viewed from there, the Earth moves in its orbit at almost 19 miles per second. Orbiting around it, the moon travels sometimes faster and sometimes slower (still as seen from the Sun, by as much as 35 miles a minute. How could one hope to hit a target that was moving so erratically and so fast? The point is, of course, that it is a great mistake to stand on the Sun for any purpose and the rocket is not being sent from there. It leaves from the Earth; the 19 miles a second doesn't make any difference. The target moves at 35 miles a minute, yes, but it is an almost constant motion around the Earth, and even in precomputer days, that problem of aiming would not have seemed too hard. One should not think that it required Einstein and Poincaré to straighten out the *London Graphic*. The matter would not have confused Copernicus for a minute, and that much of the principle of relativity is built firmly into physics that Newton set forth in the *Principia* in 1687 and that high-school students have long been supposed to understand.

Newton and Einstein and Poincaré did not claim that all motion is undetectable. Everybody has had the experience of gliding out of a railroad station so gently that it seems to be the station that is moving, but if suddenly the brakes are applied there is a lurch, and we know very well, even without looking out the window, that it is the train that is moving and that its motion has changed. Only if the train travels in a straight line at constant speed is its motion undetectable from inside; let the motion change and suddenly it is as if there were milestones in space.

The inconsistency bothered Einstein, and in about 1907, he started to think what life would be like for an experimenter living in a gravity-free box in empty space. If the experimenter releases a pair of objects, they will simply hang in midair where they are. Now a confederate outside the box gives it an acceleration in a certain direction. The objects, unconnected with the box, will stay where they were while one wall of the box moves forward to meet them. To the experimenter it will seem that they have accelerated toward the wall, both at exactly the same rate. Now another experiment is performed. Instead of accelerating the box, the confederate brings up a vast massive object—say, a planet—and sets it near the box. To the experimenter, the phenomena and sensations are the same as before. Again, the two objects accelerate toward the wall, and again, they both hit at the same time. A basic result of Newtonian physics—and Stevin knew it earlier—is that, when things are dropped, they fall at a rate independent of their size and mass as long as air resistance does not play a part. If one cannot distinguish between the effects of acceleration and gravity, then acceleration is indeed undetectable and the universe is again free from milestones.

In brief: it is impossible to distinguish the effects of inertia from those of gravitation by any physical test in a small closed room.[2] Newton's dynamics implied as much if the physical tests are mechanical ones, using weights and pendulums and such. Einstein goes further: he means *any* physical test, including all known physics and physics yet to be found. He called this statement, which is of course extremely vulnerable to experimental test, the principle of equivalence. It took him another eight years of very hard work to transform this insight into the quantitative theory of gravity and curved space-time known as the general theory of relativity. Modern developments in the quantum theory of fields suggest that certain parts of the general theory are about to be recast, but no discoveries in the last 70 years have shaken its central principle.

Impotence

- No self-acting machine will produce more energy than is put into it.

- It is impossible to make any arrangement whereby heat flows spontaneously from a cooler place to a warmer place.

- It is impossible, by observations in a closed room, to establish that the room is standing still in space.

- No experimental test conducted in a small closed room can distinguish the effects of accelerated motion of the room from those of gravity.

The statements suggest an array of lost causes, and yet each one has the power of positive fact. Does anything follow from this? The British mathematician Edmund Taylor Whittaker called statements of this kind *postulates of impotence*; I think he was the first to class them together and give them a name and show how they contribute to knowledge. Note that each statement could be phrased so as to begin "It is impossible by any means whatever. . . ." They cannot be got around by transforming oneself into a mechanic or an electrician or a chemist or a biologist. They unite wide ranges of scientific law into single statements. They also have the virtue that is most admired in a scientific assertion: they expose themselves to destruction by even a single counterexample. Here is what Whittaker says:

> A postulate of impotence is not the direct result of an experiment, or of any finite number of experiments; it does not mention any measurement, or any numerical relation or analytical equation; it is the assertion of a conviction, that all attempts to do a certain thing, however made, are bound to fail. We must therefore distinguish a postulate of impotence, on the one hand, from an experimental fact: and we must also distinguish it, on the other hand, from the statements of Pure Mathematics, which do not depend in any way on experience, but are necessitated by the structure of the human mind; such statements as, for instance, "It is impossible to find any power of two which is divisible by three." We cannot conceive any universe in which this statement would be untrue, whereas we can quite readily imagine one in which any physical postulate of impotence would be untrue.[3]

There is, of course, a great difference between a postulate of impotence and its contrary "There exist means by which one can . . . ," because disproof is more important in science than proof. If I say that such-and-such is possible and you set to work to convince me that it is not, your only hope is to show that doing it would violate some general law that I myself accept as true. Otherwise, if you simply try and fail, I can always reply that you are stupid or did not try hard enough. Your repeated failures need not convince me. But if I say that a thing is impossible and then you do it even once, I have to back down. Another feature of postulates of impotence that gives them strength is that they allow expression of very general principles in nontechnical language.[4]

In his essay, Whittaker goes on to speculate that the time may come when "any branch of physics which is in a highly developed state may be exhibited as logical deductions from postulates of impotence." He writes, of course, from a mathematician's perspective. For myself I am skeptical, on account of the vast gulf that separates the ways of thought of mathematics and logic from those of empirical science. In mathematics and logic, a word means what I say it means, whereas in science, every new discovery reacts subtly on people's sense of how the world is and therefore on the vocabulary that is used to describe it. Think of the changes in meaning that words like "heat" and "gene" and "electron" have undergone. I am not sure that any part of science has, or ought to have, a vocabulary so fixed that one could play logic with it to create a structure deduced from axioms by exact reasoning.

One can also be skeptical as to whether there are enough postulates of impotence to go around. How many scientific laws can be expressed in this way?—a surprising number, perhaps, and the rest of this chapter discusses a few more examples.

Examples of Impotence

- Every child at some moment gets the happy idea that by pushing forward on some part of the family car while seated in it he can make it move. But nothing moves, and out of this experience and others like it we derive Newton's third law of motion: to every action there is an equal and opposite reaction. That is, if I push forward with some part of my body, some other part of it pushes backward with the same force, so that no net force is exerted. That seems obvious when it is pointed out, but naive people can often be gotten to say that if they push on a wall with a certain force and it does not fall down, this is because the wall pushed back on them with a larger force. Newton's law is not obvious to everybody, and in fact many of his contemporaries flatly disbelieved it. If it were not true, we could make perpetual motion machines.

- The basic fact about electric forces is Coulomb's law, which states that the force between two electrically charged particles varies (as does gravity) inversely as the square of the distance between them. This can be expressed in several ways as an impossibility—for example: it is impossible to create an electric field inside a hollow conducting shell by any arrangement of electric charges outside it. This restatement is not obvious, and it assumes that the idea of electrical conductivity is understood, but it works. In fact, it leads to the most delicate test of the validity of Coulomb's law—far more delicate than any that are based on measuring actual forces and distances.

- A basic fact concerning electricity itself is the conservation law, which can be expressed as a principle of impotence: it is impossible by any means whatever to change the total amount of electric charge in the universe. Later we shall see how this bit of wisdom becomes transformed into positive knowledge.

Finally, certain ideas pointing toward the future of physics can be expressed as postulates of impotence. I cannot do them justice without getting a bit more technical, and so I won't be offended if you skip.

In quantum mechanics, results are often calculated in terms of a mathematical object called a wave function, which is in its simplest form a function of the coordinates of the point in space at which one is looking and the moment in time when one looks. It is a complex function; that is, its numerical value has a complex phase associated with it in the form of a factor $e^{i\phi(x, t)}$, where i is the square root of -1, ϕ is a function of the coordinates and time, and e, for profound but simple reasons, is a number about equal to 2.718. When the theory was first proposed more than fifty years ago, a number of the older physicists would have nothing to do with it, on the grounds that everything we measure in nature is expressed in terms of real numbers and that, therefore, complex numbers can play no role in physical description. That indeed turned out to be so, in the following sense: it is impossible to perform any experiment by which the value of $\phi(x, t)$ can be found. One can even choose this function arbitrarily at every point of space and time (as long as the choice is not made in too pathological a way) without changing the results of any calculation of an observable phenomenon, *provided* that one introduces an appropriate description of the electromagnetic field. Even if the field is numerically equal to zero, so that one would normally say that no field is present, something to describe it must be put in. This indifference as to phase is a symmetry, and *if you assume the impossibility of determining it,* several conclusions follow: that there exists such a thing as an electromagnetic field, that this field has its sources in charges and currents, and that these sources are conserved, in the sense that, as I mentioned above, electric charge can neither be created nor destroyed. In this way, the existence of electromagnetism and the conservation of electric charge get built into the foundations of quantum mechanics.

Recall the principle of equivalence, which asserts that there is a symmetry in space-time but that this symmetry can exist only if there is such a thing as a gravitational force and if the force has properties that we know it to have. Otherwise, an observer in a closed room would really know when the room was being accelerated. Here also, we postulated a symmetry, or impossibility, and found that it can only exist if a certain field of force exists. In fact, the symmetries in phase and in space-time are related through the general concept of what is called a gauge field, but a general discussion would lead us very far and it is better to go on to two more examples.

In the physics of elementary particles, one speaks of several distinct ways in which particles interact. The unachieved hope of theory and experiment is to show that these are only different manifestations of one basic interaction. What kind of interaction might this be, and how, in detail, does it work? Physicists think they know part of the answer to the first question. The universal interaction, like its special cases of gravitation and electromagnetism, arises from a symmetry; how this might come about was first shown in a short but celebrated paper by Chen-Ning Yang and Robert L. Mills in 1954.[5]

The particles composing an atomic nucleus attract each other strongly. We know this because nuclei are generally very stable even though there is a strong electric force that tends to disrupt them. Every two protons in a nucleus repel each other, and in a large nucleus this force reaches quite impressive values: a proton at the edge of a nucleus of uranium, for example, is repelled by the other protons in it with a force that totals about 50 pounds. The specifically nuclear force that holds the particles together in spite of this repulsion is called, reasonably enough, the strong force, and it has an interesting property. A nucleus consists of neutrons and protons attracting each other, and a long series of experiments has shown that the strong force makes no distinction between neutrons and protons. If an experimenter had no means of interacting with these particles except through strong forces, it would be impossible to tell one from the other. Thus the laws of nature, as they apply to strong interactions, have a symmetry. The nature of this symmetry had been known since 1932, when Werner Heisenberg gave it a mathematical formulation. (The technical term is "isotopic spin," or "isospin.") Yang and Mills added something new.

Even though the choice between neutrons and protons is arbitrary it must be made, since there really are two different particles involved. In Heisenberg's formulation, it is made once for all and for everywhere. Suppose that, here and now, I change my mind and reassign the names. Immediately, they must be reassigned throughout the universe. "It seems," write Yang and Mills, "that this is not consistent with the localized field concept that underlies the usual physical theories." That is, how is Nature to know, out beyond the Moon, and why should she care, what assignment I choose to make? The authors then make a new proposal: that the names can be assigned independently and arbitrarily at every point of space and time, so that it makes no difference anywhere but here and now what choice I make. This is just like choosing the phase of a wave function arbitrarily, but since two kinds of states are involved, the mathematical details are different and several new features emerge. As before, the symmetry calls forth the existence of a field, but it is of a new kind. Like the particles of the electromagnetic field which are called photons or light quanta, those of the new field have one unit of spin and no mass, but unlike photons they can bear electric charge, which may be $+1$ or -1 as well as 0. Further, the new quanta interact strongly among themselves. The new field is, in fact, the one responsible for strong interactions, just as the electromagnetic field produces electromagnetic interactions.

All this, except for the values of the electric charge and the conclusion that the new particles interact strongly among themselves, was and remains in conflict with what is known. It was pretty well established at that time that the particles responsible for nuclear forces possess mass and not spin; they are called mesons. The value of the paper is not in its detailed conclusions but in the method it proposes: find a symmetry, suppose it is local and not global, and see what field of force it calls for. This not only generalizes the arguments that had earlier explained the existence of gravitational and electromagnetic forces, but also provides a program for using new symmetries if they can be found.

Nothing about the Yang–Mills program is easy to carry out. It took ten years to understand how it is possible for the particles so introduced to have a mass, and many mysteries remain. But we know at least something of what is going on. Neutrons and protons are not fundamental particles at all, and the symmetry between them, though real, is not a fundamental property of nature. Mesons are not fundamental either. Neutrons, protons, mesons, and all the other strongly interacting particles are composites, made of quarks, and it is these that our theory, unless we learn better, must treat as fundamental. The immediate goal of the theory is to explain why quarks stick together to form neutrons, protons, and the rest, and why other particles that one might imagine are not found. The next task will be to understand how composite particles interact. The picture that emerges is similar to the earlier one except for details, but they are very important. The particles of the force field, called (obviously) gluons, are massless, and there are eight kinds. They interact strongly with quarks and with each other—so strongly that particles called glueballs are expected, made of gluons sticking together. Gluons exert a force between quarks that binds them in a new way: it does not release its grip at large separations as do all the other fundamental forces, and therefore an individual quark can never be separated out and studied in isolation as other particles are.

Does this mean that physicists are walking on the edge of disaster, building their theory out of entities that are by their nature impossible to observe? At first it seems so, but reflection shows that the situation is actually not much more precarious than it was before. Who has ever observed an electron? Something called a delta particle splits into a pion and a nuclear particle about 10^{-23} seconds after it is formed. Who can claim to have observed it in that brief instant? The particles of physics have already passed beyond the limits of direct verifiability that science usually puts on a speculative hypothesis. What is a particle? Do not expect a physicist to start talking about a little ball with certain properties. It is, wrote Heisenberg, an entity on the introduction of which the laws of nature assume an especially simple form. We should not expect that physicists on Planet Krypton have organized their explanatory arguments around particles at all—they may have found a form that is even simpler. And they may not have divided their science into fields that even remotely correspond to those most of us take for granted. The only thing we might reasonably expect is that they use some form of mathematics.

At present the picture is very complicated, and it contains gaps that must be filled in with suppositions based on experiment rather than conclusions derived from first principles. Still, there is no disagreement with experiment anywhere. I will not try to explain disconnected ideas concerning which there is not full agreement. Nearly everybody believes, though, that the unifying theories of the future must be constructed out of principles of symmetry. If not that, then the number of possibilities one could arbitrarily invent is so vast that there would be almost no probability of hitting the right one. Perhaps principles of symmetry do not generate all of physics, but in this endeavor they are the only guide.

Indeterminacy

My last example of a principle of impotence is peculiar in that it does not lead to a positive statement of natural law but rather removes an objection to one. It is Heisenberg's principle of indeterminacy, or uncertainty.

Quantum mechanics is fundamentally a theory of particles: electrons, protons, and the rest. It represents their spatial positions by waves: where the amplitude of the wave is largest the particle is most likely to be found, and the wavelength is related to the particle's speed. The representation is in terms of probabilities; it does not say just where the particle is or how it is moving. In about 1926, when the details of the description were worked out, it was found that there is a curious reciprocity: a wave representation can tell quite accurately where a particle is but then it cannot tell accurately how fast the particle is moving or, conversely, it can specify the speed but not the location in space. This reciprocity is expressed in a simple formula. Let Δp be the uncertainty in the value of a particle's momentum in a certain direction and Δq be the uncertainty in its position, measured in the same direction. Then

$$\Delta p \, \Delta q \geq \frac{h}{4\pi}$$

where h is Planck's constant, a number so small that the whole effect is appreciable only at the level of particles and small atoms. One is at first inclined to say, as many people said, that the existence of this uncertainty means that the representation in terms of waves is incomplete and that the probabilistic description is a confession of ignorance, as when we say that the probability of tossing heads is one-half because we don't know exactly how the coin will be thrown or how it will land. The implication is that we cannot predict the fall because our perceptions are coarse and our thinking is slow, and not because it is impossible in principle. Thus, the early critics held that quantum mechanics was a coarse theory dealing only in averages and that an exact theory was still to be invented.

Heisenberg's answer to this charge surprised everybody. Instead of trying to amend the theory to make it more exact, he studied some simple arrangements by which one might hope to measure quantities that the theory cannot specify. He found that simple facts of nature get in the way of exact knowledge, in the same way and to the same degree that the theory is unable to be specific. That is, the indeterminacy inherent in the theory reflects an exactly corresponding indeterminacy in the results of even our best experiments. The interpretation of this situation finally hammered out between Heisenberg and Niels Bohr is as follows. The concepts of speed and position that we seek to apply in the world of particles are derived from, and intuitively clear in, the world of our daily experience. They are not exactly applicable in the microworld, and if we want to use them, the indeterminacy relations are a tax we have to pay. Thus, what first appeared a blemish on the mathematics of the new theory turned out to express facts of nature whose importance nobody had noticed before. It is not that the particle has a position and a momentum but it is impossible for us to know what they are; rather, the concepts themselves can only be applied with limited precision in this domain.

The further implications of indeterminacy are vast. Suppose I want to predict the future course of a ball I throw. I can do it well enough, provided that I know its speed and direction on leaving my hand. This is possible because the ball is so enormously massive compared with an electron, for example, that the quantum indeterminacy is of no practical importance. But it is conceptually important. It means that the future course of the ball is impossible to predict with perfect accuracy, while that of a particle like an electron is often impossible to predict with any accuracy at all. Not just hard, not just that we can't do it, but impossible. Since the material world is made of particles, this means that its future cannot exactly be predicted by any means. Exit strict determinism. Enter free will? I don't know. Free will is part of our understanding of ourselves as human beings. The task of science is to represent the world in terms harmonious with this understanding. We do not yet know nearly enough about the mind or the brain even to sketch such a representation, and so it is much too early to know what part quantum indeterminacy will eventually play.

On Being Sure

Perpetual motion is impossible. Space travel is bilge. These statements seem rather strong, emerging as they do from a scientific tradition that once held it to be impossible that the Earth moves around the Sun. Obviously, I must now explain what I mean by impossible, for though I may assume that I know what I am thinking in my own mind, no statement I might make about the world external to it can be called absolutely certain. Science is only a systematized form of the information-gathering activities we pursue in daily life, and people involved in science do not deal in certainties any more than other people do. If I say to myself that I am writing this sentence it is probably so, but it is not impossible that I am hallucinating. Every statement of fact, unless it is about what I am thinking, has an escape clause, and Kant's judgments a priori have no longer the odor of absolute truth. Our knowledge of the external world is expressed in statements (or judgments) that have a greater or less probability of being... what? Correct? Who is to tell? What is the criterion if absolute verification is out of the question? Then of not becoming at all soon the kind of statement that begins to have a jarring and discordant relation to other statements with which, at present, we live comfortably. It seems that the best equipment a scientist can have is a good intuitive sense of how probable it is that a statement belongs to this happy set. Niels Bohr said "It is wrong to think that the task of physics is to find out how nature *is*. Physics concerns what we can say about nature."

Could Bohr have said the same of mathematics? Let me translate. Many mathematicians, perhaps most, think that mathematics consists of certain structures that are in some sense *there,* waiting to be discovered, waiting for us to find out what they are. Others prefer to think that we invent the structures, even the idea of what a structure is, as we go along. For them, mathematics consists largely of what can be said about mathematics. Anyhow, the question of absolute truth in mathematics does not much affect the question of the truth of physics, even though theoretical physics is full of mathematics, because the fundamental principles of physics are themselves liable to error and can at best be regarded as plausible guesses. I think most physicists would rate the fundamental principles of modern physics as very likely to survive, in deepened and generalized form, and if I have said that a thing is impossible, I mean that it shares in this high probability.

"But," you may ask, "how about what happened to Newtonian mechanics?" Well, it has not been superseded, only transcended. The experiments that agreed with theory in 1687 still agree today. All that has changed is that we can now do a greater variety of experiments, on objects of atomic size and on objects moving at great speeds and on gravitational effects that Newton's theory does not get quite right. The mistake was to regard Newtonian dynamics as absolute truth. That happened in the eighteenth century. There is no sign in Newton's writings that he so regarded it.

I once heard the distinguished mathematician Hermann Weyl say that if there are any a priori principles in physics they are symmetry principles, that is, principles of indistinguishability, or in the language of this book, impossibility. It would be hard to dispute so modest a claim, but it is unfortunate that the example that Weyl later chose to illustrate it[6] is nature's indifference to the distinction between right hands and left hands. He accepted as true, and argued from, the proposition that if another world were created which was the mirror image of this one, it would be impossible to distinguish one from the other by experiments in physics. Four years after Weyl's book appeared, Yang and Tsung-Dao Lee suggested that it was time to put this plausible belief to experimental test, and when that was done it failed. It turned out, as Wolfgang Pauli later wrote, that God is left-handed.[7] Of course, Weyl was not really wrong when he opined that the only a priori principles of physics are symmetry principles. Mirror symmetry was assumed on grounds that amounted to a mixture of common experience and mathematical simplicity. One could reasonably assert it. The only trouble was that it was false.

At the beginning of these pages, I crudely classified statements of impossibility according to whether they are positive or negative in content—whether they lead to significant conclusions or merely to the warning "Don't try." Let us examine the distinction a little more closely and perhaps, by doing so, learn more about impossibility. It is a scientific fact that you can't put a thousand gallons of water into a pint bottle. It is also a scientific fact that you can't detect absolute motion through space. Why is it that the first statement is in no general textbook of physics and the second is in all of them? The difference is that only the first is clearly impossible, while the second has required great effort to establish and could still just possibly be wrong. Putting it in geographical terms, the second lies near the border that runs between possibility and impossibility, whereas the first sits firmly in impossibility, miles away. What follows from the first? Well, if you can't put in a thousand gallons, then you certainly can't put in two thousand. Still, nobody is really interested. But from the other follows a rich harvest of conclusions, many of which could just possibly be wrong and therefore lie in the domain of real science. Because that narrow strip, on each side of the border, is where science lives.

Notes

1. J. R. Pierce, "Relativity and Space Travel," *Proceedings of the Institute of Radio Engineers,* 47: 1053–61 (1959).

2. The room has to be small because the gravitational field must be uniform. We know from Newtonian theory, and can even verify experimentally, that the gravitational field at the top of a building is less than at the bottom. There is no way to accelerate a building so as to produce that effect.

3. E. T. Whittaker, *From Euclid to Eddington,* University Press, Cambridge, 1949, p. 59.

4. I should mention that these points were made earlier, less quotably but with granitic clarity, by Karl Popper in *The Logic of Scientific Discovery,* Basic Books, New York, 1959, Sec. 15 (originally published in German, 1934). See also *The Poverty of Historicism,* Beacon Press, Boston, 1957, p. 61.

5. C. N. Yang and R. L. Mills, "Conservation of Isotopic Spin and Isotopic Gauge Invariance," *Physical Review,* 96: 191–95 (1954). Similar conclusions were reached at almost the same time in England by a graduate student named Shaw, but he did not publish them.

6. H. Weyl, *Symmetry,* Princeton University Press, Princeton, 1952.

7. T. D. Lee and C. N. Yang, "Question of Parity Conservation in Weak Interactions," *Physical Review,* 104: 254–58 (1956); W. Pauli, *Collected Scientific Papers,* R. Kronig and V. F. Weisskopf (eds.), 2 v., Interscience Publishers, New York, 1964, v. 1, p. xiii.

The Hydra of Mathematical Impossibility is slain by the Hercules of context extension.

WHEN MATHEMATICS SAYS NO

Experience is never limited and it is never complete.

Henry James

When all the impermanencies of the world are considered, when one thinks of vast empires that have fallen, of religious beliefs and customs consigned to the ash heaps of time, of facts and systems of science patched up as a result of body blows received from pummeling nature, when one sees day-to-day arrangements of life changing rapidly before our eyes even as we live it, in what quarter are we to find a yearned-for permanence? One answer has been—and it has been an answer for a very long time indeed—that permanence and security can be found in the realm of mathematics. It is asserted that the proven statements of mathematics are true and indubitably so, that they are universal, that their truth is independent of time and of national (or even intergalactic) origin. These are commonly held views, and since they are by no means self-evident, they have naturally been the subject of discussions for rather a long time. Such discussions have, over the years, constituted a good fraction of what is called the philosophy of mathematics. In the opinion of the writer (and of many observers of the mathematical scene), these views are naive and lead, moreover, to an inadequate picture of mathematical activity.

In this article, I shall explore these views from a particular point of view, namely, that of the statements of impossibility that occur in mathematics. Of such statements there is an abundance:

- "It is impossible for parallel lines to meet."
- "It is impossible to square the circle."
- "It is impossible that the sum of two even numbers be an odd number."
- "It is impossible to give a proof of the consistency of Zermelo's axioms."

and many, many others. We might say that since the phrase "it is impossible that" is simply the negation of the phrase "it is the case that," any statement of mathematics that asserts that something is the case can be converted to an impossibility by denying its denial. Thus, "two and two is four" converts to "it is impossible that two and two not be four." Nonetheless, some statements seem to fit the impossibility format more naturally than others. Examples: children say in subtraction "you can't take six from four," and mathematicians say that "a transcendental number is one that cannot possibly satisfy a polynomial equation with integer coefficients." Furthermore, the psychological import of a statement that asserts impossibility is different from one that asserts actuality. ("You mean that such and such is impossible? You mean that no matter what I do, no matter how hard I try, I will never succeed in . . . ?") There seems to be a time element at work in such statements. Actuality is here, actuality is now, it is complete; an impossibility seems to bargain with an uncommitted future.

Consider the following three statements:

- It is impossible for two integers p and q to exist such that $p/q = \sqrt{2}$.
- It is impossible to define the terms in an axiom.
- It is impossible to display $10^{1000000000}$ decimal digits of $\sqrt{2}$.

The first statement is an old theorem of mathematics. The second is a statement about mathematics and about the language in which mathematics is written. Since formalized mathematics proceeds by deduction from axioms to theorems, the former are arbitrary starting points and hence indefinable. In the first two statements, the action takes place within the world of the mathematical imagination. In the third statement, if we interpret the words "to display" in some physical sense, the exterior world and judgments about it now play a role. Isolated, self-contained, wholly formalized mathematics exists only as an idealization; both common discourse and the facts of the real world constantly intrude to provide meaning and direction.

The object of this chapter, then, is to present typical statements of mathematical impossibility and to discuss their epistemological status—that is, to discuss what the statements are really saying and our reasons for believing that they are meaningful and true.

Squaring the Circle

I shall begin with what is probably the most familiar of all the impossibility statements of mathematics: "It is impossible to square the circle."

This statement is very old—the playwright Aristophanes (400 B.C.) uses the term "circle squarer" as a term of derision. A circle squarer, metaphorically speaking, is one who persists in trying to do the impossible.

Much more narrowly construed, the term "circle squarer" refers to one of a group of people, operating on the fringes of mathematical activity, who persist in believing they have discovered how to square the circle despite what mathematicians tell them. The impossible exerts a lure that cannot be matched by the possible.

The meaning of the statement is complex, and I shall begin with a deliberate oversimplification. First, the problem: given a circle, construct a square whose area equals that of the circle. There is a second version of the problem whose statement is simpler: given a circle, construct a square whose perimeter equals the length of the circumference of the circle. The two problems are intimately related. If one is impossible, so is the other, and conversely. What follows relates to the second formulation. The impossibility statement, in its simplified form, is this: try as you will, you cannot succeed; it is impossible to square the circle.

If you are hearing this for the first time, you may say, "The impossibility statement is ridiculous. It goes against common sense. Suppose the circle is a beer barrel, a tire, or the trunk of a tree. Just draw a rope around the circumference tightly, snip off the length of rope, measure it, divide the length in four equal parts, and voilà!, you have the side of the square whose perimeter equals that of the circle."

Perhaps you are not experimentally inclined but are arithmetically inclined and you recall some high-school geometry. You might refute the claim of impossibility in this way. "Let us suppose the radius of the circle is 1 foot. I know from my Euclid that the circumference of the circle is therefore 2π feet. I know from my little hand-held computer that the value of π is 3.1416, to four figures after the point. Therefore, the value $2\pi/4$, which is the side of the required square, is 1.5708 feet. Go build a square whose side is 1.5708 feet and you have squared the circle!"

These arguments asserting possibility have brought in new elements: (1) the circle as a physical object, (2) measurement as a physical act, (3) construction as a physical act, and (4) approximation within mathematics itself. There is no doubt that we can "square the circle" in either of the ways just mentioned, and our solution would be a good practical solution. But these solutions are open to criticism; while they provide good approximations, they are not exact in the strict mathematical sense of the word.

If our task is to arrive at an ideal mathematical square, residing in the mathematical world, by a sequence of ideal mathematical operations of a certain specified kind, then we must pursue the task totally within the mathematical world. Our experiences with mathematics and physics have led us to two different places—"nature and artifice have collided."[1]

The Greek mathematicians of classical antiquity were rather less interested in going the way of physical measurement than in going the way of pure mathematical theory. It was they who located the problem totally and firmly within the mathematical world, and this placement becomes an essential part of the final assertion of impossibility. But we still have a job to do before the problem becomes well posed and leads to an impossibility statement. We must clarify the means by which we are allowed to "construct" line segments. Geometry is pursued in the real world by both physical and conceptual means. One draws real lines and real curves on a real piece of paper, using certain drawing instruments. The physical environment becomes a laboratory in which reasoning, constructions, and discovery can all take place. The favorite drawing instruments of the Greeks were the ruler and the compass. With these instruments, the straight line and the circle can be produced. The Greeks also had instruments for drawing other curves, and discussions of their use occur in advanced material. In view of the simplicity of the ruler and compass, the notion of ruler and compass constructions took on a distinguished status. Such a construction leads to a figure all of whose parts are built up successively by the application only of these two instruments. Euclid gives many such constructions in *The Elements*.

We must now make a mathematical model of the physical act of construction by ruler and compass. Such an act is replaced by a formalized, mathematical surrogate, which states clearly what we are allowed to do. Once we have done this, the problem of squaring the circle is located in the realm of abstract mathematics; more precisely, with the aid of the algebraization of geometry initiated by Descartes and of the calculus initiated by Newton and Leibnitz, it is taken away from geometry itself and becomes a problem within the complex of ideas now known as algebra and analysis. To argue about this problem no longer requires that you own a set of drawing instruments, but that you have a profound knowledge of theorems of algebra and of advanced calculus. The problem can now be stated precisely, and the meaning of the impossibility of circle squaring is this: it is a *theorem* of mathematics that no finite number of algebraic operations of such-and-such a type can lead to the desired result. The truth status of the impossibility of squaring the circle is identical to that of any other theorem of pure mathematics, and its acceptance is on that basis.

As a matter of historical fact, in the days when Aristophanes was laughing at the circle squarers, it was not known whether or not such a construction was possible. Repeated failures led the mathematical community to conjecture that it was not. In the course of these failures many ingenious ruler and compass constructions were devised whose accuracy was very high (but not perfect). Proof of the impossibility was not reached until the 1800s. Over the years, a stronger assertion emerged, namely, that π is a transcendental number in the sense just defined. For a long time this was considered to be the outstanding unsolved mathematical problem. Finally, in 1882, the transcendentality of π was established by the German mathematician Ferdinand Lindemann.

Impossibilities within Deductive Mathematical Structures

As we have just seen, to refine and make precise the notion of a mathematical impossibility requires that one confine oneself to a certain limited area of mathematics. Such an area will embrace its own mathematical objects, it will set forth definitions and axioms and ultimately will yield a set of true statements (theorems) relating those objects. This limitation is known as "working within a deductive mathematical structure." Historically, the details of the axiomatizations are often laid down *after* a considerable bulk of results have become clear on a more informal basis.

Let me mention a few more interesting impossibilities and the areas of mathematics in which they are now located.

1. It is impossible for the sum of two even integers to be an odd integer. (arithmetic of positive integers)

2. Given the edge of a cube, it is impossible to construct by ruler and compass the edge of another cube whose volume is twice that of the first. (Galois theory)

3. It is impossible with ruler and compass operations to trisect a general angle. (Galois theory)

   Incidentally, (2), (3), and circle squaring constitute the three classical impossibilities of Greek geometry.

4. It is impossible to find a formula that involves only a finite number of arithmetic operations and a finite number of root extractions that solves the general quintic equation (or indeed any equation of degree higher than four). (Galois theory)

5. It is impossible to solve the "Fifteen Puzzle." (two-dimensional combinatorial geometry)

   (This is a popular puzzle made of plastic. Little movable square pieces labeled 1, 2, 3, ..., 14, 15 are placed in rows and columns within a 4 by 4 frame. One space is left blank. The order of the pieces can be altered by pushing the squares successively into the blank space. The pieces are placed initially in the order 1, 2, 3, ..., 15, 14, and the object of the puzzle is to rearrange them to the usual order 1, 2, 3, ..., 14, 15. The initial order is very important.)

6. It is impossible that there exist more than five types of regular polyhedra: the tetrahedron, the cube, the octahedron, the

dodecahedron, and the icosahedron. (three-dimensional Euclidean geometry)

7. It is impossible for $\sqrt{-1}$ to exist. (arithmetic of positive and negative real numbers)

8. It is impossible to set up a one-to-one correspondence between the set of integers and the set of real numbers. (Cantorian set theory)

Each of the impossibilities 1 through 8 is a mathematical theorem and has been proved on the basis of a precise statement of conditions within the indicated mathematical structure. The truth status of each of these impossibilities is precisely the same as that of any proved theorem. It is different from that of the statements of, for example, physics, and it will pay to look into just what this truth status is.

No Probable Possible Shadow of Doubt[2]

Why are the theorems of mathematics true? There are probably more answers to this question than there are people who have thought deeply about it. Schools of mathematical philosophy have crystallized around the answers. To those of a skeptical mind, no answer may be convincing; taken as a whole, the answers may even be contradictory.

It has been said that mathematics is true because it is God given. Mathematics is true because man has constructed it. Mathematics is true because it is nothing but logic; and what is logical must be true. Mathematics is true because it is tautological. It is true because it is proved. It is true because it is constructed; its fabric is knit from its axioms as a sweater is knit from a length of yarn. It is true in the way that the rules and subsequent moves of a game are true. It is true because it is beautiful, because it is coherent. Mathematics is true because it is useful. Mathematics is true because it has been elicited in such a way that it reflects accurately the phenomena of the real world.

Mathematics is true by agreement. It is true because we want it to be true, and whenever an offending instance is found, the mathematical community rises up, extirpates that instance, and rearranges its thinking. Mathematics is true because, like all knowledge, it is based on tacit understanding. Mathematics is true because it is an accurate expression of a primal, intuitive knowledge. Mathematics is true because there are numerous independent but supportive avenues to its kind of knowledge.

It has also been said that mathematics isn't true at all in an absolute sense, it is true only in a probablistic sense. Mathematics is true only in the sense that it is refutable and corrigible; its truths are eternally provisional. Mathematical truth is not a condition, it is a process. Truth is an idle notion, to mathematics as to all else. Walk away from it with Pilate.

Rattling off this list in rat-a-tat fashion has very likely induced some vertigo in the minds of readers and a feeling that chaos must prevail in this most fundamental question of this most fundamental field. But the chaos is something that only philosophers of mathematics contend with. The majority of mathematicians hardly worry about it at all and often regard philosophical speculation with disdain or amusement. As they pursue their individual researches, inner peace and tranquillity are the rule and not the exception. The reasons for their feelings of security are hardly ever verbalized, and not the least of their reasons is that it is perfectly legitimate to do what they are doing because so many of their brilliant colleagues are doing it also.

Without in the least hoping to resolve the question of mathematical truth or even to express adequately my own feelings about it, I return to the impossibility of squaring the circle and ask: why should one believe Lindemann's theorem, which implies this impossibility?

Imagine an encounter between a mathematician M and a person P, the latter of whom believes he has found a way to square the circle. Such encounters have occurred so often that this one is not entirely fictitious. (If the reader wants amusing descriptions of encounters with flesh-and-blood circle squarers, Augustus de Morgan's *A Budget of Paradoxes* is highly recommended.) I shall assume that mathematician M is an establishment fellow and that, while P has a good opinion of his own work, he is not an utter fanatic.

P comes to M and says, "See here, I have found a ruler and compass construction that squares the circle. What do you say to that?"

M's probable reply is "No. You must be mistaken. Your conclusion must be erroneous." M asserts this on the basis of the fact that the world mathematical community has accepted, since Lindemann, the proof of the impossibility. Lindemann's work has passed through the normal processes of validation. M may not have participated personally in this validation, but the record is open, and any time M wants, he may choose to sit in judgment of Lindemann. If M is living in the 1980s, the acceptance of the impossibility is simply part of his mathematical inheritance.

Now P's claim contradicts what M and the whole mathematical community believe to be the case. If M believes further that the portion of mathematics in which the discussion takes place is logically consistent[3]—and he must make this assumption, else the whole enterprise falls to the ground—then P's construction must be erroneous.

As a matter of psychology, P will probably not be satisfied by M's reply. After all, P has worked hard to arrive at his construction. His work has the same prima facie value as the established answer, except—and this is vital—that it has not been through the validation process. P claims that his work should have its moment in court, in the course of which the validity of the established answer should be reexamined. If M is a soft-hearted individual, he will agree.

M should now do several things. M (or the mathematical community) should reexamine Lindemann's work (or later versions of it) critically. This is not likely to occur, except in the case of a severe crisis. M should therefore examine P's work critically. He must verify that P is dealing with the same problem as the established problem. (Very often, amateurs do not understand the precise statement of a problem.) Assuming that P understands the problem, M must verify that P's steps are correct in the sense that the logical inferences are correct, that appeals to other "well-established" results are made properly, and that these well-established results are themselves correct. (It is often the case that amateurs assume what they want to prove, prove it afresh, and say: QED.) Depending on the complexity of P's work, this process may be exceedingly difficult and time consuming, and in any case, M will hardly want to reopen the validations of all the "well-established" results appealed to by P.

One may write a scenario in which M, after considerable labor, points his finger at such a page and such a line and says to P, "Look. You made an error right here and it is such and such." P, being a decent and reasonable sort, reexamines his own work, agrees with M, and the encounter is terminated. But if P's work is validated and the established work is discredited, then P's work, of course, prevails. If P's work is validated and the established work is revalidated, then we are in a crisis condition.

In point of fact, what M most likely says in a typical encounter is "Go away. My belief is that (1) Lindemann's work is valid and (2) mathematical analysis is consistent. Therefore your work is invalid, and I assert it without even examining your work." What is behind this brush-off?

As regards (1), M might reason this way: I personally have not examined Lindemann's work nor any modern formulations of it, but the mathematical community has. This community operates as an open forum, in which material is constantly exposed to surveillance, criticism, revision, improvement, and extension. This forum has intellectual links to the historical record and to the informal discussions of the past and present. It also has links to forums in allied areas such as in physics and philosophy, and all this constitutes the mathematical experience. The record of this experience is good; while it does point out certain historical errors, ultimately corrected, it claims a very high batting average.

My belief in the validity of Lindemann's work is therefore not absolute but very strong. It rests ultimately on my faith in the collective judgment of the mathematical community. The margin of error that I allow to this judgment does not inhibit my personal work, nor does it create neurotic indecision. While my belief in this specific piece of mathematics may be somewhat less than, say, my belief in my own existence, my belief in the mathematical process as a whole is at the same level.

When it comes to (2), the consistency of mathematical analysis, M might reason this way: Experience has shown that it is consistent thus far and that it has possessed enough resilience to handle any seeming inconsistencies that have popped up. I am aware of work such as that of Kurt Gödel (validated by the community) that if a mathematical discipline is rich enough (i.e., contains sufficient definitions and axioms) to be able to formulate the problem of its own consistency, then that consistency cannot be demonstrated within the discipline itself. Such a demonstration might be forthcoming within an enveloping metadiscipline. My belief in the consistency of mathematical analysis rests less with the possibility of such a demonstration than in the fact that inconsistency would rob mathematics of its unique status among intellectual disciplines, a status to which I am committed. I have thus pursued the meaning of impossibility to the point where I have been compelled to formulate my acceptance as a personal commitment. The pursuit must now be terminated.

But there is more to the notion of impossibility than merely a conclusion derived within a deductive structure. For structures can give way and impossibilities can be converted to possibilities.

The Theater of the Absurd: Conversion of the Impossible to the Possible

It is an error—or, at the very least, it contributes to a misleading view of mathematics—if mathematics is seen as a set of static, formal, deductive structures, permanent in arrangement and fixed for all time. A truer picture of the subject is obtained if these structures are viewed as historic but provisional, emerging as new thinking elicits new rules and delineates their scope, and as new creative pressures alter their individual relevances. The rules may change, hypotheses may change, the order of deduction may be turned upside down to allow hypotheses to become conclusions and vice versa, new interpretations may be found within larger milieus. Consider the following impossibilities, each of which has given rise to a mathematical crisis.

1. It is impossible for $\sqrt{2}$ to exist. (the crisis of Pythagoras, discussed below)

2. It is impossible for $\sqrt{-1}$ to exist. (the Crisis of Cardano)

3. Given a straight line L in the plane and a point P not lying on it, it is impossible that there be other than precisely one straight line through P and parallel to L. (the crisis of synthetic a priori geometry, discussed below)

4. It is impossible for infinitesimal quantities to exist. (the crisis of Berkeley)

5. It is impossible to have a function that is 0 for all values of x, except at $x = 0$, and whose integral (area) is positive. (the crisis of Heaviside-Dirac)[4]

6. It is impossible to put all the real numbers into a one-to-one correspondence with the positive integers, or the independence of the continuum hypothesis. (the crisis of Galileo—considerably updated)

In a word now: all of these impossibilities have been converted into active, useful, and logical possibilities.

Impossible—and yet possible. The $\sqrt{2}$ is the first instance of the "absurd" in mathematics. Impossible, absurd, within a rigid axiomatic frame of arithmetic to which mathematics was unable to confine itself and still remain creative. Possible on relaxation or extension of the frame. The theater of the absurd has been wildly successful. Though each of the impossibilities (1 through 6), and their subsequent dissolution form large and important chapters in the development of mathematics, I shall only talk about (1) and (3) at any length.[5] These two have particular interest because the crises they engendered spilled over to the larger nonscientific world.

It is amusing to observe that, in some instances, the way out of a crisis actually emerges far in advance of a proper statement of the impossibility itself. It is impossible working with integers only to divide the integer 1 by the integer 2, or the integer 3 by the integer 2, because the results are not integers. But there is hardly a number system in which, historically, $\frac{1}{2}$ and $\frac{3}{2}$ do not exist simultaneously with 1, 2, 3. Impossibility is a status conferred by axioms.

Axiomatization has fluctuated in importance. At the moment, and since 1800, it is very strong and influential indeed. Arithmetic and analysis (calculus) were hardly axiomatized until last century. Classic Greek geometry was, of course, axiomatized. That is where it all began; that is where "were forged the chains with which human reason was bound for 2300 years."[6] Ancient Indian and Oriental mathematics were innocent of axioms.

The impossibility associated with $\sqrt{2}$ is that of finding two integers p and q such that $p/q = \sqrt{2}$ (i.e., $(p/q)^2 = 2$). The discovery that this is impossible is attributed to Pythagoras (sixth century B.C.). Since $\sqrt{2}$ exists as the palpable length of the diagonal of the unit square, and since it does not exist as the ratio of two integers (what other kind of numbers can there be?), then it both exists and doesn't exist. Here, indeed, is collision between nature and artifice.

A way out was hinted at by the Babylonians. In a tablet that has been dated approximately 1700 B.C.,[7] one finds an excellent sexigesimal approximation to $\sqrt{2}$. Greek reasoning led to a crisis in Greek mathematical thought. Ultimately, after many centuries, the dilemma was resolved when geometry was relocated within the real number system (i.e., the system of all "decimals" with infinitely many digits), a process already begun in the Babylonian tablet. The impossibility of $\sqrt{2}$ as the ratio of two integers becomes a dead issue in the reformulated geometry but remains a very live issue, though nonparadoxical, within the theory of numbers.

The crisis of Pythagoras had important implications beyond mathematics itself. Coming at the time of, or just prior to, the development of axiomatic deduction, this discovery was conceivably instrumental in the promulgation of deduction as a device for arriving at truth. Sir Karl Popper speculates that the crisis and its residue went far deeper than mathematics: "[The Platonic theory of forms and ideas] cannot be understood except in the context of the critical problem situation in Greek science (mainly in the theory of matter) which developed as a result of the discovery of the irrationality of the square root of two."[8] One wonders what the subsequent history of Western thought would have been if Plato had not dreamed up ideal forms to keep us enthralled and in thrall.

Yesterday's shocks are often the bases of today's stabilities. Every undergraduate in mathematics and physics knows that there are three principal systems of continuous geometry. The most famous is Euclidean geometry. Then, there are two kinds of non-Euclidean geometry: the hyperbolic geometry of Bolyai and Lobatchevsky and the elliptic geometry of Riemann. It is now hard to realize that in the early nineteenth century the possibility of a geometry alternate to that of Euclid was approached with fear and indignation. Undoubtedly, the authority of the ancients was at stake, as were ancient views of the relationship between the world and a mathematical description of the world. Euclid's geometry was held to provide an accurate description of the way the spatial world is. It had a priori truth, and this being the case, an alternate geometry was unthinkable, impossible.

The matter may now be viewed as a conflict between axiomatics and experience. Geometry, in the hands of Euclid, was built up from certain common notions and "self-evident" axioms. His fifth axiom, the famous parallel axiom, asserts that if a straight line is given in a plane and if a point not on the line is given, then one and only only line may be drawn through the point parallel to the given line— proposition (3), above. Of course, this may be rephrased dramatically as an impossibility: it is impossible that there be other than one parallel through a given point.

To subsequent generations, this axiom seemed rather less transparent than the others, and there is a long history of attempts to deduce it from them. These attempts failed, and when something fails over a period of time, common sense, if you can call it that, would seem to say that what you're trying to do is impossible to do. At any rate, common sense of one sort was in conflict with that of another sort, and out of the conflict emerged the impossibility of the deduction.

How does one prove impossibility in this case? It is done by finding a set of mathematical objects, together with an interpretation that links the objects to the terms appearing in the axioms, that satisfy all the axioms of Euclid other than the fifth. The objects may be part of conventional Euclidean geometry, but the basic terms such as "point," "line," "intersect," and "parallel," are given special meanings. This process, which has since become commonplace in mathematical logic and set theory, is known as finding a "model" for the axioms. People have found a number of models—in fact, infinitely many—none of which satisfy axiom 5. In this way, its independence is established. The possibility of more than one parallel is established by the geometry of Lobatchevsky and Bolyai and that of no parallels by the geometry of Riemann.

Will now the real geometry please stand up? None can answer this request, for in the wake of the new discoveries, there is now no logically privileged geometry. Each non-Euclidean geometry is as logical and as consistent as Euclidean geometry. What remains is not the essential truth of geometry in some mystic sense, but questions of utility, simplicity, and convenience. What geometry is useful? In the small arena of terrestrial and planetary measurements, Euclidean geometry is the shoe that fits the foot; over the vast reaches of intergalactic space-time, Riemannian geometry appears to be what is wanted.

When Bells Ring and Lights Flash

It is not uncommon for today's lecturer in mathematics to begin by saying something like "Let X be a function space of such and such a kind and let f be a typical function in X." Later on, the lecturer might say, "Since f is *living* in X, such and such is true." This current colloquialism underscores the formal limitations to which f has been subjected and because of which certain consequences flow. It also underscores the fact that f is prior to X, and that X may not be the natural habitat for f—indeed, there may be no natural habitat, and residency in a particular spot may carry a price.

This is familiar from the larger world. We live in a room, the room is in a house, the house is on a lot, etc. What is impossible to do in a room may be quite possible in a house, what is impossible in the house may be quite possible in the backyard. Of course, the reverse may be equally true in that structures may evolve precisely to bring about desired impossibilities (e.g., that it be impossible for rain to fall on our heads or for thieves to lift our video recorders).

Now, one of the major contemporary tendencies in mathematics is to view it as the science of deductive structures. This view has reinforced analogous views in fields such as anthropology, psychology, education, and literary theory. As mentioned above, a structure is a set of objects together with a set of rules that govern the combination or interaction of the objects. For the most part, the objects in their primitive conceptualization predate the formation of the rigorous structure, and a given object may reside in many, many structures. Thus the mathematical object 2 may be an element of the set of integers, of a group, a ring, a field, etc. The operation of squaring a number (the function $y = x^2$) may be an element of many different sets of functions.

Structures are something like social clubs whose laws of admission are set up on the basis of exclusion principles. Thus, the infinite sequence of ones $(1, 1, \ldots)$ is excluded from membership in the Hilbert space called ℓ^2 because the sum of its squared components is infinite. The elements that are allowed in the structure ℓ^2 are "good," or at least in Dr. Johnson's terminology, eminently "clubbable." The purpose of club formation is to insure that members may interact properly. Within the club, some things are possible for members and others impossible. The structural emphasis of twentieth-century mathematics has taken the limelight off the individual members (numbers, vectors, functions, permutations, etc.) and placed it on the structure itself as an entity within which one looks for such features as closure, substructures, and homomorphisms.

Insofar as mathematical objects have an existence apart from the structure in which they are temporarily living,[9] questions may be asked of them in their wider, unstructured character. The answers may be various. Are there any members, x, of my structure for which $x^2 = 2$? No, if all the x are residing in the set of positive integers. Yes, if the xs comprise the real numbers. Does the equation $x^2 = -1$ have a solution? No, if x is a real number; yes, if x is a complex number.

Do you really want to solve the Fifteen Puzzle? Then act like Alexander cutting the Gordian knot: lift the little squares out of their frame into the third dimension, and rearrange them properly. This is what you would do if your life depended on getting the desired arrangement.

Impossibilities are converted to possibilities by changing the structural background, by altering the context, by embedding the context in a wider context. It is very likely the case that all mathematical impossibilities may be altered in a nontrivial way so as to become possibilities. With regard to such conversion, a number of very important questions can be raised. First, why does one want to do it?

What are the internal or external pressures for it? Surely one would require a better answer than merely that the stuff of mathematics is sufficiently pliable to allow it. Second, what are the larger consequences of the act? While there are many instances of conversion, of which, perhaps, examples (1 through 6) of the last section are the most famous, to my knowledge there has been no general critique of the act.

When bells ring and lights flash, we are duly warned. Presumably, we are skirting on the edge of what is dangerous. When we shove a piece of plastic into the bank slot and ask for a hundred dollars at a time when our balance is seventy, mathematics says no and an error message is returned. When we take our scientific computer in hand, read in 1, and attempt to divide it by 0, those flashing lights remind us of our impossible, desperate, meaningless act.

Yet, tomorrow, the bank manager might have his machine programmed to allow everybody a line of credit of one thousand dollars. Washington does it all the time. It's called deficit financing, and giants of economic theory are associated with this structural change.

Do you want to divide by zero? Well, maybe not 1/0, but 0/0. This absurd ratio, when properly interpreted as the limit of legitimate ratios, is the very stuff out of which differential calculus is built. But why have we excluded 1/0? Sorry, an oversight. There was no need to exclude it, for within projective geometry or modern matrix theory, answers are given routinely, usefully, and without shame. (*Every* rectangular matrix has a Moore-Penrose generalized inverse.)

When bells ring and lights flash, you may indeed want to pay attention. Then again, you may only want to look at the mechanism that has set them ringing.

A Summing Up

When placed within abstract deductive mathematical structures, impossibility statements are simply definitions, axioms, or theorems, as the case may be. If theorems, then assessments of their validity are arrived at by the standard processes and criteria of mathematical validation. These include an examination of the intuitive, deductive, and interactive bases of the theorems.

In mathematics there is a long and vitally important record of impossibilities being broken by the introduction of structural changes.

Meaning in mathematics derives not from naked symbols but from the relationship between these symbols and the exterior world. This relationship is established through the mediation of the mathematical community. Insofar as structures are added to primitive ideas to make them precise, flexibility is lost in the process.

In a number of ways, then, the closer one comes to an assertion of an absolute "no," the less is the meaning that can be assigned to this "no."

Notes

1. Stuart Hampshire, *Modern Writers and Other Essays*, Knopf, New York, 1970.

2. W. S. Gilbert, "The Gondoliers."

3. Allow one contradiction and any assertion becomes logically true. For example, suppose that $0 = 1$. Suppose, further, you would like to show that $4 = 11$. Multiply both sides of the first equation by 7. This produces $0 = 7$. Now add 4 to both sides of this. Although the world wouldn't collapse if such a mathematics were introduced, what role could it conceivably play?

4. This was a crisis—of sorts—in the mathematical community that physicists, in their naiveté, hardly noticed. Physicists wisely reserve their energies for crises in physics.

5. The transformation of (6) to a possibility is less familiar, even to a professional. It is embodied in the Löwenheim-Skolem theorem of set theory. See, for example, Thomas Jech, *Set Theory*, Springer Verlag, New York, 1971, p. 81.

6. Eric Temple Bell, *The Search for Truth*, Williams and Wilkins, Baltimore, 1934.

7. See Asger Aaboe, *Episodes from the Early History of Mathematics*, Random House, New York, 1964, pp. 26–27.

8. Karl Popper, *Conjectures and Refutations: The Growth of Scientific Knowledge*, Basic Books, New York, 1962.

9. This separate existence is up to a point, of course. The number 2, as mere symbol, can serve only to distinguish, as with a hat check. Mathematics begins when 2 is related somehow to 1 and 3. In this relationship we would have a very primitive structure.

MISCELLANEA

That Professor Goddard with his "chair" in Clark College and the countenancing of the Smithsonian Institution does not know the relation of action to reaction, and of the need to have something better than a vacuum against which to react—to say that would be absurd. Of course he only seems to lack the knowledge ladled out daily in high schools.

—*New York Times,* January 1920

(Apparently, the *New York Times* thought that rockets, which had been in existence for centuries, are propelled in the same way as a punt.)

• • •

Dr. Lee De Forest predicted today that man would never reach the moon "regardless of all future scientific advances."

—*New York Times,* February 25, 1957

(De Forest was the inventor of the vacuum tube.)

• • •

It is a peculiar property of instinctive knowledge that it is predominately of a negative nature. We cannot so well say what must happen as we can what cannot happen, since the latter alone stands in glaring contrast to the obscure mass of experience in us in which single characters are not distinguished.

—E. Mach, *Science of Mechanics,* p. 36

It is impossible for a pitcher in baseball to throw a fourth strike.

• • •

It is impossible that the infinite should move at all. If it did . . . there would be another place, infinite like itself, to which it would move. But that is impossible.

—Aristotle, *de Coeli* 274b30

• • •

[Choice is not] wish, though it seems near to it; for choice cannot relate to impossibles, and if anyone said he chose them he would be thought silly; but there may be a wish even for impossibles, as for immortality.

—Aristotle, *Nicomachean Ethics* 1111b20

• • •

For the purposes of poetry a convincing impossibility is preferable to an unconvincing possibility.

—Aristotle, *Poetics* 1461b11

• • •

In framing an ideal we may assume what we wish, but should avoid impossibilities.

—Aristotle, *Politics* 1265a17

(Nowadays we would say "In proposing a model.")

• • •

It is certain because it is impossible.

—Tertullian, *De Carne Christi* 5

("I believe because it is absurd" is attributed to St. Augustine.)

• • •

It is as impossible for a man to be cheated by anyone but himself, as for a thing to be, and not to be, at the same time.

—R. W. Emerson, *Compensation*

One cannot devise a successful gambling system to be used against a fair coin.

—P. J. Davis and R. Hersh, *The Mathematical Experience*

• • •

The sphere of poetry does not lie outside the world as a fantastic impossibility spawned by a poet's brain; it desires to be just the opposite, the unvarnished expression of the truth, and must precisely for that reason discard the mendacious finery of that alleged reality of the man of culture.

—Nietzsche, *Birth of Tragedy*

• • •

The poorest man may in his cottage bid defiance to all the forces of the Crown. It may be frail—its roof may shake—the wind may blow through it—the storm may enter—the rain may enter—but the King of England cannot enter—all his force dares not cross the threshold of the ruined tenement.

—W. Pitt, speech in the House of Commons

• • •

It is possible to divide up the space inside a sphere the size of a pea and rearrange it so as to fill a sphere the size of the Sun.

—Banach–Tarski theorem

• • •

It is impossible to make an antigravity device.

• • •

Faced with the riddles of the material world the scientist has long been used, with manly resignation, to admit "*ignoramus*," but looking back over the long trail of victories he can be confident that the thing he does not yet know he can under certain circumstances find out, and perhaps some day he will. Faced, however, with the riddle of what matter and energy are, and how they combine to create a thinking organism, he must forever resign himself to the unchangeable fact:

"*Ignorabimus!*"

—Closing words of an address, "On the Limits of Our Knowledge of Nature," by Emil du Bois-Reymond, delivered in 1872 before the Congress of German Scientists and Physicians at Leipzig.

• • •

For the mathematician there is no *ignorabimus,* nor, in my opinion, for the natural scientist either. Trying to identify one problem that could be called insoluble, August Comte once said that science would never find out the chemical constitution of the heavenly bodies. A few years later this problem was solved by Kirchhoff's and Bunsen's techniques of spectral analysis, and today even the furthest star can serve as a laboratory for studying physics and chemistry that we cannot learn on Earth. In my opinion the real reason why Comte failed to find an insoluble problem is that no insoluble problems exist. Instead of a foolish *ignorabimus* let our watchword be

> We must know,
>
> We shall know.

—David Hilbert

(These lines close his last public address, delivered in 1930 at a banquet honoring his retirement. It was later broadcast over the radio, and listeners say that when he had finished, and before the microphone was turned off, they heard him laugh.)

• • •

The exact sciences start from the assumption that in the end it will always be possible to understand nature, even in every new field of experience, but that we may make no *a priori* assumption as to the meaning of the word "understand."

—Werner Heisenberg

• • •

My own pet notion is that in the world of human thought generally, and in physical science particularly, the most important and fruitful concepts are those to which it is impossible to attach a well-defined meaning.

—H. A. Kramers

When you have eliminated the impossible, whatever remains, however improbable, must be the truth.

—A. Conan Doyle, *The Sign of Four*

• • •

An omelet cannot be made without breaking eggs.

• • •

A silk purse cannot be made from the ear of a female pig.

• • •

Extrasensory perception is impossible.

• • •

It is impossible for a thing to be in two different places at the same time.

• • •

The president of the United States has an impossible job.

• • •

We will never know the true story about Mayerling.

• • •

Communication with the dead is impossible.

• • •

A telegram cannot be sent into the past.

—Einstein

• • •

A cat can have kittens in the oven but that doesn't make them biscuits.

• • •

Nullam rem e nihilo gigni divinitus umquam. Nothing comes from nothing by divine power.

—Lucretius, *De Rerum Natura* I. 150

(Lucretius thus argues that the creation of the world was a gathering together, not a making from nothing. Echoed in *King Lear*, I. i: "Nothing will come of nothing, speak again.")

• • •

Everything that comes into being must arise either from what is or from what is not, and it is impossible for it to arise from what is not (on this point all physicists agree).

—Aristotle, *Physica* 187a33–34

(It follows from this that the world is infinitely old. Aristotle makes the point in the course of refuting Anaxagoras on another matter.)

• • •

Omnia fint ex nihilo & ex nihilo nihil fit—non contradicant. Everything is made of nothing and nothing is made of nothing—these do not contradict.

—Thomas Hariot, *Mathematical Papers*, v. 3, fol. 375

(Hariot is one of the first English atomists. Atoms are the nothings that everything is made of, but *they* are not made from nothing.)

• • •

Three pawns cannot give mate.

• • •

The Devil said "I can do anything." Chaim said "Prepare a magnificent feast." The Devil waved his finger and muttered something and the grass around them was loaded with linen and fine food. "Not bad. Can you take that mountain over there and put it on top of this one here?" The Devil gestured and it was done. Chaim thought a moment. "Whistle a tune." The Devil whistled. "Now sew a button on it."

• • •

Jesus answereth again, and saith unto them, Children, how hard it is for them that trust in riches to enter into the kingdom of God! It is easier for a camel to go through the eye of a needle, than for a rich man to enter into the kingdom of God. And they were astonished out of measure, saying among themselves, Who then can be saved? And Jesus looking upon them saith, With men it is impossible, but not with God: for with God all things are possible.

—Mark 10:24

• • •

The aim of the theatre is to get people to imagine what is not possible.

—Gregory Moser

• • •

Something impossible does not follow from something possible.
From an impossibility anything follows.
What is necessary follows from everything.
Therefore this follows: "You are a donkey, therefore you are God."
This also follows: "You are white, therefore God is triune." But these consequences are not formal ones and they should not be used much, nor, indeed, are they used much.

—William of Occam, *On Terms*

• • •

It is folly to inquire into the consequences of an impossibility.

—Galileo, *Dialogo*

• • •

That the purified language of science, or even the richer purified language of literature, should ever be adequate to the givenness of the world and of our experience is, in the very nature of things, impossible.

—Aldous Huxley, *Literature and Science*

CHAPTER ELEVEN • THOMAS E. FOSTER

PROMISES AND IMPOSSIBILITY

T his chapter discusses impossibility as an excuse in the law of contract—its historical development, its place in modern contract theory, and its relation to other commonly held principles. Looking primarily at reported cases, but also at legislation, legal scholarship, and even works of literature, we will attempt to understand how a system of obligations is both illuminated and limited by the concept and fact of impossibility.

In Anglo-American law, contract liability is strict liability; as expressed in the ancient maxim *pacta sunt servanda,* contracts are to be kept. In this view, a person who promises performance is liable in damages for breach of contract even if he is without fault[1] and even if existing or supervening circumstances render the contract more burdensome and less desirable than anticipated or, for that matter, altogether impossible to perform. Of course, the prudent promisor investigates carefully and does not make absolute promises. He may protect himself by limiting his obligation, through, for example, a clause committing him only to use his "best efforts" or through a force majeure clause.[2]

Unfortunately, few of us, when contemplating a contractual relationship, thoroughly explore existing facts and conditions, realistically assess our own abilities, or plan for every eventuality. We do not consider that performance of our promise, when required, may have become vitally different from what we expected, that circumstances may have altered its essential nature. And, yet, it is possible that something will have occurred or been revealed that has "so radically altered the world in which the parties were expected to fulfill their promises that it [would be] unwise to hold them to [their] bargain."[3] In this event, someone—the parties themselves, an arbitrator, or a court or other tribunal—must determine whether justice requires a departure from the general rule that puts the risk of such a sea change on the promisor.

> Basically, the law has two alternatives: [It] must adopt either a strict rule which will require the parties, when they form a contract, to foresee its consequences as accurately as possible, though at the expense of serious hardship to one of them if unforeseen circumstances render it impossible to perform his promise, or a rule giving an excuse under such circumstances. The early cases accepted the former alternative; the later cases tend to adopt the other.[4]

Implied in this formulation is an element of Anglo-American law that is essential to keep in mind, the all-or-nothing rule. Traditional analysis of impossibility has assumed, as does this chapter, that either the promisor gets stuck or he gets off scot-free. While the wisdom of *sharing* losses caused by unknown or changed circumstances has been eloquently argued,[5] it has simply not been adopted in the United States or in England.

At the outset we must note the obvious: only in a system in which promises are routinely and strictly enforced is an elaborate doctrine of excuse necessary. Anglo-American commercial contracts are quite definitely such a system. In the United States, contracts even have constitutional stature. Article I, Section 10 provides that "no State shall ... pass any ... Law impairing the Obligation of Contracts." The commercial men who framed the Constitution were reacting against the anarchic situation of the early postindependence period, when "a course of legislation had prevailed in many, if not all, of the States, which weakened the confidence of man in man, and embarrassed all transactions between individuals by dispensing with a faithful performance of engagements."[6]

James Madison had argued that the Contract Clause would not only protect against the vagaries of state legislators, but also educate the public as to the importance of observing contracts, "inspire a general prudence and industry, and give a regular course to the business of society."[7] This broad purpose was evidently well served.[8] Thus, a mere two generations later, Chief Justice Taney extolled "the great and useful purpose" of the clause, which "had maintain[ed] the integrity of contracts, and [secured] their faithful execution throughout this Union, by placing them under the protection of the Constitution of the United States."[9]

Systems in Which Promises Are Unenforceable

To illustrate the effect of excuse on the general enforceability of contracts, we will first consider two contract-related systems built on the premise that promises ought *not* to be enforced: divorce and bankruptcy. Both systems were created by legislatures to relieve the rigor of the common law, which did not recognize divorce and which had once held that a person who did not repay his debts was a thief. In recent decades, both systems have been greatly "liberalized." Each now allows escape from solemn promises on the bald statement by one party that performance is impossible.

Divorce

In Massachusetts and many other states, to obtain a "no-fault" divorce a spouse need only declare that the marriage has suffered an irretrievable breakdown. The noncomplaining party has no power to affect or alter this declaration.[10] The marriage will be automatically dissolved. A judge may become involved to divide up property or provide for alimony or child custody but cannot enforce the marriage vows or penalize their breach or even effectively inquire why the breakdown is irretrievable.

The dissolving reach of divorce laws extends beyond the marriage contract itself. When New York adopted "no-fault" divorce in 1966, for example, the courts applied the law retroactively to make it impossible to enforce preexisting separation agreements.[11] To allow such nonenforcement, New York courts first concluded that marriage was not in fact a contract within the protection of the Contract Clause.[12] Such a conclusion flatly contradicted early American jurisprudence. For example, Chief Justice Marshall, although clearly understanding the special contractual nature of marriage and accepting the states' general right to legislation on the subject of divorces, wrote: "When any State legislature shall pass an act annulling all marriage contracts, *or allowing either party to annul it without consent of the other,* it will be time enough to enquire whether such an act be constitutional [under the Contract Clause]."[13]

Bankruptcy

In bankruptcy, the debtor becomes eligible for court protection by merely declaring to the court that it is impossible for him to pay his debts when due.[14] The court then acts to adjust rights among creditors, but it has no power to force the debtor to keep his original promise to repay debts or perform other obligations. On the contrary, the whole purpose of a bankruptcy proceeding is to effect a discharge of all debts and obligations so the promisor may start over. For, as Justice Johnston observed in *Ogden v. Saunders* (when laws for the relief of debtors were in their infancy), there comes a point where pursuing a debtor merely destroys him without benefitting the creditor.[15]

Unlike domestic relations law, bankruptcy law has far-ranging commercial consequences, and there is an uneasy relationship between the bankruptcy system and normal commercial relations. The usual commercial rule that contracts are to be performed was forcefully expressed in 1968, by the New York Court of Appeals: "[W]here impossibility or difficulty of performance is occasioned only by financial difficulty or economic hardship, *even to the extent of [causing] insolvency or bankruptcy,* performance of a contract is not excused."[16] Once bankruptcy is declared, however, entirely new rules come into play. The court appoints a trustee to assume the affairs of the bankrupt. Section 365(a) of the Bankruptcy Code gives this trustee in bankruptcy an almost absolute power to "assume or reject any executory contract or unexpired lease of the debtor."[17] As recently interpreted by the Supreme Court, this authority is broad enough to swallow up all normal contractual rules, not to mention other important federal concerns such as the national labor laws.[18] The Court held that "the authority to reject an executory contract is vital to the basic purpose [of] a Chapter 11 reorganization, because rejection can release the debtor's estate from burdensome obligations that can impede a successful reorganization."[19] In other words, freely made promises have been transformed into burdensome obligations and may be disregarded. Clearly such alchemy obviates any need for an impossibility excuse, or any other defense, once the bankruptcy system is entered.[20]

Antecedent Impossibility: Promises to Do the Impossible

Assuming a system in which contracts are generally enforced, the need for an excuse due to impossibility usually arises in one of two situations. A promise may become impossible to perform because of a change in circumstances or a supervening event (a painter dies before he has completed a promised portrait) or it may turn out that the promise could not have been performed because of existing, antecedent circumstances (a building cannot be put up on unstable land).[21] Although many authorities on contract law lump these two situations together,[22] there are in fact some important differences between them. Let us look first at existing, or antecedent, impossibility.

Is a Contract to Do the Impossible Void?

Traditionally common law lawyers regarding themselves as eminently practical men, would have nothing to do with impossible things.[23] This attitude is perfectly expressed by Chief Justice Coke in the celebrated *Dr. Bonham's Case* (1610): "When an Act of Parliament is against common right and reason, or repugnant [*i.e.*, internally inconsistent], *or impossible to be performed, the common law will control it, and adjudge such Act to be void.*"[24] A fortiori, a contract (being a matter of private law-making) based on a promise to do an impossible thing would fail and have no consequences.

Hobbes, who was well versed in the common law, in his *Leviathan* (1651), states that the "subject of a covenant [i.e., an informal contract] is always ... understood to be something to come; and which is judged possible for him that covenanteth, to perform. And therefore, to promise that which is known to be impossible is no covenant."[25] Consequently, as John Powell concluded in an eighteenth-century treatise on contracts, no "obligation [can] be incurred, from a contract to perform things naturally impossible."[26] Powell argued that should one man be "absurd enough to covenant with another to build him a large house in a day; or to go to Rome in the same time; or to overturn Westminster Hall; or to drink up the sea; or touch the sky with his hand or such like impossibilities: such contracts would be void."[27] In our own century, one English contract textbook regarded a contract to do the impossible (in this instance with respect to the sale of nonexistent goods) as an "agreement [that] can be nothing but a phantom since there is nothing upon which it can fasten. If a contract may be discharged by subsequent impossibility of performance, then a fortiori its very genesis is precluded by present impossibility."[28]

Although this view prevailed for many years, it is subject to attack because it ignores the motivations, intentions, and actions of the parties, who must have had something in mind when they made their agreement. The parties may have intended to warrant that a certain state of facts exists or to wager on an outcome unknowable to both. One party may have specifically assumed the risk that the admitted impossibility could be overcome, perhaps by advancing the state of the art, or may simply have been mistaken or used bad judgment. Why should he be let off the hook at this late date?

The countervailing view, that impossible promises were not to be totally disregarded, was expressed as early as the beginning of the eighteenth century, in a case in which the defendant, on payment by the plaintiff, became obligated to deliver two grains of rye the next Monday, double the amount the next Monday, and so on for a year.[29] Counsel for the defendant claimed "that the agreement appeared upon the face of it to be impossible, the rye to be delivered amounting to such a quantity, as all the rye in the world was not so much, and being impossible was void."[30] The judges, however, expressed a different view. Thus, Chief Justice Holt responded that "where a man will for a valuable consideration undertake to do an impossible thing, though it.cannot be performed, yet he shall answer damages," and Justice Powell thought that "the defendant ought to pay something for his folly."[31] Because the case was settled before judgment, the tension between these two views on a promise to perform the impossible was not judicially resolved.

American cases contain the language of the English precedents, but American judges were not as venturesome as Lord Coke and his successors in voiding statutes or contracts because of antecedent impossibility. Shortly after the Civil War, for example, the Supreme Court held:

If a condition be to do a thing which is impossible, as to go from London to Rome in three hours, it is void; but if it be to do a thing

which is only improbable or absurd, or that a thing shall happen
which is beyond the reach of human power, as that it will rain tomorrow, the contract will be upheld and enforced. . . . It is the province of courts to enforce contracts—not to make or modify them.
*When there is neither fraud, accident, nor mistake, the exercise of
dispensing power is not a judicial function.*[32]

Despite the ambiguous verbal formulations, it appears that in nineteenth-century America the tendency was to uphold the contracts.
Thus, in a subsequent case, the same court while stating that "where
there is obvious physical impossibility, or legal impossibility, which
is apparent on the face of the contract, the latter is void," ignored an
obvious legal impossibility and upheld the contract.[33]

The contrast between language (seeming to allow excuse) and result (upholding contracts) in American cases led the eminent lawyers
who drafted the first Restatement of Contracts (1932) [an attempt to
formulate what the common law was] to take the view that the
common law rule was as follows: Parties may bind themselves by
contract to perform what is in fact impossible. It is only where the
promisor has no reason to know of the facts to which the impossibility is due, and where he does not agree to bear the risk of their
existence, that the formation of a contract is prevented.[34] Under this
rule, a court would look at the language of the promise and the
circumstances under which it was made to determine whether a
promisor must pay damages for his failure to perform an impossible
promise.

The view that even impossible promises ought to be a valid basis
for obligations comports with common notions of the relationship
between individual responsibility and justice. We reward people who
take certain risks, including the risk of failure, but expect them to
shoulder the responsibility for any negative consequences. In a typical government contract action, for example, a bidder is awarded the
contract *based on his low bid.* If he then encounters difficulties, expected or unexpected, most people would say that he should have
bid higher or not at all. As one court held, when a government contractor was found not only to have believed it could advance the
state of the art, but even to have "promised to perform under its
own substituted specifications [with] full knowledge of the perils of
performance, [the contractor had] fully assumed the risks of impossibility of performance."[35]

Courts are even less sympathetic in situations in which a promisor
asserts that a risk of impossibility was taken (or allocated) when the

only real risk was one of being found out, such as bigamy. Few courts will relieve a promisor who has merely closed his eyes and hoped for the best. In an illustrative case, a company entered into a conciliation agreement with the Equal Employment Opportunity Commission that was impossible to implement consistently with the seniority provisions of the company's existing labor contract. The Supreme Court scoffed at the company's attempt to excuse the violation of its labor contract by appealing to the conciliation agreement: "The Company committed itself voluntarily to two conflicting contractual obligations. [In such a situation], it is far from clear that the defense [of impossibility to justify its breach of the labor contract] is available to the Company *whose own acts created the condition of impossibility*."[36]

If such cases stand at one extreme, at the other is quite another kind of impossibility case, in which a promise is made in a spirit of daring, where the stakes are high, even infinite, and someone is led to test with his own strength and judgment the all-or-nothing rule. Some of the best examples are perhaps in works of literature. Consider the Grimm brothers' "Twelve Dancing Princesses." The princesses disappear every night. In the morning they return exhausted, with holes in their dancing shoes. The king announces that whoever discovers where they dance will receive the hand of one of his daughters in marriage but that anyone who tries and fails will be executed. Our hero arrives and with some supernatural assistance (a cape to make him invisible) discovers their nocturnal haunt. In the meantime, however, many have undertaken the deed, with full understanding and acceptance of the consequences, and have failed and suffered the penalty. No suitor was allowed to save his head with the plea "But it was impossible." In such a tale, impossibility adds spice to the challenge and validates the heroic nature of the one who succeeds.

In *All's Well That Ends Well*,[37] Shakespeare explores the consequences that follow when promisors promise the impossible. Helena, orphan daughter of a renowned physician, loves a young count, Bertram, but she realizes the impossibility of her love: "'Twere all one / That I should love a bright particular star / And think to wed it, he is so above me" (I. i. 85–87). When Bertram, whose father has just died, is called to Paris as ward of the king, Helena secretly follows. The king is suffering from a supposedly incurable fistula—but Helena believes that her father has left her a remedy.

Recognizing both the difficulty and the possible reward, she muses:

> *Impossible be strange attempts to those*
> *That weigh their pains in sense, and do suppose*
> *What hath been cannot be. Whoever strove*
> *To show her merit, that did miss her love?*

[I. i. 224–27]

As she hoped, she is allowed to propose a bargain with the king, venturing her life on the cure. The king is impressed enough to risk his self-esteem, though he believes his case is hopeless. He accepts Helena's offer:

> *Methinks in thee some blessed spirit doth speak*
> *His powerful sound within an organ weak:*
> *And what impossibility would slay*
> *In common sense, sense saves another way....*
> *Thou this [your young life] to hazard needs must intimate*
> *Skill infinite, or monstrous desperate.*
> *Sweet practicer, thy physic I will try*
> *That ministers thine own death if I die.*

[II. i. 174–77, 183–86]

If, however, she succeeds, the king agrees that she may choose any husband whom it is within his power to bestow.

Helena's cure works, and the king forces Bertram to marry her. Another situation involving impossibility immediately arises. Bertram hates Helena for trapping him and deserts her for foreign wars, leaving as her only hope two seemingly impossible conditions, which he sets in a letter:[38]

> *When thou canst get the ring upon my finger,*
> *which never shall come off, and show me a child*
> *begotten of thy body that I am father to, then*
> *call me husband; but in such a 'then' I write a*
> *'never'.*

[III. ii. 57–60]

Helena follows her feckless love to Florence, tricks him into giving up the ring, and bears his child. At last they are reconciled and the contract based on the impossible promise is completed.

While Helena and Bertram are in Florence, a third variation on the theme of impossibility is played out. Parolles, a follower of Bertram and soldier manqué, declares that he will undertake to recover a regimental drum captured by the enemy. Bertram and Parolles form a contract: If Parolles brings "this instrument of honor again into his native quarter," Bertram guarantees that "the duke shall both speak well of it and extend to you what further becomes his greatness" (III. vi. 61–62, 65–66). Bertram is willing to believe Parolles ("to the possibility of thy soldiership [I] will subscribe for thee" [III. vi. 78–79]), but the other soldiers are skeptical. One comments, "Is this not a strange fellow, my lord, that so confidently seems to undertake this business, which he knows is not to be done" (III. vi. 81–84).

Parolles realizes he has trapped himself and laments: "What the devil should move me to undertake the recovery of this drum, being not ignorant of the *impossibility*, and knowing I had no such purpose?" (IV. i. 34–37; italics added). He contemplates a ruse to make it appear he has attempted the exploit, but Bertram's friends, in a stratagem of their own, ambush him and let him damn himself with his own words. His failure to perform his impossible promise leads to exposure of his essential cowardice and to his disgrace.

All three promises are in the form, "If you do this [impossible task] for me, then I will reward you. You must promise in return that you will perform the task. Your failure will justify punishment for breach of promise." A modern instance of this form of promise appears in cases involving doctors' promises of cure.

Impossibility in Medicine

Although, in contrast to Helena, physicians do not, as a general rule, play "You Bet Your Life," there does appear to be an absolute obligation of successful performance with respect to doctors' promises of cures. In Michigan, for example, there is a statute that binds doctors to their written promises of cures.[39] And every law student is familiar with *Hawkins v. McGee*, the successful contract action against Dr. McGee for a botched skin transplant that left his patient with a hairy hand.[40] The strict rule seems to operate under two presumptions: first, that doctors know what they are doing and, second, that they deliberately assume the risk of failure, even if a "promised" cure turns out to be beyond their power or altogether impossible. As one court has said, "If a doctor makes a contract to effect a cure and fails to do so, [he] is liable for breach of contract even though [he] used the highest possible professional skill."[41]

In actuality, most if not all contractual actions against doctors do not really involve promises at all, at least not written promises, and are simply malpractice actions in disguise.[42] These actions usually arise in one of two situations: either the patient has already lost a malpractice action in tort and is casting about for another form of remedy[43] or the patient has delayed filing a claim so that the statute of limitations has run on tort actions but not on contract actions.[44] While courts acknowledge that "it may be unusual for a physician to enter into a special contract to cure rather than to undertake only to render [his] best judgment and skill,"[45] they do find such contracts and when found, no excuse for impossibility is considered. In the leading case in New York, for example, the court was able to twist the patient's allegations into the semblance of a contract claim: "The gist of the action here is defendant's failure to perform his *promise* to cure plaintiff within a specified time by a specified method."[46]

A New Hampshire case[47] squarely addressed the excuse of antecedent impossibility and found it was irrelevant in an action on an oral contract against a physician. The defendant claimed that "the *mutual* understanding of the parties [was] that a cure [for patient's skin disease] was impossible." Based on plaintiff's contrary testimony, however, the court held it "not important that the *defendant* believed or knew that there was no chance of cure. *If he agreed to cure, and the plaintiff thought he would, he is held, although he knew he could not.*" As long as the *plaintiff* believed (and what patient doesn't?), even if only partially, the court reasoned "[w]hen a thing is promised, it is of no consequence whether or not the promisee expects performance," and stated:

> Obligations are often taken when the obligee does not expect their . . . observance. He may pay a price for one, considering it worth while to take the chance that the outcome may be realized in spite of his belief that it will not be. *He buys, not performance, but the promise of performance,* and, if the promise is broken, remedy is not to be denied merely because performance was not expected when the promise was taken.

Supervening Impossibility: The Promise Becomes Impossible

We have seen that the doctrine of excuse by reason of antecedent impossibility is fairly straightforward. There has been some shift from treating relevant contracts as void from inception to treating them as either enforceable or excusable as circumstances warrant. The primary problem becomes one of proof. Unless the promisor can prove, in the face of the impossibility appearing in the contract itself, that he has not knowingly assumed the risk, he will have to pay damages. And, as we saw in the special case of physicians, in some situations, once the promise is proven, assumption of risk is conclusively presumed. Enforceability seems to be reasonable in a system based on promises. This movement *toward* liability on impossible promises probably comports with long-standing common understanding of what a promise means, as exemplified in the literary works we examined.

In the case of supervening impossibility, there has been some movement *away from* the early English rule of absolute liability and a widening of allowable excuses. This relaxation of absolute liability has received extensive coverage in the popular press. We shall see, however, that the shift is probably more one of emphasis than a fundamental realignment of contractual duties and obligations.

Absolute Liability: The Rule of Paradine v. Jane

The absolute rule is often called the rule of *Paradine v. Jane*[48] from the mid-seventeenth-century case, but in fact it can be traced to the very beginning of English law. Obligations under covenants (i.e., contracts under seal) and for debts, actions that long preceded modern contracts, were never excused. For example, Glanvill, writing in 1187 of a debt due on a thing borrowed, says that when the time for return has come, "if the thing itself be destroyed, or has by any means been lost, whilst in your Custody, *you are absolutely bound to return to me a reasonable price.*"[49] The translator refers to Exodus 22:14,15.[50]

When actions to enforce simple, unwritten or unsealed promises developed in fifteenth- and sixteenth-century England, there seemed to be no question that liability would be as absolute as in actions on written or sealed promises such as covenant and debt. At the time of *Paradine v. Jane,* Hobbes, in the continuation of the passage quoted here earlier, set forth this general understanding: "But if [performance of a Covenant] prove Impossible afterwards, which before was thought possible, the Covenant is valid, and bindeth, (though not to the thing it selfe,) yet to the value. . . ."

In *Paradine v. Jane* itself, the defendant was a tenant who had been evicted and dispossessed during the English civil wars and refused to pay rent. The tenant's plea for relief, however, was held insufficient because he had not reserved any rights in his lease to protect himself from ouster. The court distinguished between obligations created by law and those created by private agreements:

> Where the law creates a duty or charge, and the party is disabled to perform it without any default in him, and hath no remedy over, there the law will excuse him. As in the case of waste, if a house be destroyed by tempest, or by enemies, the lease is excused ... *but when the party by his own contract creates a duty or charge* upon himself, he is bound to make it good, if he may, notwithstanding any accident by inevitable necessity, *because he might have provided against it by his contract.*[51]

Later cases take this language as the starting point on the question of impossibility.[52] If the party did not provide for his own excuse, why should the court step in after the fact? *Paradine v. Jane* seems to have been canonized as a leading case simply because its often-quoted language perfectly expressed nineteenth-century concepts of fair dealing, inflexible honesty, and individual autonomy—the moral and cultural underpinnings of the developing regime of "freedom of contract."[53] Courts pontificated: "He that agrees to do a thing should *do it* [even if impossible]. . . . Where one of two innocent persons must sustain a loss, . . . the law leaves it where the agreement of the parties has put it."[54] Application of the rule was seen as protecting the integrity of contracts. As Justice Noah Swayne wrote at the time of the American Civil War:

> The principle [of *Paradine v. Jane*] rests upon a solid foundation of reason and justice. It regards the sanctity of contracts. It requires parties to do what they have agreed to do. If unexpected impediments lie in the way, and a loss must ensue, it leaves the loss where the contract places it. *If the parties have made no provision for a dispensation, the rule of law gives none. It does not allow a contract fairly made to be annulled,* and it does not permit to be interpolated what the parties themselves have not stipulated.[55]

Relaxation of the Rule of Paradine v. Jane

Attractive as the rule was, its source of power—inflexibility—was finally seen to create more hardship than necessary. The burden placed on the promisor was simply too great. The first relaxation of the rule occurred in the mid-nineteenth century when English courts developed the theory of implied conditions. In *Hall v. Wright,*[56] an action for breach of promise to marry, the absolute rule was applied, but only over strong objections. The dissenters cogently argued that a contract to marry was subject to certain implied conditions, such as the continued health and chastity of the parties. The defendant had claimed that because of a sudden disease of the lungs he could not marry without greatly endangering his life. Counsel for the plaintiff successfully countered that "the incapacity merely brings the case within the rule laid down in *Paradine v. Jane*: a contractor may, by the common law, break his contract; but *he must pay damages for doing so.*[57] A divided court on appeal upheld a jury award in favor of the plaintiff for 100 pounds damages.

Although the dissenters in *Hall v. Wright* lost the battle, they seem to have won the war. Just four years later, in *Taylor v. Caldwell*,[58] the court interpreted the absolute rule as applying only "when the contract is positive and absolute, *and not subject to any condition express or implied.*" The plaintiffs in this case had arranged for the use of a music hall for the presentation of four concerts. But, before the first concert had been given, and through no fault of any of the contractors, the hall burned down. The plaintiffs sued to recover "divers moneys paid by them for advertisements and expenses incurred by them in preparing for the concerts." The court, however, taking the hint from the dissenters in *Hall v. Wright* on implied conditions,[59] held that the obligation of the defendants to provide the music hall was subject to the implied condition of its continued existence. Just as the death of a promisor bound to a personal services contract, such as the painting of a portrait,[60] discharged the contract by the impossibility of an implied condition, so the destruction of a chattel or thing on which a contract depended nullified all obligations. The court relied solely on the obscure seventeenth-century case of *Williams v. Lloyd,* in which a court held that the death of a horse discharged the promisor's obligation to redeliver it to its owner:

> "Let it be admitted," say the Court, "that he promised to deliver it on request, if the horse die before, that is become impossible by the act of God, so the party shall be discharged, as much as if the obligation were made conditioned (on the continued existence of the horse)."[61]

Significantly, the only authority cited by the *Williams v. Lloyd* court was Exodus 22:10,11,[62] which contrasts with the absolute rule of

Exodus 22:14 discussed above. Even a defaulting promisor can quote scripture.

There is also a third generally implied condition of "impossibility" in addition to death and destruction that affects the absolute rule: certain supervening governmental interferences discharge all obligations. "The law will not permit an action against a party to a contract for failing to perform an act that a subsequent [governmental] enactment forbids, in the absence of circumstances showing contributing fault or that he assumed the risk of enactment."[63] This excuse appears as early as the sixteenth century,[64] and it is discussed in *Hall v. Wright*.[65] As a modification of the absolute rule, excuse by reason of governmental action clearly involves practical rather than actual impossibility, because the promisor is free to violate the law. However, no court will force a person obligated under the privately created law of his contract to break the public law of the state. As the Supreme Court recently stated: "Obedience to judicial orders is an important public policy. . . . A contract provision the performance of which has been enjoined is unenforceable."[66]

Modern Responses to the Rule of Paradine v. Jane

The rule of *Paradine v. Jane* has been relaxed beyond these three well-recognized implied conditions by both statute and case law, but perhaps not as much as its fervent opponents claim. The Uniform Commercial Code, adopted in some form by all states in the United States in the 1960s to govern relationships among merchants, contains an explicit excuse for impossibility. It provides that a seller may not be in "breach of his duty under a contract for sale if performance as agreed has been made *impracticable* by the occurrence of a contingency the non-occurrence of which was a basic assumption on which the contract was made."[67] The code adopts the test of "commercial impracticability (as opposed to 'impossibility') . . . in order to call attention to [its] commercial character."[68] The doctrine of impossibility of performance contained in the code "ultimately represents the ever-shifting line, drawn by courts hopefully responding to commercial practices and mores, at which the community's interest in having contracts enforced according to their terms is outweighed by the commercial senselessness of requiring performance."[69] "Impracticability" has also been chosen as the standard in the Restatement (2d) of Contracts,[70] which purports to state the common law applicable to *all* contractual relationships, not merely commercial agreements.

This change in nomenclature from "impossible" to "impracticable," however, is more evolution than revolution. Even the first Restatement of Contracts fifty years ago cautioned that the concept of "impossible" must be given "a practical rather than a scientifically exact meaning. Impracticability rather than absolute impossibility is enough, and the words 'impossible' and 'impossibility' are used [herein] with that meaning."[71] As one court recently wrote:

> Although a strict rule [of *Paradine v. Jane*] was originally followed denying any excuse for accident or "inevitable necessity," it has long been assumed that circumstances drastically increasing the difficulty and expense of the contemplated performance may be within the compass of "impossibility." By adopting the term "impracticability" rather than "impossibility" the drafters of the Code appear to be in accord with Professor Williston who stated *that the essence of the modern defense of impossibility is that the promised performance was at the making of the contract, or thereafter became, impracticable owing to some extreme or unreasonable difficulty, expense, injury, or loss involved, rather than that it is scientifically or actually impossible.*[72]

Furthermore, the liberalization of the verbal formula has not significantly increased the number of cases in which the excuse for impossibility has been granted. In a large majority of the reported cases involving the "impossibility" section of the code, it has been found that the conditions for the excuse have *not* been met, perhaps because the code itself is ambivalent. A number of judges have referred to a comment to the "impossibility" section of the code that states:

> The exemptions of this section do not apply *when the contingency in question is sufficiently foreshadowed* at the time of contracting to be included among the business terms which are fairly to be regarded as part of the dickered terms . . . as a matter of reasonable, commercial interpretation from the circumstances.[73]

Courts have used the "foreshadowed" language to add a foreseeability test to the doctrine of impracticability—in effect recreating common law impossibility. If the contingency was *possible* to foresee, then the strict rule of *Paradine v. Jane* will be applied, because any foreseen risk must have been allocated.[74] This approach has been criticized. As Judge Wright held in one of the cases arising out of the 1956 closure of the Suez Canal, "foreseeability, or even recognition of a risk, does not *necessarily prove* its allocation."[75] But, in this case, the longer, more expensive voyages required when the canal was closed were *foreseeable*. Thus, the court judged "the impracticability of performance . . . in stricter terms than [had] the contingency [been] unforeseen,"[76] and it ultimately concluded (as did all other courts, English and American, considering similar cases) that performance of the contract was not rendered legally impossible. The case is a fine example of a court using latitudinarian language to reach the same old puritanical result.

Cook v. Deltona Corp.[77] provides an excellent summation of the issues involved in impossibility by reason of supervening events. There the court considered whether a land development company could be excused from its contractual obligation to dredge and fill underwater land it had sold in Florida. As awareness of environmental matters had grown greatly since the time of sale, the defendant land company found itself unable, at the time for performance, to get the necessary permits from the Army Corps of Engineers. Judge Hill wrote:

> There is a fascinating contradiction inherent in the judicially created impossibility defense which reveals a basic tension in the law. Contracts are born of the need for certainty. They are the merchant's exchange of serendipity for serenity, [his] insurance against change. The early common law enforced the policy by making contractual liability absolute on the theory that a contractual duty . . . is tailored by the party for himself and any eventuality might be provided for in the contract. *Paradine v. Jane.* But change is what impossibility is about. By recognizing impossibility as a sort of "escape hatch" from the self-made chamber of contractual duty, the courts have recognized that absolute contractual liability is economically and socially unworkable. Impossibility accommodates the tension between the changes a party bargains to avoid and the changes, unbargained for and radical, that make enforcement of the bargain unwise.[78]

Unfortunately for the defendant, the court held that foreseeable changes, such as stricter environmental controls, were among those that were part of the bargain and therefore rejected the claim of excuse.

The Eclipse of Paradine v. Jane

The rule of *Paradine v. Jane* may have lost much of its allure. Today the case seems to be cited mainly as a whipping-boy for the bad old days of "sanctity of contracts." And there is indeed a widespread perception that times have changed. Even the popular press is asking, "Are Contracts Obsolete?"[79] Nonetheless, the *result* in *Paradine v. Jane* would certainly be the same today in England, and probably in many jurisdictions in the United States as well. In England, in 1981, the doctrine of "frustration" (an alternate phrase for excuse by reason of impossibility) was for the first time applied to a lease (similar to the one in *Paradine*), as matter of principle, but it was rejected as not applying to the case at hand.[80] The majority thought that a proper case of excuse on a lease would be "exceedingly rare."[81] Similarly, in one of the leading cases in the United States, the doctrine of frustration of a lease due to supervening events was thoroughly and sympathetically examined by the Supreme Court of California and then held not to apply in the particular circumstances.[82]

What, then, accounts for the perception that the contract is becoming obsolete, that its obligations no longer hold? For this view is held by its supporters as well as its opponents. In an almost Spenglerian lament, Professor Harold Berman of Harvard writes:

> Liberalization [of excuse] is due to the breakdown of our faith in contract itself. A jurisprudence of adjustment, entirely appropriate in the realm of remedies, has been applied to the realm of substantive rights as well. Considerations of social policy have been introduced in matters that in the public interest ought to be left to determination by the parties themselves. The decline of faith in contract has been accompanied by an increased faith in general overriding principles, and this, too, has contributed to an unwarranted liberalization of excuse. Courts and writers have sought to develop general business doctrines ["a few loose formulae"] applicable to the most diverse kinds of business activity. The solution, it is submitted, lies in the opposite direction.[83]

There appear to be several reasons for the perception in legal circles and elsewhere that excuse is now granted readily and that the value of the contract has been weakened.

First, there have recently been a few well-publicized cases of excuse. In the most notorious, the trial judge released ALCOA from the burdens of a long-term contract under which it processed alumina.[84] This was controversial enough, but the judge went further and attacked the all-or-nothing rule. Scorning *Paradine v. Jane,* the judge, with the benefit of "hindsight" far superior to that which the parties had when they made their contract, imposed a new price term to save ALCOA from millions of dollars in losses. Why not, the court asked, let increased wisdom undo past foolishness? For some legal commentators, cases like *ALCOA* illustrate "the decline of the sanctity accorded to contracts since the heyday of laissez-faire in the last century."[85] But it is hard to view *ALCOA* as illustrative. Although the decision has its supporters,[86] it has been uniformly rejected by other federal courts[87] and termed "grotesque" and "bizarre" by otherwise even-tempered legal scholars.[88] One federal court, adhering to the traditional line and announcing itself "respectfully at odds with the reasoning and result in *ALCOA,*" stated: "The willingness of courts to reform contracts on the basis of subsequent knowledge may undermine the policy of finality which is so essential and revered in contract law."[89] [Perhaps most significant of all, the businessmen who took the case to court in the first place were so astounded at the court's "reformation" that they reached an out-of-court settlement, mutually abandoning the court-created price term.[90]] Unfortunately, the widespread rejections of *ALCOA* by legal scholars, courts, and businesspeople do not seem to be the stuff from which news articles are made.

A second reason for the general perception may lie in the narrowly averted collapse of the international banking system, in the wake of a wholesale sub-rosa adoption of the impossibility defense. Brazil, Mexico, Argentina, and a host of other countries simply could not, and cannot, pay their debts. For political and accounting reasons, creditors have not forced these countries into bankruptcy and the debtors have not explicitly repudiated their debts; but the various payment moratoria, negotiated and otherwise, bear daily witness to the fact that some contractual obligations, if the scale is large enough, need not be honored.

Third, it is also well known that contracting parties in trouble find other avenues of escape than through litigation. The closing of Ohio thrift institutions early in 1985 by executive order is a good example. The contractual obligation of those state-regulated savings banks to repay their depositors on demand was simply abrogated by the executive power of the state. Similarly, Congress, in the Federal Timber Contracts Modifications Act of 1984, rewrote burdensome contracts that imprudent timber operators in the Pacific Northwest had entered into in the inflationary early 1980s. Although such naked displays of political power may increase cynicism toward the obligations of contract, it is noteworthy that in each instance *judicial* relief was not available for "impossibility."

Fourth, courts have figured out other ways to abrogate contracts, even though the analysis does not explicitly refer to the doctrine of impossibility. In the Washington Public Power Supply System litigation, for example, the Supreme Court of Washington ruled that the creditors holding defaulted bonds did not have to be paid because municipalities and participating utilities had exceeded their authority in incurring the debt. The contracts involved, which were "take or pay" or "dry-hole" contracts, obligated the borrowers to repay come hell or high water. Only in the dissenting opinion did the court come close to an analysis of impossibility. One dissenting judge thought the "contracts are best characterized as a purchase of a "possibility" of power. In return for consideration in the form of guaranty of the revenue bonds, the participants received not guaranteed power but an exclusive right to power which might or might not materialize."[91] That is, he believed that the risk had clearly been allocated to the participants. On rather weak reasoning and hypertechnical legal arguments, however, the majority held that such risk was legally impossible for the participants to assume, so the bondholders became bagholders.

Finally, the whole issue of enforceability of contracts is a subject of very hot debate in academic legal circles. Some scholars regard the institution of contracts as an instrument of oppression.[92] Others merely want to do away with promise as a basis for obligation, so that *expectations* based on another's word are never protected and only actual *reliance* is recompensed.[93] That is, a party is protected against breach of promise only to the extent it has acted on the faith in that promise, and not for *"lost profits"* or other expectations. To the extent that "impossibility" offers a tool for undermining the traditional rule of enforcement of contracts, such writers vociferously magnify its importance. The Restatement (2d) of Contracts, while not joining in this general attack on the use of contracts, has both embraced "impracticability" and introduced a rule designed to mitigate the harshness of the all-or-nothing rule, inviting the court when "impossibility" is claimed to "grant relief on such terms as justice requires."[94] It remains to be seen whether these voices decrying the institution of contracts and their strict enforcement will be listened to by the ordinary promisor or the average judge.

Conclusion

As in Mark Twain's obituary, the reports of the demise of strict contract liability are greatly exaggerated. While courts in general have recognized that an excuse by reason of impossibility is appropriate in many circumstances, more often than not the particular facts being considered have not justified the excuse. The Uniform Commercial Code's adoption of an excuse for impossibility (or "impracticability") due to the occurrence of supervening events has had little impact. Moreover, in one respect, the defense of impossibility is being narrowed, as courts enforce rather than negate promises that were impossible from the beginning. Therefore, promisors should remain wary. As Lord Buckley, the American comedian, used to say: "If you come to it and you can't do it, well there you jolly well are, aren't you." Despite enticing language to the contrary, most courts in both England and America still hold that there you jolly well will stay.

Notes

1. For reasons of style, masculine pronoun forms have been used. Throughout this chapter, in indefinite contexts, read "he" as "he or she," etc.

2. A clause that protects the parties in the event the contract cannot be performed because of causes outside their control. See *Black's Law Dictionary,* rev. 5th ed., 1979, p. 581.

3. Cook v. Deltona Corp., 753 F.2d 1552, 1558 (11th Cir. 1985).

4. Hawkins v. First Federal Savings and Loan Association, 280 So. 2d 93, 95 (S. Ct. Ala. 1973), quoting 6 Williston on Contracts, §1931 (rev. ed., 1938). Here "early" cases refer to pre-twentieth-century cases in America.

5. See, for example, Fried, *Contract as Promise,* Cambridge University Press, 1981, pp. 69–73.

6. Dartmouth College v. Woodward, 17 U.S. (4 Wheat.) 518, 628 (1819) (Marshall, C. J.).

7. *The Federalist No. 44,* C. Rossiter, ed., 1961, p. 283. Madison believed that the mere expression of certain rights, as in the Bill

of Rights, served an important educative function. Such "paper barriers have a tendency to impress some degree of respect for them, to establish public opinion in their favor, and rouse the attention of the whole community." (Speech proposing the Bill of Rights, June 8, 1789, quoted in "Note: The Origins and Original Significance of the Just Compensation Clause of the Fifth Amendment," Yale Law Journal, 94: 694, 710 (1985).

8. See generally Horowitz, *The Transformation of American Law*, Cambridge University Press, 1976. Horowitz discusses the increasing rigor of contract enforcement evident as the nineteenth century progressed.

9. Bronson v. Kinzie, 42 U.S. (1 How.) 311, 318 (1843) (invalidating a state law that protected a defaulting mortgagor beyond his covenant).

10. *Massachusetts General Laws*, Chapter 208 §1 provides "a divorce from the bond of matrimony may be adjudged for . . . an *irretrievable* breakdown of the marriage." §1B provides for a one-year waiting period before the divorce becomes final if the noncomplaining spouse objects. A disagreement between estranged spouses as to whether the marriage has suffered an irretrievable breakdown only proves the point.

11. Gleason v. Gleason, 26 N.Y. 2d 28 (1970).

12. Ibid., 42 ("Marriage is not a contract within the meaning of the provision of the Federal Constitution which prohibits the impairment by the States of the obligations of contracts.").

13. Dartmouth College v. Woodward, 17 U.S. (4 Wheat.) 518, 629 (1819) (emphasis added).

14. Under the rehabilitation chapters of the Bankruptcy Act in effect prior to 1978, the petition had to state that the debtor was insolvent (a balance sheet test) or unable to pay his debts as they matured (§§130(1), 323, 423, and 623). The Bankruptcy Code now allows a petition to be filed before any act of bankruptcy is committed.

15. 25 U.S. (12 Wheat.) 213 (1827) (separate opinion).

16. 407 East 61st Garage, Inc. v. Savoy Fifth Ave. Corp., 23 N.Y. 2d 175, 281 (1968) (emphasis added).

17. 11 U.S.C. §365(a). The legislative history to §365(a) indicates that Congress intended "executory contract" to mean a contract "on which performance is due to some extent on both sides." 95th Cong., 1st sess., 1977, H.R. Rep. No. 595, p. 347.

18. National Labor Relations Board v. Bildisco and Bildisco, 104 S. Ct. 1188 (1984). A 1984 amendment requires court approval for termination of labor contracts (U.S.C. §1113). In the first test of this section, the court allowed the labor contract to be abrogated. *In Re Wheeling Pittsburgh Steel Corp.*, Lexis Slip Op. (W.D. Pa., July 17, 1985).

19. National Labor Relations Board, supra, 1198.

20. The awesome power of bankruptcy has not been lost on the business community. See, for example, the *New York Times*, Nov. 6, 1983, Section 4, p. 9, col. 1. ("For the Manville Corporation ... bankruptcy has meant a way to freeze thousands of worker lawsuits related to ill effects of asbestos exposure. For Wilson Foods and Continental Airlines, bankruptcy has been a route to slashing the wages established in union contracts. And for HRT Industries, a retailer, bankruptcy provided a way to delay payment for the Christmas inventory it had just stocked before filing.")

21. See, for example, Stees v. Leonard, 20 Minn. 494 (1874). "A contractor encountering unexpectedly swampy terrain, almost completes a promised structure, but it collapses. He rebuilds. It collapses again. Finally, he throws up his hands." (As described in Fried, *Contract as Promise*, p. 64.)

22. See, for example, 6 Williston, Contracts (rev. ed. 1938) §1933. ("If unknown to both parties there is little reason to distinguish existing impossibility from supervening impossibility.")

23. See, for example, St. Germain, *Doctor and Student*, 1530, reprinted by the Selden Society, T. F. T. Plucknett and J. L. Barton, eds., pp. 228–29, where the student claims that a promise to be binding at common law must be possible to perform.

24. Dr. Bonham's Case, 8 Co. Rep. 114a, 118a, 77 Eng. Rep. 645, 652 (1610) (emphasis added).

25. Hobbes, *The Leviathan*, C. B. Macpherson, ed., London, 1968, part I, chapter 14, p. 198.

26. Powell, *Essay Upon the Law of Contracts and Agreements,* London, 1790, p. 160.

27. Ibid., p. 161.

28. Chesire and Fifoot, *Law of Contracts,* 8th ed., London, 1972, p. 207.

29. Thornborow v. Whitacre, 2 Lord Rey. 1164, 92 Eng. Rep. 270 (1705).

30. 92 Eng. Rep. 270.

31. Ibid., 271.

32. *The Harriman,* 76 U.S. (9 Wall.) 161 (1869) (contract to carry material into a war zone: failure held not excused) (emphasis added). See also Parsons, *The Law of Contracts,* 4th ed., Boston, 1855, pp. 185–86 ("If one for a valid consideration promises another to do that which is in fact impossible, but the promise is not obtained by actual or constructive fraud, and is not on its face obviously impossible, *there seems to be no reason why the promisor should not be held to pay damages for the breach of contract; not in fact, for not doing what cannot be done, but for undertaking and promising to do it.*") (emphasis added); and Holmes, *The Common Law,* Howe ed., 1963, pp. 234–35 (When "a man convenants that it shall rain tomorrow . . . he only says, in a short form, I will pay if it does not rain.").

33. Jacksonville etc. Railway v. Hooper, 160 U.S. 515, 528–9 (1895) (defendant railway held liable for damages arising out of its failure to perform contract to insure building, even though procuring insurance was not within its statutory powers).

34. Restatement of Contracts §456, Comment c at 847. In a typical oil exploration investment, for example, the investor buys a chance and pays for any dry holes. The possibility of profitably recovering hydrocarbons is antecedent to the drilling.

35. Austin Co. v. United States, 161 Ct. Cl. 76, 314 F.2d 518, *cert. denied,* 375 U.S. 830 (1963). (Company believed it could design and build a "better" range finder than the government had requested. It failed due to unforeseen technical problems.)

36. W. R. Grace and Co. v. Local Union 759, 461 U.S. 757, 103 S. Ct. 2177, 2183–4 (1983) (emphasis added).

37. *The Riverside Shakespeare*, Evans, ed., Boston, 1974. Act and scene references are to this edition.

38. In Shakespeare's main source, Painter's *Palace of Pleasure*, the impossibility is explicit: "the hard condition of two things *impossible*" (*All's Well That Ends Well*, Hunter, ed., 1959, Appendix).

39. Michigan Compiled Laws §566.132(g).

40. 146 A. 642, 84 N.H. 114 (1929). (The doctor was found to have said: "I will guarantee to make this hand a one hundred percent perfect hand.")

41. Safian v. Aetna Life Ins. Co., 260 A.D. 765, 24 N.Y.S. 2d 92 (1940), aff'd., 286 N.Y. 649 (1941).

42. No litigant would choose a contractual action if a tort action were available. Recovery in contract is limited, precluding, for example, payment for pain and suffering.

43. See, for example, McQuaid v. Michou, 157 A. 881, 882 (N.H. 1934).

44. See, for example, Robins v. Finestone, 308 N.Y. 543, 546 (1955).

45. Ibid., 546.

46. Ibid., 547.

47. McQuaid v. Michou, 157 A. 881, supra, 883 and 885 (emphasis added).

48. Aleyn 26, 82 Eng. Rep. 897 (1647).

49. Glanvill, *De Legibus*, 1187, Beames, trans., 1812, book 10, chapter 13.

50. "When a man borrows a beast from his neighbor and it is injured or dies while its owner is not with it, the borrower shall make full restitution."

51. Paradine v. Jane, supra, 82 Eng. Rep., 897 (emphasis added). The "remedy over" would have been unavailable in this instance be-

cause the despoiler was an alien. The phrase "if he may" refers to the traditional distinction between a house and a wood if either is destroyed by tempest. In the latter case, the "lessee *cannot* make the woods grow again as they were before" (Thornborow v. Whitacre, supra).

52. See, for example, John Williams' notes to Walton v. Waterhouse, 2 Wms. Saunders 420, 422, n.2, discussing *Paradine v. Jane. Walton* is reported at 85 Eng. Rep. 1233 (1684) (action on a covenant to repair a dwelling which was "wholly fallen down and ruinous"). Williams' edition of Saunders was first published in 1799.

53. In one sense the case *was* almost of the nineteenth century—a leading contracts textbook traces its "modern vogue" to John Williams' note to the old case of *Walton v. Waterhouse* in an edition first published in 1799, and comments that *Paradine v. Jane* had up to then not been particularly famous for 150 years (Kessler and Gilmore, *Contracts,* Boston, 1970, p. 758).

54. School Trustees of Trenton v. Bennett, 27 N.J.L. 513, 519–20 (1859) (emphasis in original).

55. Dermott v. Jones, 69 U.S. (2 Wall.) 1, 8 (1864) (emphasis added). Later, the same justice noted in *The Harriman*, 76 U.S. (9 Wall.) 161, 173 (1869), that the rule comported with a proper view of the judicial sphere: "[The rule of] *Paradine v. Jane* . . . has always been the rule of the common law. It is the province of courts to enforce contracts—not to make or modify them. When there is neither fraud, accident, nor mistake, the exercise of dispensing power is not a judicial function."

56. El. Bl. & El. 758, rev'd El. Bl. & El. ·765, 120 Eng. Rep. 688, 695 (1859).

57. El. Bl. & El. 767, 120 Eng. Rep. 696.

58. 3 B. & S. 826, 122 Eng. Rep. 309, 312 (1863) (emphasis added).

59. The connection between *Hall v. Wright* and *Taylor v. Caldwell* was pointed out in Simpson, "Innovation in Nineteenth Century Contract Law," 91 L. Q. Rev. 247, 270–71 (1975).

60. Taylor v. Caldwell, 122 Eng. Rep. 313, citing *Hyde v. Dean of Windsor,* Cro. Eliz. 552; 78 Eng. Rep. 798 (1597). The notion

that death releases all obligations is an ancient one but this is true at law only if there has been no breach in the lifetime of the promisor. See 2 Wms. Exors., 6th ed., p. 1593.

61. Taylor v. Caldwell, 122 Eng. Rep. 314 (translating the law French of Williams v. Lloyd, W. Jones 179; 82 Eng. Rep. 95 [1629].

62. "When a man gives . . . any beast into his neighbor's keeping, and it dies . . . , there being no witness, the neighbor shall swear by the Lord that he has not touched the man's property . . . and no restitution shall be made."

63. Restatement (2d) of Contracts, §458 Comment a at 852.

64. Abbot of Westminster v. Clarke, 1 Dy. 26b, 28b, 73 Eng. Rep. 59, 63 (1536). The court assented to the proposition of counsel that "if the condition of an obligation be, that if the obligor carry twenty quarters of wheat before a certain day in a foreign country . . . and before the day a statute be made, which prohibits any man from carrying corn into a foreign country; that is a dispensation with the condition."

65. Hall v. Wright, supra, 120 Eng. Rep. 695.

66. W.R. Grace & Co. v. Local Union 759, 461 U.S. 757, 103 S. Ct. 2177, 2184 (1983) (citing Restatement (2d) of Contracts).

67. Uniform Commercial Code §2-615(a).

68. Ibid., Comment 3.

69. Transatlantic Financing Corp. v. U.S., 363 F.2d 312, 315 (D.C. Cir. 1966) (footnote omitted).

70. Restatement (2d) of Contracts §261. (The Second Restatement was adopted to reflect changes in the common law of contracts since the 1920s and 1930s.)

71. Restatement of Contracts §454, Comment a.

72. Mishara Const. Co. v. Transit-Mixed Concrete Corp., 365 Mass. 122, 310 N.E. 2d 363, 366 (Mass. 1974) (emphasis added; citations omitted) (the presence of a picket line made delivery of concrete "impossible").

73. Uniform Commercial Code §2-615 Comment 8 (emphasis added).

74. See, for example, Eastern Air Lines, Inc. v. Gulf Oil Corp., 415 F. Supp. 429 (S.D. Fla. 1975) (Arab oil embargo and subsequent price rise foreseeable at time of contract formation: no relief from fuel supply contract).

75. Transatlantic Financing Corp. v. U.S., 363 F.2d 312, 318 (D.C. Cir. 1966) (footnote omitted; emphasis added).

76. Ibid., 319.

77. 753 F.2d 1552 (11th Cir. 1985) (citations omitted).

78. Ibid., 1557-8.

79. *Forbes,* April 29, 1985, p. 101 (specifically discussing *Paradine v. Jane*).

80. National Carriers Ltd. v. Panalpina Ltd., [1981] A.C. 675.

81. Ibid., 692.

82. *Lloyd v. Murphy,* 25 C. 2d 48, 153 P. 2d 58 (1944).

83. Berman, "Excuse for Nonperformance in the Light of Contract Practices in International Trade," Col. Law Review, 63: 1413, 1438-9 (1963).

84. Aluminum Co. of America v. Essex Group, Inc., 499 F. Supp. 53 (W. D. Pa. 1980).

85. *New York Times,* Jan. 8, 1985, D2, Col. 1.

86. See, for example, Speidel, "Court-Imposed Price Adjustments under Long-Term Supply Contracts," Northwestern University Law Review, 76: 369 (1981).

87. See, for example, *Wabash, Inc. v. Avnet, Inc.,* 516 F. Supp. 995, 999 (N.D. Ill. 1981), and *In re Westinghouse Elec. Corp.,* 517 F. Supp. 440, 458 (E.D. Va. 1981).

88. Dawson, "Judicial Revision of Frustrated Contracts: United States," Boston University Law Review, 64: 1, 26, 28 (1984) (hereinafter *Dawson*).

89. Printing Industries Assoc. v. International Printing and Graphic Communications Union, 584 F. Supp. 990, 998 (N.D. Ohio 1984).

90. *Dawson,* supra, p. 28.

91. Chemical Bank v. Washington Public Power Supply System, 99 Wash. 2d 772, 666 P. 2d 329, 348 (1983) (dissenting opinion) (emphasis in original); reviewed, 102 Wash. 2d 874, 691 P. 2d 524 (1984).

92. See generally, Kennedy, "Form and Substance in Private Law Adjudication," Harvard Law Review, 89: 1685 (1976).

93. See, for example, Atiyah, *Promises, Morals and the Law,* Oxford, 1981.

94. Restatement (2d) of Contracts §271.

CHAPTER TWELVE • ADAM YARMOLINSKY

IMPOSSIBILITY IN GOVERNMENT AND FOREIGN POLICY

Politics has been described as the art of the possible. If discerning the possible in politics is so chancy a venture that it cannot be reduced to a science, but remains an art, then politics must consist of islands of possibility in a sea of impossibilities. Yet the phrase suggests that politics is more than the art of distinguishing the impossible, but requires an effort to achieve what is within the politician's reach, if not his (or her) grasp.

This essay will address two questions: What are the principal sources of impossibility in politics? And what are the qualities that enable some politicians to achieve goals in spite of impossibility?

To begin with, politicians don't put quite the same meaning, or meanings, into the word "impossible" that those in other professions do. Where the diplomat's "yes" means "maybe" and "maybe" means "no," the politician very seldom says "yes," and a "maybe" generally means "something can be done," while a "no" is a conditional no—circumstances can always change. "Finality," said Disraeli, "is not the language of politics." It may be surprising to some readers to learn that, at least in dealings with peers, a politician's word is to be trusted more than that of most people. A bargain may be unconscionable, but it is binding. If a committee chairman tells the majority leader he has the votes to bring a bill out of committee, the majority leader can generally rely on that statement, because the committee chair, in turn, can count on the commitments he has obtained from individual legislators. This is so not because politicians are inherently more honest than other people, but rather because a commitment represents a necessary point of certainty in the rapidly shifting, very uncertain universe that surrounds the politician.

When a politician says something is impossible, he means that it can't happen unless certain conditions change—and conditions do change, sometimes even at the behest of the person who wants them to. What makes a political event possible or impossible is the behavior of other people, and almost always of more than one other person; even a dictator is influenced by his expectations of how various elements of the population will react. At first, predictability can be expected to decline as the number of relevant actors increases. When a bill has to get through the authorization and the appropriations committees of the House and the Senate, it is at least twice as much work as when there is a permanent authorization and all you need this year is an appropriation. But early on, the predictability curve turns upward, as random variations in individual behavior begin to cancel each other out. Overall, the curve turns out to be shaped like the Big Dipper, and it becomes asymptotic at a point far from certainty—as the results of national election polls demonstrate.

Accordingly, most political outcomes are not achievable (impossible) at least in the terms originally proposed, but few if any political outcomes are really impossible, given enough energy and ingenuity—although you may be sorry you tried and sorrier still if you succeed. It is generally conceded that President Kennedy was fortunate that the misery of the Bay of Pigs was not prolonged and magnified, and I believe President Carter was fortunate that the hostage rescue attempt aborted in the desert outside Tehran, as, had it reached its goal, it might well have resulted in the death of all the hostages and in reprisals against other Americans living in Iran.

William Morris, the Victorian socialist poet-printer, put these propositions more elegantly when he wrote: "Men fight and lose the battle, and the thing they fought for comes about in spite of their defeat and when it comes it turns out to be not what they meant, and other men have to fight for what they meant, under another name."

The art of the possible, then, is the art of recognizing what is within the existing political capacities of those who desire a particular outcome; but it is also the art of dissolving—or, more likely, dodging—the obstacles in the path of achievement, so that a particular outcome moves from the "impossible" column to the "possible" column. This art is practiced at all levels of government—local, state, and national—and in politicoeconomic intercourse among nations. It is an essential skill in elective and appointive office, and in the career services—civil, military, and diplomatic.

Physical impossibility is not a major problem for politicians. This is so, not because politicians are faster than a speeding bullet or can leap over tall buildings with a single bound, but rather because political problems are not, by and large, physical problems. Indeed, politicians are able to accept physical impossibilities as political realities with remarkable equanimity. Both our government and the Chinese government(s) agree that there is only one China and that it occupies both the mainland and the island of Formosa. Bei Jing and Taipei disagree as to which one of them represents China, but we are willing to pretend that both of them are correct, thus denying the validity of the principle I learned in high-school physics that two bodies cannot occupy the same space at the same time. Theoretical physicists may not accept the principle today, but, not, I suspect, for the same reason that prompts us to recognize two congruent Chinas.

Politicians are inclined to take physical limitations as givens. Political alternatives are generally not physical alternatives, and there are almost always political ways around physical obstacles. There is a sharp difference of opinion as to whether our economic difficulties are primarily in the realm of distribution or of production, but in either case the problems are seen as organizational rather than technological. Even the most vocal supply-side enthusiasts don't argue that we are short on technological innovation. Their incentives are designed to motivate managers, not scientists. The important questions about the hot line between Washington and Moscow are not how rapidly it can operate, but how rapidly it *should* operate in order to keep up with crisis developments while allowing leaders time for second thoughts before they send a reply.

Physical impossibility enters into political calculations only when politicians neglect the physical facts—the hot line was in need of electronic upgrading for a long time before both sides got around to renegotiating their agreement in 1983. An industrial policy to revitalize the United States steel industry must find a political means to accommodate the need to relocate steel production facilities in order to shorten transportation distances. For economic reasons, it is clear that new steel mills should be located on the two coasts; but the political obstacles to moving the mills out of the Middle West are practically insuperable. If you don't want acid rain to ruin our relations with Canada, you have to find a way to finance scrubbers in Ohio factories or to live with the economic and political consequences of closing those midwestern plants. To say there is no free lunch only means you have to find the money—yours or someone else's—to pay for it.

The politician's problem of physical impossibility is thus transformed into problems of economic impossibility—or, rather, problems of choice among various economic possibilities. Again, most economic choices turn out to be unaffordable, but no particular purchase appears impossible. A zero-sum game can always be transformed by bringing in more players, who must ante up at least some of their assets, for the benefit of all the players who got in first. Even unlikely combinations are not out of reach, given enough political ingenuity, or political muscle, and a willingness to accept the political costs—as the Reagan administration has demonstrated by combining a tax cut with an enormous increase in the defense budget. Unprecedented deficit financing may be economically dangerous—at least on the current scale—but it is not politically impossible.

Of the three principal sources of impossibility in politics—bureaucracies, factions, and elections—the single greatest source of impossibility is bureaucracy. Bureaucracy, a word not intended in any pejorative sense, is what makes things actually happen as a result of political decisions. Truman's observation about Eisenhower is classic: "He'll sit here and he'll say, 'Do this! Do that!' And nothing will happen. Poor Ike—it won't be a bit like the Army. He'll find it very frustrating." The only thing Truman got wrong was that the Army doesn't always respond to a direct order either. A case in point: Early in the Kennedy administration, the secretary of defense issued a directive instructing base commanders to "make every effort to promote desegregation off-base." Nothing happened. Most base commanders never even heard about the directive. It was only when the secretary saw to it that specific responsibilities were assigned, when a follow-up mechanism was devised, and when achievement in eliminating or reducing off-base discrimination was made an element in the periodic evaluations of a base commander's performance that results began to become visible.

None of the foregoing is intended to deny the critical importance of individual acts. Rosa Parks may have done more for civil rights by refusing to sit in the back of the bus than Lyndon Johnson and the Congress of the United States together. But to translate Rosa Parks' action, to translate Martin Luther King's dream, into specific results, bureaucracies had to change their day-to-day practices.

Bureaucracies always have the last word, because it is only through the bureaucracy that anything can actually be accomplished: it is the bureaucracy that drafts the detailed instructions, that hires the people to carry them out—and buys the tools and rents the space and meets the payroll—and checks up to make sure that the job was done the way the instructions called for. If the bureaucracy doesn't want to do it your way, it can frustrate you at every turn.

Bureaucracies have two other strategic advantages over those who would be their masters. They sit astride the channels of communication between would-be decision makers and the actual operators, and the routes to advancement for those who have to carry out the orders.

Everything a politician can find out about what is actually going on within the bureaucracy amounts to not much more than the bureaucracy is willing to tell him. He can try to read between the lines of their reporting, but he will always be short of the detailed knowledge needed to interpret what tale is told; he can rely on his own staff to try to ferret out the truth, but staff members' access to the interior of the bureaucracy will be very much a function of how well they get along with the people from whom they are seeking information. When Secretary of Defense McNamara, in the early days of the Kennedy administration, called on the RAND Corporation, an Air Force think tank, to help with analysis of Air Force operations, the RAND people pointed out that there were definite limits on what they could do for the secretary without being cut off from the firsthand sources of information within the Air Force on which the usefulness of their analysis depended. Some of the most useful information for politicians develops when two factions within a bureaucracy disagree; but the factions will go to great lengths to reach a compromise, in order to avoid disclosing their disagreements, and the underlying facts, to their masters. The alleged Vietnam era conspiracy to inflate figures on North Vietnamese troop strength, discussed in a recent CBS documentary, really arose out of an apparently desperate effort within the bureaucracy to compromise on conflicting estimates and present a united front to President Johnson.

Every public bureaucracy has its own promotion system—civil service, military service, foreign service—which is designed, so far as possible, to exclude outside influences. Military officers from all four services serve on the staff of the secretary of defense and in the office of the Joint Chiefs of Staff, where single-service interests should be subordinated to common concern. In the jargon of the Pentagon, they wear purple suits. But these officers know that their promotions depend on decisions by their own service promotion boards, whose members wear Army olive drab, Navy blue, Air Force light blue, or the bright plumage of the Marines. That there is at least a potential conflict of interest must be clear.

It is a cliché that change comes hard to bureaucracies, so much so that it is sometimes easier to create a new bureaucracy rather than try to change an existing one. And, even then, the new bureaucracy may be coopted by the old one. When the Department of Housing and Urban Development was created out of the old Federal Housing Administration and a number of other smaller agencies, the idea was that HUD would find new answers to the new problems of housing urban populations. But for a long time it continued to be dominated by the old ideas of the FHA, which knew all there was to know about insuring residential mortgages, because that was something it had been doing since it was set up, a generation earlier. For decades, the Army, Navy, and Air Force refused to recognize that they had been incorporated into a new Department of Defense and continued to plan separately and independently, even for combined operations. Thus, the Air Force stockpiled a different number of days' supply of ammunition for its close support of the Army than the Army stockpiled for operations that depended on close air support.

It is only natural that a bureaucracy will go on doing what it started out to do, even if what it does is no longer relevant to the purposes for which it was created. If a new organization, still dominated by the people and the ideas of the old Federal Housing Administration, is asked to address the problems of ghetto housing, it will come up with plans for bigger and better mortgage insurance programs. What the bureaucracy knows how to do must be the best way to deal with whatever task is assigned to it. Impossibility is trying to change a bureaucracy's direction rather than just effect incremental changes.

From their dealings with bureaucracies, politicians learn to recognize that bureaucracies, not unlike elected officials, have their constituencies. These constituencies are generally industrial or professional rather than geographical—although it is no accident that secretaries of the interior come from the West and secretaries of agriculture from the Middle West. The Air Force Systems Command necessarily has a symbiotic relationship with the aerospace industry, as does the Bureau of Public Roads with the trucking industry and the Federal Home Loan Bank Board with the savings and loan industry. There is almost always a triangular relationship among a bureaucracy, its constituents, and the relevant congresspersons and congressional committee staffs. The astute politician must take proper account of these relationships. During the fight over the proposed Immigration Reform Bill of 1984, the Agriculture Department bureaucracy, acting (informally) on behalf of western growers, who wanted a continuing supply of cheap Mexican labor, sought to add a "guest worker" amendment, which was opposed with equal vigor by the Labor Department bureaucracy on behalf of the U.S. labor unions, who are the Department's primary constituency. Each bureaucracy worked with its committees in the Congress to secure appropriate representatives on the Senate-House conference committee that would settle the differences between the Senate and House versions of the bill. The inability of the politicians in the White House to resolve the dispute between the underlying constituencies added critically to their difficulties in trying to secure passage of the bill.

Politicians prefer to deal with bureaucratic obstacles in an indirect fashion. If they can split the bureaucracy by taking sides with an internal faction, before the opposing factions have managed to reconcile their differences, they may be able to neutralize the opposition of the overall organization. If they can set up a new bureaucracy oriented toward a new program, leaving the old bureaucracy to wither on the vine, it may cost less than it would to convert the existing organization. This device, a favorite of Franklin Roosevelt's, has become more difficult in an era of rising costs and cost-consciousness.

If bureaucracies force new ideas into old forms, whether or not they fit, factions—our second principal source of impossibility—split the force that drives the new idea. It is characteristic of the canny politician that the first question he will ask about a cause in which he has been enlisted is "Who will be against us?" He knows that politics is at least as much the art of neutralizing one's enemies as it is of mollifying one's friends. It is really a matter of arithmetic: there may be several reasons for supporting a particular cause or goal; but there are always more reasons for opposing it, since there will be as many such reasons as there are other causes or goals that some see as more important. It is almost unheard of for a political idea to capture the popular imagination to such an extent that it can over-whelm the opposition. The idea of a nuclear freeze, of ending the war in Vietnam, or of extending fundamental rights to blacks—these are ideas that swept the country. But most ideas—even very good ones—cannot succeed against the host of other ideas—good, bad, and indifferent—that are all competing for the same scarce resources of money or time or public attention. The only way a less-than-over-whelming idea can come out on top is if its proponents make judi-cious alliances with the proponents of other ideas and share the spoils. The antipoverty legislation of the sixties was enacted, against heavy odds, in part because its advocates enlisted the support of the conservation lobby, by agreeing to make half the Job Corps training centers conservation camps—although there was not much of a job market for young people trained to do conservation work.

But most of the time good ideas fail, because no one is able to put together a coalition strong enough to pull one idea out of the mass of contending proposals and make it happen.

This is not the case, however, with negative ideas. It does not take large numbers to keep something from happening. A small group of true believers can almost always stymie the positive efforts of a clear majority, as the National Rifle Association has amply demonstrated. Most politicians, most of the time, are looking for reasons not to support most causes—or at least not to support them actively, in a way that brings one cause into conflict with others competing for the same scarce resources. Like Sam Goldwyn, the career politician will refuse to pick more than nine of the ten most beautiful women in Hollywood. In fact, the politician may refuse to pick even one, for fear of offending all the rest.

Political parties are, more than anything else, mechanisms de-signed to maintain workable coalitions, shifting goals while preserv-ing some degree of continuity. American political parties are the least ideological political organizations in the world. Republicans can move from being sworn enemies of deficit spending to denying the significance of unprecedented deficits, without any embarrassment. Democrats may be for or against big defense spending, depending on the season. But each party still maintains a kind of internal equilibrium that enables its members to offer mutual support for a set of propositions that are politically if not logically consistent. In recent years, however, with the decline of party power—for all the well-rehearsed reasons—and the rise of single-interest groups, our simplest mechanism for creating and preserving coalitions is in eclipse. Ironically, the dominance of the single-interest groups has made it less likely—more nearly impossible—that any of them will achieve their intensely pursued goals. All they can do is to stop other groups from achieving *their* goals.

Elections are, paradoxically, yet another obstacle to positive political accomplishment. A newly elected administration may have a brief period in which it can do great things: pass laws, change policies, initiate new programs. This immediate postelection period is the time when some problems can actually be resolved, either by the political force of the new people, as with Lyndon Johnson's Great Society programs, or by a tacit agreement to suspend political infighting, as was the case with Social Security reform at the outset of the Reagan administration. But the shadow of impending elections induces a kind of paralysis that sets in many months before the actual event. The incumbents are reluctant to do anything controversial, since they tend to believe that the status quo gives them an edge over their opponents—or, if their record has not met with general approbation, they are too busy defending it to push new ideas into actions. At the same time, the outs find that it is more effective to attack the record of the ins than to propose specific alternatives, which are likely to garner opponents as well as supporters. It is easier, and generally more effective, for a presidential contender to declare in favor of new ideas, even to announce the areas in which he believes new ideas are needed, than to specify the actual content of those ideas.

The increasing importance of money in electoral campaigns (as television ads have displaced party organization canvassers) exacerbates the negative effects of elections. If candidates have to spend at least as much time soliciting dollars as they do soliciting votes, they have even less time to spend on the substance of their jobs. Keeping contributors (even more than constituents) happy becomes a matter of helping to resolve individual problems (real or imagined) rather than of initiating or facilitating social change.[1]

All these sources of impossibility are magnified when political problems cross national boundaries, as they do more and more often. Again, it is easier to frustrate the aims of another national sovereignty than to achieve one's own aims. Governments are generally quite respectful of each other's interests, once they are satisfied that a particular interest is a matter of real concern to the other sovereignty. They will try, up to a point, to refrain from offending their neighbors. This is especially the case if they can do so by not acting, rather than by taking positive action, as Schelling pointed out in making his classic distinction between deterrence (if you step across that line, I'll knock you down) and compellence (unless you step across that line, I'll knock you down). Deterrence is easier.

The practical determinants of behavior between sovereignties involve a calculation of how far what I propose to do will affect what you see as your vital interests—interests for which you are prepared to upset the apple cart of peaceful international relations—always provided there is not too wide a disparity between the relative power positions of the two countries or of their great power patrons. There is a range of activities in which separate sovereignties will involve themselves, beyond not stepping on each others' toes, to reach out to cooperate with each other, where cooperation is not a zero-sum game. The range extends from the International Postal Union to the control of airplane hijacking. Here impossibility gives way to mutual self-interest. But even these agreements can be hostage to the special interests of constituencies within one country, who may be adversely affected by a proposed agreement. Witness the failure of the United States, after years of painstaking negotiations to agree to the Law of the Sea Treaty, although it clearly offered a net gain, including significant national security benefits, apparently because certain mining interests believed they could exploit undersea mineral resources more profitably without the treaty.

The availability of a mutually advantageous resolution of international differences clearly does not guarantee its acceptance. The result may be a tacit (or explicit) agreement to disagree for the time being. Thus, in the case of the Law of the Sea Treaty, the United States has refused to sign the treaty without (so far) taking any specific action in violation of it. Disagreement may even escalate into armed conflict. At some point peaceful resolution becomes an impossibility. What began as a miscalculation of how the other side would react may jell into a determination to risk war, if necessary, to achieve national objectives.

There is a choice of strategies here: A nation may choose to appear intransigent, in the hope that the other side will back down; or, it may choose to appear accommodating, in the hope that a peaceful accommodation can be achieved. It is not unlike the classical paradox of the prisoner's dilemma. If one side is intransigent and the other side is accommodating, the first side will come out ahead. But if both sides are intransigent, the consequences will be worse for each one than if both sides are accommodating. The worst position is to resist settlement but to appear unlikely, or unprepared, to resist the use of force—as the British learned to their sorrow in the Falkland Islands dispute.

The threshold of impossibility for the peaceful resolution of international disputes remains relatively high, at least until the outset of actual hostilities. Once blood has been shed, the calculus of possibilities changes radically; political survival is now at stake—not necessarily the survival of the countries involved in the conflict, but the survival of their governments. The party in power may not be able to remain in power after compromising the nation's position vis-a-vis another nation. Although John Kennedy could survive the Bay of Pigs, a party in power has little hope of surviving if it loses a war. Lyndon Johnson chose not to run again in 1968, and his chosen successor, Hubert Humphrey, lost the election to the man Kennedy had beaten in 1960. For this reason, the possibility of compromise is sharply reduced once fighting has begun.

The entire calculus of possibility and impossibility changes again with the appearance of nuclear weapons. At this point, physical and political impossibility may coincide. It is, insofar as we can discover, physically impossible for civilization, or perhaps even life on earth, to survive a general nuclear exchange. Therefore, it is politically impossible to use nuclear weapons for any purpose except to discourage the other fellow from using nuclear weapons for any purpose except to deter us from using them. So long as both sides have enough weapons that can survive the most powerful attack that can be launched against them and still inflict "unacceptable damage" on the aggressor, neither side can attack without bringing on its own destruction. And we can be sure that the Russians will spend their last ruble—as we would spend our last dollar—to be sure of retaining the capacity to retaliate in that devastating fashion.

From here the circles of impossibility spread out. Nuclear war becomes impossible as a political concept. Indeed, the expression itself is an oxymoron. A war must have a political object, and a nuclear war can have none. Nuclear weapons that have very accurate warheads and can reach their targets very rapidly—so-called first-strike weapons—have no political utility. Since there is no possible political advantage in initiating a nuclear war, because both sides will be destroyed in the process, there is no advantage in having the physical capacity to strike first. In fact, these weapons increase the risk of a nuclear exchange by accident or miscalculation. Indeed, any direct military confrontation between the nuclear superpowers runs so great a risk of escalation to a nuclear exchange that, ever since the Cuban missile crisis, responsible politicians have shuddered to contemplate such confrontation.

Unhappily, the circles have not spread far enough to persuade some political figures that any nuclear conflict is impossible to manage and dangerous to contemplate, or to bring Americans and Russians back to the bargaining table to consider seriously how to increase the possibility of avoiding Armageddon. Instead, the Reagan administration chooses to pursue the illusion—physically, politically, and economically impossible—of a perfect defense against a nuclear attack. Admitting that impossibility can significantly increase the probability of human survival in a dangerous world.

Notes

1. I remember a distinguished member of the Senate Foreign Relations Committee explaining to me, after I had testified on some major policy issue, that he wished he had more time to spend on the matters I had discussed, but, of course, he had to give priority to the problems of (individual) constituents.

CHAPTER THIRTEEN • JUERGEN G. BACKHAUS

AN IMPOSSIBLE ECONOMIST

It is indeed true that, in contrast to the exhilaration
which the discoveries of the physical sciences tend to
produce, the insights which we gain from the study of
society more often have a dampening effect on our
aspirations.

Friedrich von Hayek, *The Pretense of Knowledge*, 1978, p. 30.

The assignment to discuss impossibility statements in economics would have been straightforward albeit somewhat difficult if I had been allowed to concentrate on such subjects as Arrow's impossibility theorem.[1] The editors of the present volume, however, have claimed the branch of economics to which the theorem belongs (mathematical economics or economic theory) as a branch of applied mathematics (and this is probably an apt characterization). I am therefore directed into the more treacherous domains of political economy and applied economics, where agreement in the profession is scanty and almost any treatment is bound to breed misunderstanding.[2]

My discussion will unfold in two parts. The first gives examples of simple impossibility statements with which, I think, most economists would agree; the second offers some generalizations about these examples. My interpretation owes much to the writings of Friedrich von Hayek, who, although a Nobelist in economic science, commands wide but not unanimous respect in the profession. Hence I cannot expect to be in agreement with all my fellow economists when offering these generalizations.

Impossibility Statements in Economics

When economists say no, the general public is likely to be both tired and irritated by their arguments, an attitude all too easy to understand. While one economist says no, another vigorously attacks his colleague's reasoning, yet cannot bring himself to say yes, and a third may at best be willing to say maybe.[3] What is so confusing and tiresome to the layman is the consequence of at least three tendencies that are characteristic of contemporary economics (at least when discussed in the public marketplace of ideas).

First, economists tend to disagree less about outcomes than about theory to explain those outcomes.[4] A recent series of studies by Bruno S. Frey and his collaborators shows that the consensus among economists is actually quite strong. Indeed, remaining variances can be accounted for by cultural differences or, more precisely, by the economic systems economists tend to assume as defining the set of assumptions under which they work. These differences are no mere historical accidents. Instead, we are looking at institutional differences that significantly influence the performance of the economy and the incentives policy makers respond to. For example, in Austria the state has a long history of involvement in the economy, whereas in the United States public and private sectors are separate. Not surprisingly, then, Austrian economists tend to see the state as an important and potentially stabilizing agent in the economy, whereas American economists see it as the likely source of disturbances in the market economy.[5]

Second, economists, when they are asked to argue in public, tend to disagree with laymen about the likely outcomes of particular policy measures. As we might expect, this disturbs and annoys laymen, especially if they have vested interests in the measures. In such cases, economists cannot be expected to make impossibility statements at all. For example, economists hardly disagree that there are disincentive effects of compensation policies such as unemployment compensation. On the one hand, it is by no means impossible that these policies achieve their desired goal, if this goal is taken as easing the burden of the unemployed. On the other hand, they are useless if one considers that their goal is to reduce the number of people "out of work and looking for a job"; quite the contrary, most schemes to disburse unemployment benefits tend to increase the number of unemployed workers in the economy at any particular moment. In such a case, the economist emphasizes consequences of public policies that may otherwise be overlooked, but he does not deny, at least not altogether, the possibility of achieving the stated goal with the means under consideration. Typically, any public policy measure has multifarious consequences upon society, but only very few of these effects lend themselves to public debate. When the economist's tale is different from the politician's, the reason need not be that one is right and the other wrong. The reason may very well be that different aspects are being emphasized.

Third, economics is not a science that seeks to account for the idiosyncratic behavior of every individual; rather, it explains and predicts the broad characteristics of behavioral patterns of many individuals, as they are reflected in observable variables. The proposition that when car prices decline, the number of cars demanded will increase is not rendered untrue by observing that Aunt Mabel sells her car and starts riding her bike at precisely the same time that car prices drop. It is also irrelevant whether Aunt Mabel knows about the fall in car prices. The proposition is disproved if it can be observed that (1) the prices of cars fell, (2) the demand schedule (indicating prices and respective quantities) remained unchanged, and (3) the number of cars demanded declined while (4) all other (relevant) data remained unchanged.[6] This statement, really a bread-and-butter proposition in economics, cannot be readily turned into an impossibility statement. It is not at all impossible that car sales decline consequent to price decreases. Many Aunt Mabels may very well have caused a glut in the second-hand car market—perhaps because (1) while the absolute prices of cars declined, their prices relative to the prices of other goods did not; (2) a tax on cars not applicable to bicycles has caused the demand schedule to shift toward the origin; (3) riding cars has come to be considered un-American, since it contributes to air pollution; or (4) riding bikes has become less dangerous since Congress passed a law mandating bike lanes along every public road as well as requirements to enforce leash ordinances (to protect cyclists from straying dogs), with a loss of highway subsidies as penalty for sluggish enforcement. Thus, the example shows that typical statements in economics, rather than excluding any particular occurrence, are often designed to suggest an array of alternative outcomes, with the most likely suggested in the main statement and the other alternatives hidden in the assumptions.

We are therefore not at all surprised to learn that economists, in general, do not think in terms of impossibilities. The notion is actually alien to their discourse. They like to analyze situations in terms of trade-offs, alternatives to preconceived notions, and individual adaptations of behavior in response to alternative constraints. To take another example straight from the elementary course: If the price of whiskey rises, will it be impossible for the poor drunkard to sip his bourbon? No, the economists will answer, he is unlikely to reduce his consumption of alcoholic beverages to zero. If whiskey is the only alcoholic beverage available, and if he is a drunkard as we assume, his demand for whiskey is likely to be inelastic; his response to a price increase may be small in terms of alcohol but perhaps large in terms of respect to other goods such as housing, clothing, or food. We would say that he faces a trade-off between food and liquor, given his limited means, and he is unlikely to decide for one while eliminating everything else. Such a response, consumption of either food or alcohol, is termed the "corner solution."[7] Again, the proposition is not disproved by pointing to a single alcoholic who, jolted out of his compulsive habits by the price increase, stops drinking altogether. To stop drinking would amount to a change in his preferences.[8]

Economics became a professionalized discipline when rulers of independent states turned to experts for advice on economic policy. Typically, this advice was positive; a particular policy measure would be demonstrated to have some desired outcome, such as an increase in state revenues, in population, or in precious metals entering the country, or a decrease in state expenditures, etc. Rarely do we find impossibility statements in the early literature. But the rule is not without an exception. The German and Italian cameralism, a sideline to the more prominent mercantilist economics of France, England, and Spain, distinguished itself by cautioning against the excessive use of taxation. Anticipating the Laffer curve,[9] cameralists insisted that an increase in the rate of taxation would reduce the tax yield, or: You cannot further increase the tax revenue by increasing the tax rate. Assuming the existence of a Laffer curve, a smallest tax rate can be established beyond which increases in the rate will reduce the tax revenue. This rate maximizes tax revenues if the tax base is constant. Historically, this insight spurred the search for new revenue sources and the invention of new types of taxes, notably the excise tax, which would yield the desired revenues. Here the impossibility statement, as in economics generally, is made subject to the condition that other things remain the same (ceteris paribus). The example fits the situation described in Davis' chapter on mathematics, where impossibility is seen as a starting point for its conversion to a possibility.

In this century, there is a prominent instance of an economist making an impossibility statement whose dramatic impact on the practice of economic policy has lasted to the present. When Hitler assumed power in 1933, he was presented with legislative drafts for the continuation and expansion of deficit-financed reemployment programs begun under the two chancellors immediately preceding him. Wilhelm Lautenbach, the economist responsible for drafting the programs, was sent to explain them to Hitler. The chancellor, who had not yet achieved dictatorial powers, was anxious to reduce unemployment, which at the time idled more than a quarter of the German work force; but he feared inflation no less, and he objected accordingly. Lautenbach is said to have retorted: "You are now the most powerful man in Germany. But there is something you cannot do: you cannot bring about inflation under the present conditions, as hard as you may try."[10] Of course, Lautenbach was right, and the result was that Hitler agreed to the first large-scale, successful experiment in Keynesian economic policy. An economist had impressed an audience of politicians with a macroeconomic argument.

In the interest of balance, let me recount a second example in which an economist said no, this time on the basis of microeconomic insights and, again, was right. About fifteen years after Lautenbach's no, another German economist changed history by saying no way. After the severe winter of 1947–48, shortages of food and coal were rife in the American and British zones in Germany. A stringent system of rationing had been imposed by the military government, but Ludwig Erhard, an economics professor who later became first minister of economic affairs and then chancellor of the West German republic, advocated abolishing bureaucratic allocation systems and proposed introducing a new currency. Questioned whether he was not about to cause further chaos and suffering from hunger and cold, he denied even the possibility, let alone the likelihood, of such an outcome.[11] Again, he was perfectly right.

Why were these men so sure of their convictions? Was this the certainty with which Moses led his people through the Red Sea? Was it intuition? Scientific truth?

Consider the following examples of impossibility statements borrowed at random from the standard core of an economics curriculum.

1. It is impossible to ensure the protection of domestic jobs by imposing a tariff on foreign goods. That statement turns on emphasizing the costs of a particular public policy. While it may very well be possible to protect particular, identifiable jobs already held by specific people in a given industry, other jobs are likely to be endangered and some new jobs unlikely to be created (where otherwise they could have been) as a consequence of the foreign trade policy. Hence, secondary consequences may defeat the avowed policy purpose.

2. It is impossible to ensure a sufficient supply of housing for low-income families by imposing rent controls. Rent controls are likely to have the opposite effect by creating a shortage in the housing market.

3. It is impossible to ensure that a tax imposed on a firm will be borne exclusively by that firm, unless its supply schedule is perfectly inelastic (i.e., "unresponsive"). This statement again emphasizes that repercussions of a particular policy measure on other market agents' activities may at least partly offset the intended result.

4. In the long run, it is impossible for trade unions to raise the average income of the worker household. The statement, again, emphasizes the multifarious consequences of cartelization in a particular market—here the labor market—on exit and entry into the market and the intergenerational distributive effects stemming from this cartelization. For example, trade unions benefit older workers with job protection rights and seniority, while they harm younger workers without such rights by reducing the number of jobs available. The statement certainly does not exclude the possibility that particular households may very well gain from trade union activity, a contingency that creates a constituency for the union.

The preceding statements are examples of applied microeconomics. We can have impossibility statements, as we have seen before, in macroeconomics as well. One is the famous fallacy of composition suggested by Keynes, which, if turned into an impossibility statement, might read:

5. It is impossible for everyone in a closed economy to save more if there is no compensating investment. (But will there not be some compensating investment if everyone really wants to save?)

We can generate impossibility statements by starting from a particular empirical observation that we hold to be the case. One such observation is the Phillips curve.[12] It suggests a relationship between unemployment and inflation. If we assume the curve exists, we suggest:

6. It is impossible to permanently reduce both unemployment and inflation by means of fiscal policy. Therefore, there is a trade-off between unemployment and inflation, an idea that is widely disputed but that agrees well with economists' parlance in terms of alternatives that may be weighed against each other.

If the Phillips curve is treated as a temporary phenomenon, we might write:

7. In the long run, it is impossible to achieve lower unemployment by increasing inflation.

Recently, a school of economists has gained widespread recognition by inquiring how expectations about state economic policies change the behavior of key decision makers in the market toward which public policy is directed. The formation of these expectations may render state economic policy making (at least in part) ineffective by anticipation. The story goes like this:

8. Economic agents are able to form rational expectations about the effects of permanent macroeconomic stabilization policies. Hence, there will be no surprise in the policy effects that can be anticipated. It follows that any policy *rule* that is systematically related to economic conditions—for example, one designed with stabilization in mind—will be perfectly anticipated and therefore have no effect on either output or employment.[13] Alternatively stated, it is impossible for systematic stabilization policies to bring about deviations from the natural rate of unemployment. This example is important in emphasizing the creation of knowledge about economic conditions and the use that economic agents make of this knowledge. Rational expectations economics cer-

tainly does not reduce government economic policy to insignificance, nor does it relegate the government to policies that can only be successful to the extent that they are unsystematically related to economic conditions. As we shall see in the next part of our discussion, this impossibility notion points to the importance of governments creating mechanisms through which rational agents may generate desired economic outcomes.

9. We conclude this list of examples by mentioning the Coase theorem.[14] It holds that if two parties are engaged in potentially conflicting activities and if they can freely negotiate at no cost (i.e., the transactions costs of negotiating, monitoring, and enforcing contractual agreements are zero), then it will make no difference for the allocation of resources which party is liable to the other in compensation for potential damages and injuries. For example, if there are ranchers and wheat farmers, then, says Coase, the allocation of resources will be unaffected irrespective of whether the rancher is liable for the farmer's loss caused by his straying cattle or whether the farmer has to either suffer this loss or protect his land (by fencing it). Please note that the theorem is silent about the distribution of wealth. It talks only about the allocation of resources, namely, how much land will be devoted to ranching and farming respectively. What does the theorem really amount to? We all know that transactions costs are (almost) never zero. Hence, the statement focuses our attention on the extent and incidence of transactions costs and on particular types of these costs as they are determined by the institution of different property arrangements on the allocation of resources. Although this impossibility statement covers an (almost) empty set of real world occurrences, it is fruitful in pointing toward the causes of particular effects under consideration.

Statements That Are Impossible for the Economist to Make

As the first part of this chapter was devoted to typical impossibility statements as they might appear in everyday discourse among economists, I should now like to draw some generalizing conclusions to point out what kinds of statements economists can make on the basis of their science and what kind of knowledge they do not possess. Hence, we are now concerned with what is impossible for the economist to say. A large part of economics, notably in the field of theoretical economic policy, discusses the relationship between means and ends, between policies and desired (or undesired) policy outcomes. This area of research is rich with impossibility statements of the following type: Policy x will, under present circumstances (ceteris paribus), not lead to (undesired or desired) outcome y. The Lautenbach and Erhard examples are of this kind. They exclude undesired outcomes. Examples (1)–(4) emphasize desired outcomes and the futility of certain means to achieve them. The other four examples are more complex. Example (5) is, first of all, more specific. It establishes an equality between savings and investments and, in conjunction with Keynes' particular theory of interest, allows for the possibility of a permanent state of underemployment. We realize that the relevant information contained in statement (5) is actually a possibility statement: the unemployment equilibrium situation classical economics had felt so confident in excluding is here reintroduced as a genuine possibility, and an important one at that.

Example (7), in the neoclassical tradition, again excludes a particular policy as a sensible means to a specific end (an increase in the money supply will *not* permanently reduce unemployment). But the converse, example (6), by excluding the possibility of a joint reduction of unemployment and inflation, opens the possibility of achieving one by giving up the other. Again, the Keynesian version introduces a possibility that the neoclassical counterpart denies.

Example (8), by establishing an entire class of economic policies as an ineffectual means to the desired end of stabilization, remains within the neoclassical means-ends paradigm, but more systematically so. The important advantage over the earlier examples, of course, lies in establishing an entire class of means as ineffectual, instead of just one or a selected number of such means.

Finally, the Coase theorem is an impossibility statement that applies to an empty set. Still, the statement is not empty in itself, since it establishes the cause of one type of outcome by assuming it away (zero transactions costs) and postulating its absence. Hence, the impossibility statement establishes a cause-and-effect relationship between a class of causes (property rights arrangements or "institutions" that give rise to transactions costs) and a class of effects in the allocation of resources.

Economics, as we can see, is a science of complex phenomena. Its complexity lies in the multiplicity and diversity of possible outcomes and in the difficulty, not only of establishing cause-and-effect relationships, but even of observing many of the relevant outcomes. The precision with which economists can work is affected by the data that is accessible. Many important outcomes are not unequivocally reflected in data: the same data may be consistent with widely different occurrences. Relatedly, many important data are unavailable, often because they are unobservable. The availability of data is not systematically brought about by the needs of the science. It is irrational from the point of view of economic research to rely only on those data that are available and to exclude nonquantifiable evidence or theoretical knowledge for which there are no data (for refutation); nothing suggests that fortuitously available data are more relevant than the precise, nonquantifiable insights.

When we discuss means-ends relationships, we typically talk about an economic policy measure, the means that will affect many different individuals in different ways. The effect will elicit different reactions from each individual, and their responses will vary accordingly. We are unable to determine what their responses will be in any particular case, since we lack the relevant information that only they have about their individual situations. This information can never be available to any outsider, and certainly not to any one policy maker. The economist's only recourse in predicting policy outcomes is to establish certain patterns of reactions and to refrain from predicting precise outcomes. Hayek, in his Nobel lecture, puts it this way:

> Organized complexity here means that the character of the structures showing it depends not only on the properties of the individual elements of which they are composed, and the relevant frequency with which they occur, but also on the manner in which the individual elements are connected with each other. In the explanation of the working of such structures we can for this reason not replace the information about the individual elements by statistical information, but require full information about each element if from our theory we are to derive specific predictions about individual events. Without such specific information about the individual elements, we shall be confined to what on another occasion I have called mere pattern predictions—predictions of some general attributes of the structures that will form themselves, but not containing specific statements about the individual elements of which the structures will be made.[15]

Under these circumstances, economists' reliance on the market is readily explicable. The market is one of the very few organizations that we know can process the individuals' circumstantial information. This information will always remain inaccessible to an outsider.

Consequently, economists and those who seek their opinion must clearly understand the limits of their discipline. Hayek, again, underscores those limits, when he talks about a "theory of a somewhat limited content, because it allows us to make only very general predictions of the *kind* of events which we must expect in a given situation."[16] If we follow this reasoning and accept economics as a theoretical attempt at understanding and predicting complex phenomena, we can only conclude that (10) it is impossible for an economist to predict individual outcomes with precision and impossible in economics to predict particular outcomes as contrasted to general patterns of events.

Acknowledgments

I should like to thank the editors and my colleagues at Auburn, R. Garrison, R. Holcombe, J. Long, and E. Toma, and W. J. Samuels (Michigan State University) for their helpful comments, and B. Yellen again for her invaluable assistance in improving the prose of this essay.

Notes

1. Arrow's impossibility theorem states that, given certain plausible assumptions, there can be no ideal rational aggregation device of individual preferences, the so-called social welfare function. The conditions are (U) unrestricted scope, (P) Pareto principle, (D) nondictatorship, and (I) independence of irrelevant alternatives. See Kenneth Arrow, *Social Choice and Individual Values,* 2d ed., Yale University Press, New Haven, 1963, chapter 8, section 2. For a book-length discussion see Alfred F. MacKay, *Arrow's Theorem: The Paradox of Social Choice—A Case Study in the Philosophy of Economics,* Yale University Press, New Haven, 1980.

2. A colleague of mine suggested that the only impossibility statement in economics he could think of was this: It is impossible to write intelligibly about impossibility statements in economics.

3. This scenario has become such a commonplace that a recent textbook uses the constant disagreement among economic advisers as a teaching device. The textbook is cast in the form of a detective story, and the students, by reading the murder mystery,

are exposed to competing theories in macroeconomics. I am referring to Murray Wolfson and Vincent Buranelli, *In the Long Run We Are All Dead: A Macroeconomics Murder Mystery*, St. Martin's, New York, 1984. While this book draws on the diversity of opinions among economists as a rule, there are now two other murder mysteries available that by drawing on the more homogeneous body of microeconomic theory can present a unified view, which is the key to solving the mystery. The reader is referred to Marshall Jevons, *Murder at the Margin*, Thomas Horton & Daughters, Glen Ridge, N.J., 1978, and Marshall Jevons, *The Fatal Equilibrium*, MIT Press, Cambridge, Mass., 1984.

4. Their disagreement is even sharper when they debate *what should be* accomplished. It is hard for economists, even harder for the layman, to separate civic conviction from scholarly reasoning. The difficulty is compounded by the fact that economics is not completely silent on normative issues; but what can be said by way of prescription is very general and follows from assumptions that have to be accepted beforehand.

5. See Werner Wolf Pommerehne, Friedrich Schneider, and Bruno S. Frey, "Quot Homines Tot Sententiae: A Survey among Austrian Economists," *Empirica*, 2: 93–127 (1983). See also their international study, Bruno S. Frey, Werner Wolf Pommerehne, Friedrich Schneider, and Guy Gilbert, "Consensus and Dissension among Economists: An Empirical Inquiry," *American Economic Review*, 74: 986–94 (1984), where Austria and France are set apart from Germany, Switzerland, and the United States, countries with more market-based economies.

6. This condition (4) is called the "ceteris paribus" clause.

7. Given the usual convexity characteristics of indifference curves in the two good two model and a standard budget constraint, the likely outcome of a price increase in alcoholic beverages, which amounts to a shift in the budget constraint, does not lead to a corner solution. The corner solutions are positioned on indifference curves that are closer to the origin and hence reflect a lower level of utility.

8. With liquor ceasing to be an element in the drunkard's utility function, the indifference curve would become a straight line parallel to the horizontal axis on which liquor was depicted.

9. The Laffer curve is a backward-bending function relating tax revenues to the tax rate. Tax revenues increase as the tax rate increases from the origin (zero) toward an optimal tax rate; from then on, revenues decline with further increases of the rate, reaching zero as the rate climbs to 100 percent.

10. The story is related in Wilhelm Roepke, *Wilhelm Lautenbach: Zins, Kredit und Produktion*, Mohr (Siebeck), Tübingen, West Germany, 1952, p. 10, and Gottfried Haberler, "Critical Notes on Rational Expectations," *Journal of Money, Credit, and Banking*, 17: 834 (1980).

11. Asked about the reasons for his certainty, he is reported to have simply said: "I know it with the certainty of a somnambulist." This statement was not meant to be arrogant. It reflects a widespread conviction among economists that the operation of a market economy, although basically simple, is yet too complex to be explicable in terms of political discourse.

12. The Phillips curve suggests a relationship between inflation and unemployment and is named after A. W. Phillips, who in 1958 suggested a stable relationship between wage inflation rates and unemployment rates for the United Kingdom between 1861 and 1913. An early formulation was, however, suggested already by David Hume in 1752, and there have been numerous variations ever since. See Thomas M. Humphrey, "The Early History of the Phillips Curve," *Economic Review*, 71: 17–24 (1985).

13. For a nontechnical introduction see Rodney Maddock and Michael Carter, "A Child's Guide to Rational Expectations," *Journal of Economic Literature*, 20: 39–51 (1982).

14. Ronald H. Coase, "The Problem of Social Cost," *Journal of Law and Economics*, 3: 1–44 (1960).

15. Friedrich August von Hayek, "The Pretense of Knowledge," in *New Studies in Philosophy, Politics, Economics, and the History of Ideas*, University of Chicago Press, Chicago, 1978, pp. 26–27.

16. Ibid., p. 29.

PARADOXES OF PARENTHOOD: ON THE IMPOSSIBILITY OF RAISING CHILDREN PERFECTLY

When my son was born I had hoped he would become president. Now I will feel relieved if he does not become an ax-murderer.

My parents spoiled the first half of my life, and my children the second half.

Voices of parents

I entered young parenthood with the certainty that I would rear my children in the best possible way. I felt myself to be loving and generous and infinitely patient. I would read the right books and follow their advice most faithfully. Under my guidance my children would become mentally healthy, happy, and productive human beings. I would avoid all the mistakes my parents had made. I had unbounded confidence in my own ability to become a perfect parent.

Little did I realize at that distant time what hubris was involved in these presumptuous goals. Not trying to be a perfect parent, or at least the best possible within one's limited ability, seems thoughtless, unkind, and irresponsible. Yet, this reaching for perfection in the rearing of one's children is a self-destructive ambition, which can only lead to disaster.

My thoughts on this subject are meant to explain to readers who are young parents why the road ahead, however well paved with the best intentions, will be a thorny one. My thoughts are also meant to comfort myself and other middle-aged parents. I hope to dispel our guilt for not having succeeded quite as well as we had hoped. I want to comfort all of us who tried both too hard and yet not hard enough to be a good enough parent and to convince us that it was not our fault if we failed in the impossible task of rearing our children perfectly.

Several problems come into play. To begin with, there is the irksome matter of elusive goals. For we have no clear image of the ideal human being who might be the result of such perfect rearing. Moreover, even if we could devise such an image, we currently have no effective techniques to reach it, and even if we could invent such techniques, it is a grave question whether we should use them. In addition there is the problem that unconscious forces may interfere with our conscious intentions. Our efforts to correct our parents' mistakes by doing the opposite may curiously backfire, since opposite actions tend to have similar results.

Kundera has suggested, in *The Unbearable Lightness of Being,* that we are actors playing the first rehearsal of the drama of our life. No one can expect a first rehearsal to be an accomplished performance.

Parents are asked to provide discipline *and* acceptance; firm guidance *and* encouragement toward autonomy; a commitment to high values *and* a willingness to compromise and conform to societal expectations. I shall argue that the parental role involves a series of incompatible demands, which defy satisfactory resolution.

Some Historical Reflections

The question arises whether the ambitious goal of becoming a perfect parent could occur only in this individualistic Western culture, at this moment when rapid cultural change and extreme cultural diversity create both uncertainty and new opportunities regarding our child-rearing efforts. There is a climate of anxiety in the air: our children may not survive in this complex and difficult society unless we equip them so well in every way that they can defeat every obstacle short of nuclear annihilation.

We may look with mixed nostalgia and scorn at our forebears, believing that they lived in stable, predictable times, and needed to devote little thought to the rearing of children, because they were scarcely conscious of their parental responsibilities or because the cultural prescriptions for parental conduct were so clearly outlined.

Recent historical research contradicts such notions, suggesting that an awareness of childhood as a special developmental period is not a recent cultural acquisition. Linda Pollock argues convincingly that people have known since antiquity that children had particular needs and vulnerabilities and required special protection. The evidence that "parents have always tried to do what is best for their children within the context of their culture"[1] might be a blow to our twentieth-century ethnocentricity. But we are gradually learning that we are not unique, that across different time periods and different cultures, there have always been some parents who treated their children with great tenderness and cared deeply about them and other parents who were harsh, cruel, and neglectful.

There is also evidence that parents throughout history have assumed responsibility for their children's conduct and, in many cases, even for their future well-being. Sigmund Freud has been credited with establishing the impact of early child rearing on adult emotional health; yet the idea that parents are responsible for instilling the most important values of a culture—whether these be concerned with religion, moral conduct, or mental health—is age-old. Thus, in the Bible we find proverbs such as that urging parents to "train up a child in the way he should go and when he is old he will not depart from it" (Proverbs 22:6).

Pollock demonstrates that at least from the sixteenth century onward parents were concerned with all the functions that we associate with parenthood today, such as educating, protecting, disciplining, providing, advising, training, and helping. She quotes one mother's diary from the eighteenth century to illustrate the dedication and keen sense of responsibility felt by certain parents: "There is scarcely any subject concerning which I feel more anxiety, than the proper education of my children. . . . The person who undertakes to form the infant mind, to cut off the distorted shoots, and direct and fashion those which may, in due time, become fruitful and lovely branches, ought to possess a deep and accurate knowledge of human nature."[2]

From this short historical excursion we must conclude that striving for "perfect parenting" has existed in some form for a very long time, that it is by no means a problem unique to our age. Yet, it is possible that the striving has recently become more complex, perhaps more self-conscious and hopeless, than in former times.

Elusive Goals

When we imagine the wonderful human being that our perfect parenting efforts are designed to bring forth, we immediately focus on the good values that such a person should embody, and we find ourselves on slippery ground. With respect to values, I think our ancestors had a clearer vision than we have. For centuries, people hoped to raise children who loved and feared God. Until quite recently we had few questions about the desirability of premarital chastity, lifelong fidelity to one marital partner, valor in battle, patriotism that included a willingness to die for one's country, obedience of and respect for one's elders, religious faith, self-sacrifice, ambition, and achievement through very hard work. Yet all of these values have now been questioned and at times violently rejected, not just by isolated nonconformists but by significant groups in the society. Parents who hope to do a perfect job will have to sift and choose among competing values and decide which ones they will at least try to transmit to their children.

You have noticed that I included both masculine (valor) and feminine (self-sacrifice) values in my list. Indeed, not long ago it was taken for granted that boys and girls would adopt different values in adult life. Now many people, but certainly not the majority of Americans, would advocate androgynous values, with equal standards of sensitivity, assertiveness, courage, and warmth for both boys and girls, women and men. I know mothers who set out to raise androgynous sons but were defeated in their attempt to do so. In many cases the defeat came early on. When the little boys started to play with dolls in kindergarten, they were taunted by other boys and they cried. They had also been told not to fight. Clearly they had been raised to be sissies. The mothers did not want their sons to be outcasts. They told them to stop playing with dolls and pointed out how much fun it was to ride a nice red fire truck. The fathers did not want their sons to be teased. They showed their sons how to punch anyone who teased them.

Another mother went on peace marches with her son and taught him to speak up against injustices. A group of Green Berets came to his high school to glorify the Vietnam war. He stood up and protested and created a dangerous situation for himself. "Don't speak up foolishly," his anxious mother told him afterward. "You must learn to hold your tongue." Later, in college, he participated in student sit-ins. "Don't get yourself in trouble," she told him, "think of your future and attend to your studies." It is hard for parents to imbue their children with values that are rejected by the culture of the majority.

Parents are not really free to choose their own values; their wish to teach their children certain values may conflict with their even more urgent intent to help their children secure a safe and respected place in the society in which they will live. We could, then, give up the attempt to teach children the "right values" and merely seek out "useful" values, which will promote their happiness. We could, then, settle on the goal of raising happy human beings. The problem is that we live in such a rapidly changing society that even pragmatic values become unpredictable. The generation of women to which I belong was raised to the tune of "Cinderella and the Prince"; they "lived happily ever after," only to find themselves at midlife obsolescent, bewildered, and often alone.

Yet, let us remember eternal verities and ethical principles and assume that we could agree on *what* to teach our children. The question then arises of *how* we teach it.

Teaching and Learning

Loevinger has pinpointed a major problem in the area of teaching values.[3] She suggests that learning takes place in three major ways: through cognitive understanding, through watching models, and through rewards and punishments. The problem is that parents may choose to teach by one method and children may perversely choose to learn by a different method. As a result, what is learned may be other than what was intended. Parents may choose to punish their children for a misdeed, acting on a reward-and-punishment theory, while children might decide in this instance to learn in a modeling framework and conclude that power rests with whomever is stronger. Or, alternatively, a parent may *explain* to a child what she has done wrong, and the child, adopting a reward-and-punishment framework, may conclude that misbehavior will bear no consequences beyond words.

I think the problem can be posed in more general terms. All our behavior can be seen as forms of communication with various levels of messages, including the levels of content and relationship. Those who observe us, or listen to us, can attend at whatever level they choose or happen to notice, and often that level is not the one we intended to be noticed or even one we were aware of transmitting. A scolding may be viewed at the relationship level as "caring" or "paying attention" and thus become a reward. Praise may be perceived as pressure for future performance and thus felt as a threat. Whenever we help someone, for example, our help may be interpreted as an act of kindness, or, alternately, a form of condescension, or perhaps as a message that the person is too weak or too incompetent to help himself.

While I think I am teaching students psychological theories, they may be more interested in observing whether I am fair, critical, or approving, attentive, open, or defensive, and that is what they will learn from me. Kegan[4] tells the amusing story of a father who indignantly confronts his adult son for being lazy and without ambition. The father thinks that he was a model of hard work for his son, but the son has paid attention only to the father's many stresses and complaints along the way.

The Right Discipline

How to teach children is clearly as much of a problem as *what* to teach them. Many parents continue to imagine that "the right discipline" is the key to parenting success. They have somehow lost that key and turn to experts to find it again. Thus, it is ironic and instructive that two prominent contemporary writers, both of them parents and educators, and both claiming to be advocates of children, give us completely contradictory advice. Alice Miller, in three consecutive books,[5] accuses parents through the centuries of having been bent on breaking their children's wills, humiliating them, robbing them of any sense of control over their lives, and destroying their spirit, their curiosity, and their vitality, all for the sake of shaping obedient, conforming, nonfeeling adults. Miller has contempt for every form of "Erziehung" (a German word conveying socialization, pedagogy, discipline, and education), viewing it as inevitably coercive and manipulative. She argues that only if the child and the care giver each respect the other as a separate human being, and each allow the expression of and recognize the other's authentic feelings, will the development of a humane and whole and vital human being be assured.

Marie Winn, on the other hand, is alarmed at the premature exposure of children to the ugly realities of adult life.[6] She deplores the permissiveness of the current generation of parents, viewing lack of rules, structures, and firm expectations as destructive and dangerous neglect and an abdication of the protective obligations of parents. In direct contrast to Miller, Winn locates the problem in too little parental control. She appears nostalgic for the "benign dictatorship" of parents of olden days and calls for more adult authority and less egalitarianism.

Both these authors are passionate and convincing in their arguments. Where does this leave a well-meaning young mother or father in search of the key to perfect parenthood?

The New Good Enough Mother

Before I get carried away with the impossibility of the parental task, I need to stop and attend to the other side of the possibility-impossibility boundary. Current research on the development of infants[7] is providing new guidelines for the parent-infant relationship and redefining the meaning of Winnicott's concept of a "good enough mother."[8]

Mothers of my generation, who in many cases grew up under the shadow of maternal deprivation and thus felt a need for uninterrupted love and attachment, were often in danger of losing sight of the equally urgent need for some separateness. Yet this latter need is present from the very beginning of a child's life. Although no one would deny that infants and children are in need of love, today we are learning more precisely about the essence of such love.

We know about the infant's need for *contact*. This starts with a need for physical contact and soon expands into the realm of emotional and intellectual contact. In the new literature there is much emphasis on *contingent responsiveness*. This refers to the ability to tune in to the emotional readiness of the child so as to create a synchronous dance. Instead of approaching children with our own agenda, we try to follow their lead. Attachment grows through interpersonal sensitivity and attentiveness. Attention and stimulation that is not geared to the needs and readiness of the young child is either useless or overwhelming and in danger of provoking the child's anxious protective withdrawal. There is a need for reliability and predictability, and we must pay attention to face-to-face interactions and the nourishing of an intimate relationship.

Yet the good enough mother also turns around the child on her lap and, together, they look outward, exploring the world at large. The child is allowed her natural movement toward individuation and autonomy. There needs to be respect for her use of gaze aversion to break contact and create private space and distance. It is important to encourage and promote her attempts at self-regulation. Most important is an acknowledgment of the child as separate and as "other." The willingness to get to know a child in all her complexity and to respect her uniqueness is perhaps the highest expression of parental love.

We congratulate Winnicott for asking mothers to be merely "good enough" rather than perfect. In contrast to the very best mother, the merely good enough mother is not always attentive. Sometimes she is casual, or she is preoccupied and turns her back to attend to her own needs. Sometimes she is in a hurry and imposes her own agenda, overlooks subtle cues, and becomes unreliable and unpredictable. Too much predictability might even create stagnation in a relationship. I like to think we need unpredictability in a framework of predictability. Flaws in caretaking introduce novelty and new learning. The child needs to learn that his mother is still there, even if she does turn her back, and that both goodness and badness belong to one and the same mother. The good enough mother might ultimately be better than the very best mother, since it is one of the paradoxes of parenthood that loving too well ultimately means not loving well enough.

Overloving Parents

We have learned that children are more often damaged by too much loving than by too little. Overloving implies overinvolvement with the child in the expectation that the child will give meaning and reason to one's own life. It involves possessiveness, anxious overprotection, and inability to see the child's needs as separate and different from one's own needs. Some readers may protest the use of the word *overloving* to connote narcissistic overinvestment. You may object to having "love" associated with destructive interactions. Yet, we are learning that any virtue sufficiently escalated turns on itself.[9]

Even child abuse may be a form of overloving. Parents who are indifferent to a child who cries may close the doors or turn on the TV. It is only when there is intense involvement with the child and her crying is heard as a personal accusation that she may need to be beaten into silence.

Helm Stierlin, a German psychoanalyst and family therapist, discusses two modes of parental overloving.[10] Some parents *bind* a child by infantilizing him, giving him contradictory messages, or making him feel very guilty, so that the child cannot separate and live an independent life. Other parents let their children leave home, but they *delegate* the accomplishment of certain missions to them. Such children may need to achieve goals that the parent would have liked to achieve but, because of inner or outer constraints, could not. These goals might include professional advancement, sexual adventures, crimes, or even acts of revenge or atonement. The child of overloving parents may run away in a futile attempt to escape the parent's physical or psychic control.

Overloving parents are those who have not been able to separate from their children. They intrude narcissistically on their children's life space, interfering with the formation of a separate sense of self. Parental intrusiveness takes many different forms; in any of these forms, it can endanger a child's healthy growth and development.

Who Is in Charge?

I am thus suggesting that we have to protect our children against our narcissistic needs if we are going to be perfect parents. Yet the demands of being a parent are so relentless that we could hardly be expected to take on such a burden without some narcissistic investment—by which I mean staking one's self-esteem on the success of the outcome.

Although Miller and Winn come to different conclusions, they both zero in on the parent's psychic vulnerability: the dilemma of having to discipline children while also needing their love and approval. Miller thinks most parents are unwilling to acknowledge their children's pain, anxiety, sadness, or rage because such feelings would imply their own imperfections as parents, an intolerable possibility. The parent demands that such feelings remain unacknowledged, and the feelings become split off—only to reappear in adult life as self-destructive tendencies and antisocial projections.

Winn believes that some single parents are unable to exert adequate discipline because they are, in these times of high divorce rates, so overwhelmed by their own survival struggle that they turn to their children for emotional comfort and support, thus undermining their parental authority.

I believe that both writers make valid points, but I see the dilemma between the need to discipline and the wish for love and approval as a universal dilemma of the parent-child relationship, rather than as stemming from particular pathological conditions. We have come upon another paradox in the parenting role: parents' ability to discipline their children is based on a positive loving bond between parent and child, yet discipline forever threatens disruption of that bond.

The parent-child relationship can be viewed as the prototype of a "complementary relationship"[11] in which two partners have unequal social power but intermeshing needs. Indeed, during the formative period of her life, the child depends on the parent for her very survival, as well as for her physical, emotional, and social welfare. It seems clear, at least at first sight, that the parent is in the dominant position in this relationship. Yet, the parent's self-definition as a good parent—or even as a good person, since the parenting role is quite central for most people—is a crucial aspect of his or her identity. Whether one has succeeded in "being a good parent" in one's own eyes, as well as in the eyes of other people, is usually judged on the basis of the child's ongoing welfare and happiness *and* of the relationship that is maintained with the child.

Thus the child's dependency on the parents for physical and emotional welfare is matched by the parents' dependency on their children for self-regard, creating an almost equal emotional vulnerability for both partners in the parent-child relationship. The recognition of this need for mutual affirmation shifts the locus of potential blame when a dysfunctional interaction gets established. Rather than holding parents solely responsible, we have a more profound respect for the interlocking reciprocity in the relationship.

Parents of all ages feel deeply dependent on their children's well-being. A young mother thrives when her infant develops well, and her pleasure enhances her nurturing capacity. On the other end of the life-cycle, mothers and fathers in late midlife frequently evaluate their lives by "how well they have done" with their children.[12] Children who fail in some important way in their parents' eyes become a major threat to their parents' ability to invest their later lives with positive meaning.

Both partners often tend to feel in retrospect that regardless of outward appearances, the *other* partner was *really* in charge of the relationship. The dilemma regarding who is in charge has several dimensions. I view the parent role as one of "responsibility without authority" and every administrator knows that this creates a no-win situation. Parents are held responsible and hold themselves responsible for their children's ongoing life and ultimate fate. That belief is indeed the grandiose premise of this whole essay.

As parents we tend to ignore the innate emotional and intellectual dispositions of our children. We also tend to ignore the larger socio-cultural context, which constrains, distorts, and shapes our ability to be wise and loving parents. We insist that regardless of circumstances, it is our parental responsibility to raise our children perfectly. I applaud such a view. Responsibility is the essence of parenthood. Yet, responsibility ought to entail authority and control; and the more responsibility one feels, the more control one wishes to have. I believe the problem of parental control and overcontrol, which easily merges into oppressive intrusiveness, arises from this dilemma.

"I have to protect you against your own mistakes," a friend of mine used to say to her children. "I have to control you for your own good." She would hound them into doing their homework, bribe them into good academic performance, coerce them into practicing their musical instruments, shame them into learning foreign languages. She would only show them affection if they met her expectations. Her children have become accomplished and successful professionals. Yet their sense of self-worth depends on their achievements, and although they pursue these relentlessly, it continues to remain elusive. They will never forgive her for loving them conditionally and for having been such a controlling mother.

Parents who have grown up under conditions of great hardship, who have, for example, survived the Holocaust or suffered from poverty or discrimination, are especially determined that their children should lead better lives. No sacrifice will be too great to achieve such a goal. They set out to control their children for their own protection, perhaps unconsciously using guilt as their major weapon. It is part of the drama of social relationships that excessive determination and too much love defeat their purposes.

Now that I realize that respect for the otherness of the child is the most important requirement for becoming a perfect parent, I harbor a secret conviction that I could do an excellent job if I were given another chance. It is too bad that my children insist on making their own mistakes with my grandchildren. I can recognize that they have goals quite similar to my own when I started as a young mother: to repair all the mistakes that my parents had made with me. As I now look back on my years of imperfect child rearing, I am deeply aggrieved that my attempts at doing the opposite from my parents had somewhat similar end results, because opposites join each other on the emotional continuum. On my next life journey I shall be so respectful of my children's autonomy that I will appear to be an irresponsible mother.

Another friend of mine believed in the importance of self-regulation above all. She was extremely respectful of her children's decisions. She allowed them to discontinue their hobbies whenever the efforts seemed to outweigh the rewards. She allowed them to drop out of school where they learned meaningless things and to follow their own stars. I don't know what became of her children. We quarreled because I reproached her for being an uncaring and neglectful parent.

Letting Go

How can parents fill the requirements of a role in which they must learn to release control while responsible for the success of the enterprise? We should not delegate our own unfinished life tasks to our children; yet children need some firm guidance, lest they lose their way.

"How have you changed as a parent as you grew older?" we asked the midlife mothers and fathers that we interviewed for a research study.[13] Many of the parents then said they had learned to accept their children as they are, rather than continuing to involve them in their own dreams and expectations. This process of letting go of expectations needs to start at a child's birth and continue as a lifelong parental task. A parent (at least until the advent of amniocentesis) must accept the gender of his child, even if it disappoints his expectations. My black-haired mother and father wanted a blonde daughter. For three years my mother tinted my black hair as quickly as it grew; my early photos show a blonde little girl. Later they had to resign themselves to a dark-haired child. Accommodations, resignations, and compromises occur in every area of the child's life. "My son, the future doctor" who becomes a nurse is only one obvious example. One of my friends looked forward to being a grandparent. Her son became gay, and her married daughter decided to remain childless. The epigraph about the ax-murderer at the beginning of this chapter refers to the unexpected and astonishing process of having to give up one's expectations and adapt to and accept one's real child.

Solnit and Stark have written about the mourning that needs to take place at the birth of a handicapped child.[14] But the despair about a handicapped child only highlights more subtle mourning processes that are an inevitable part of all parenting. Some parents are conscious of their need to mourn; most parents do so intuitively, yet without deliberate intent, in their own different and creative ways.

Mourning involves facing one's loss—each disappointment being the loss of some hope—and admitting one's sad and angry feelings, rather than denying and suppressing them. Acknowledgment of feelings may involve sharing them with an intimate confidant who will accept them with understanding and without judgment. Sometimes sharing disappointments may be done in a group with similarly mourning parents, who will provide support and validation to one another. Other parents might express their grief artistically, or they may write an essay about parenthood.

If a child grows to be very different from one's expectations, the resolution process may involve important changes in one's values and perceptions of the world. In order to preserve the bond with an unexpectedly "different" child, a parent might need to change in important ways.

Sometimes it takes years to achieve such a new perspective. Other parents never achieve it; they become chronic mourners. Other parents avoid mourning altogether and just cut off their children in anger. They never learn to let go and never learn to love their imperfect children in imperfect ways. They die without having forgiven their children for repudiating their religious upbringing, for having married a partner of the wrong race, for having adopted a deviant sexual orientation. When parents experience such behavior as personal and unforgivable betrayals, it means that they have not learned to view their children as separate from themselves. When parents and children cut each other off emotionally, it is never because of excessive detachment, but rather because of overwhelming fusion. One needs to have separated from someone to complete one's mourning and forgive them.

The dilemma of simultaneously fostering attachment and separation is perhaps the most difficult parental task. It involves promoting individuation and autonomy, apparently essential life goals, while also offering the child an experience of attachment that is profound and meaningful enough to evoke a lifelong capacity to love, to feel, and to care.

I referred earlier to parents' double wish to see their child succeed and to maintain an affectionate bond. The second part of this wish faces us with yet another paradox of parenthood: disenchantment with and rebellion against parents is a necessary aspect of the relationship; the relationship is flawed if it remains conflict-free and apparently harmonious.

The process of disillusionment with formerly idealized parents is a necessary developmental step of adolescence, and some form of self-assertive differentiation should be an ongoing aspect of the good enough parent-child relationship. We would be worried about a two-year-old who does not oppose parental demands and develops her own growing willfulness; we would be concerned about a school child who never values her teacher's or her peer's opinions above those of her parents.

The most permissive and tolerant parents are in the worst position. Their children have to go to greater length to be critical, disapproving, and provocative. Moreover, such parents may have such good will that they may even wish to help their children become rebellious (!), an effort doomed by its own internal contradiction.

I stressed earlier the parental task of mourning disappointed expectations. Separation and loss, with its necessary mourning, is built into the very core of the parental role. The goal of the parent-child relationship from the very beginning involves a gradual separation and loosening of bonds. Parental love must be demonstrated by not loving too much and by introducing a measure of detachment into a relationship that is totally involving. The most devoted parent will send her child out into the world, applaud the child's new attachments, and recede into the background. Success in the area of the child's well-being might mean defeat in holding onto a close and primary bond. It is the child who experiences defeat in the world who continues to cling to her parents as her primary attachment. Unfortunately, such relationships then become corroded by the mutual guilt and blame caused by the child's failure.

In later life parents may sometimes feel neglected and superfluous. They feel like discarded transitional objects. Children get married; they start their careers; they move to another part of the country; they do not seem to need their parents anymore. However, appearances may be deceptive. The parent-child relationship, with its ambivalent feelings of love and hate, dependency, denial of needs, and the wish for approval and acceptance continues throughout life and beyond. Even after parents die, the relationship remains alive and active in the children's minds. Every parent is assured this form of immortality.

Failed Intent

It will be forever impossible to be a perfect parent, because our actions do not always match our intent. Our internalized parents interfere with our intention to be the most enlightened and responsible parents. We tend to project these internalized figures upon our children, eventually repeating, in some form, old and familiar relationship patterns. Sometimes we even turn our children into our parents, saving us the pain of saying good-bye to our parents.[15]

My students beg me to show them how to avoid this somber fate. There is evidence in the family therapy literature that honest conversations between parents and children could promote the needed separation. They should be conversations in which difficult questions can be asked and authentic feelings exchanged. An attempt must be made to settle intergenerational accounts so that children are not forever burdened with paying the emotional debts that their parents have incurred. I believe such conversations would be useful.

My parents are both dead, and I did not have the courage to engage them in such conversations. My children care about me; they know how vulnerable I am to their opinions of me; they don't want to hurt me; and they also do not engage me in such conversations. Such conversations are too difficult.

Conclusion

I want to make a last attempt to redress the balance between the impossible and the possible. Not everything is possible. We must learn to respect impossibilities. The reckless determination of our technical culture to achieve the impossible has led us to the edge of an abyss. Excessive tenacity of purpose has disturbed the delicate ecology of our planet.[16] The very idea that we are in charge of our own perfections, let alone that of our children, is grandiose and presumptuous. The goal of becoming a perfect parent carries the seeds of guilt, blame, disappointed expectations, and defeat.

I think, on reflection, that it is *possible* to become a perfect parent by tolerating, forgiving, and transcending imperfections, our own and those of our children. We shall become perfect parents by accepting the impossibility of such a goal.

Notes

1. L. Pollock, *Forgotten Children*, University Press, Cambridge, 1983, p. 64.

2. Ibid., p. 117.

3. J. Loevinger, "Patterns of Child Rearing as Theories of Learning," *Journal of Abnormal and Social Psychology*, 59: 148–150 (1959).

4. R. Kegan, *The Evolving Self*, Harvard University Press, Cambridge, Mass., 1982.

5. A. Miller, *Prisoners of Childhood*, Basic Books, New York, 1981; idem, *For Your Own Good*, Farrar, Strauss & Giroux, New York, 1983; idem, *Thou Shalt Not Be Aware*, Farrar, Strauss & Giroux, New York, 1984.

6. M. Winn, *Children without Childhood*, Pantheon Books, New York, 1981.

7. The material on infant research leans heavily on the following books: R. Schaffer, *Mothering*, Harvard University Press, Cambridge, Mass., 1977; D. Stern, *The First Relationship*, Harvard University Press, Cambridge, Mass., 1977; V. Hamilton, *Narcissus and Oedipus*, Routledge & Kegan Paul, London, 1982.

8. On the concept of "the good enough mother" see, for example, D. W. Winnicott, *The Family and Individual Development*, Basic Books, New York, 1965.

9. Examples of this phenomenon abound. Throughout history, believers have been willing to torture and kill to glorify the name of God. In our own times, we find well-meaning citizens so invested in the sanctity of life that they are ready to throw bombs

at abortion clinics, perhaps thereby endangering lives. And countries participate in an arms race, in the hope of preserving peace.

10. H. Stierlin, *Separating Parents and Adolescents,* Quadrangle Books, New York, 1972.

11. P. Watzlawick, J. Beavin, and D. Jackson, *Pragmatics of Human Communication,* W. W. Norton, New York, 1967.

12. S. F. Loewenstein, J. B. Goss, B. G. Donham, W. B. How, S. M. Huss, E. L. Kaplan, and J. Koppman-Fried, *Fathers and Mothers of Midlife,* masters thesis, Simmons College School of Social Work, May 1983.

13. Ibid.

14. A. J. Solnit and M. H. Stark, "Mourning and the Birth of a Defective Child," *Psychoanalytic Study of the Child,* 16: 523–37, International Universities Press, New York, 1961.

15. These ideas are drawn from object relations theory and family system theory.

16. B. P. Keeney, *Aesthetics of Change,* Guilford Press, New York, 1983.

IS EDUCATION A SCIENCE? NO WAY!

I f we claim to know that something is impossible, then we are implicitly claiming to know that something else is the case. If we claim to know that it is impossible for elephants to live underwater, then we are claiming to know that elephants need air. Moreover, claims to know that some things are impossible because other things are the case are strong claims—they are claims to know with certainty. Similarly, claims to know impossibilities within a discipline, craft, or practice imply that one has a body of knowledge that is well articulated and certain. Such well-articulated and certain knowledge is most commonly associated with the natural sciences. And it is just this kind of knowledge that many educators have been striving to achieve since at least the beginning of this century.

In contrast, most of what we know or believe with respect to everyday living is far from certain, so that instead of using the term "impossible," we more often rely on such terms as "doubtful" or "unlikely." Everyday living is filled with the uncertain, the unpredictable, and the ambiguous. The same is true of the everyday world of educational practice. Yet many educators have been trying to turn this uncertain world of educational practice into a world of definitive knowledge. Generally, these educators have attempted to place educational practice on a "scientific basis" and to establish lawlike regularities and generalizations of wide applicability by following a model of inquiry that they perceive as similar to the one followed in the natural sciences. If following this model of inquiry had established such scientifically based knowledge and lawlike regularities for educators, then they could certainly make claims to knowing educational impossibilities.

Many educators have taken another tack. They concede that, being a practice, education cannot itself become a science but argue that nevertheless it can draw on the social-behavioral sciences to provide it with a scientific basis. However, this procedure has no more led to the achievement of a well-defined body of knowledge in education than has the procedure of treating education as a science. Moreover, the social-behavioral sciences seem themselves to have come into a state of crisis, or at least of fundamental reconceptualization,[1] so that it is not at all clear just how at present these sciences can or should be drawn on.

Alas, educators have so far been unable to approach anything like the theoretical and methodological advances that have been made in the natural sciences. There are no powerful educational theories or methods of investigation that command commitment of educators or guide their inquiries, and there are no well-established, lawlike regularities of practice or dependable generalizations of wide applicability. Yet this state of affairs may be viewed with a certain optimism. The recent and growing recognition among educators that the natural science model of inquiry has not had the desired results in education may set the stage for a more fruitful development. To begin with, the scientific ideal in education may in good part be understood as a consequence of the positivist ideology that dominated Anglo-American thought on knowledge and science throughout most of the first half of this century.[2] Since mid-century, the hold of this positivist ideology has considerably weakened, and a variety of "postpositivist" views of knowledge and science have emerged. Thus, the breakdown of positivism may open new ways to think about education and its development. And, by studying why a scientific basis for education is impossible, we may hope to gain a clearer understanding of education and how it may be studied and developed.

Let us first look at how the attempt to achieve a scientific base of knowledge has proceeded in education. Positivism here has assumed a particularly crude form, promoting a view of science that emphasizes the aims of prediction and control over those of theory construction, explanation, and understanding. This crude form of positivism has also promoted an instrumental and technical view of education. Consequently, research in education has mostly been directed toward arriving at generalizations that could be used to predict and control educational events and outcomes. Specifically, the generalizations would concern the relationships between educational means, such as teachers' methods, strategies, or actions, and educational outcomes, such as students' learning or behavior.

Generally, those involved in this research observe, measure, and record teachers' and students' verbal and behavioral actions. These actions are determined by teachers' and students' traits, dispositions, skills, knowledge, beliefs, intentions, and so on. The researcher generally wants to find out which actions of teachers, as means, are "associated with" or "produce" which actions of students, as outcomes. To accomplish this aim, the researcher typically studies teachers' means and students' outcomes across numerous teaching-learning settings, comparing and contrasting different means and their outcomes. In this kind of natural science approach to research, the actions of teachers and students must be conceived as capable of being observed and then formulated as lawlike regularities that apply across the different settings. Thus, these actions have been conceptualized as "variables" that recur over and again in different times and places and with different people. Usually, the researcher preselects the categories of variables to be studied and "operationally defines" them in terms of criteria based on observation and measurement. Once the preselected variables are labeled and defined, then every action or event a researcher observes in the various settings is recorded as an instance of one of the variables.

For example, the researcher may have decided to study the effects that a certain type of question asked by teachers has on the responses of students. The type of question asked is considered the "independent variable" and the responses of students the "dependent variable." The criteria used in setting up the two kinds of variables are then used to identify and record instances of their occurrence. Supposedly, through studying the patterns of occurrence, the researcher can obtain data on how this type of questioning by teachers relates to or affects the responses of students.

There are, however, grave difficulties with this tactic of treating actions as if they could be converted into fixed and abstracted variables. Let us now examine four of these difficulties.

First, using abstracted categories of "variables" to represent the actions of teachers and students so tears these actions from their concrete origins that they lose much of their original meaning. The treatment of these phenomena as capable of being operationally defined and fixed makes it appear that the same phenomena can recur in different times and settings with the same effects. However, once we consider these phenomena in their concrete settings—in the full context of teaching and learning—we see how dubious such treatment is. Far from being fixed and stable, the actions involved in teaching and learning are open in their qualities and their effects. That is, the qualities and effects of any given action are constantly open to the influence and interaction of other actions or events in the setting.

Let us consider "teacher praise," a type of action generally held by educators to be both desirable and effective in motivating students. Even an action as simple and ordinary as this cannot be considered fixed and stable across different settings, times, and people. The meaning of the praise and its effects will depend on the maturity of the students, how they feel about the teacher, what kinds of activities are being praised, what events immediately preceded the praise, how the teacher combines praise with other actions, and so on indefinitely. One teacher may be held in high esteem by students, so that praise from this teacher is highly prized and sought after; another teacher, who is not respected or who is disliked, may find himself completely unable to motivate students through praise. A third teacher may use praise so frequently and indiscriminately that it loses its effectiveness. Yet another teacher may communicate praise in a very unorthodox or subtle manner, so that it is not readily observable and recordable through standard techniques. Clearly, the researcher's objectifying procedure can greatly distort what actually occurs in the individual settings, either through recording under the category of "praise" actions that differ significantly in their meanings and effects or through failing to record as "praise" subtle and unorthodox actions that have gone unidentified.

Moreover, if we consider any typical setting of teaching and learning, it does not appear that actions and events occur in anything like a lawlike manner or otherwise lend themselves to prediction and control. Indeed, recent "naturalistic" studies of full and ongoing contexts of teaching and learning[3] concur in finding these settings characterized by a great deal of openness and unpredictability. These studies find that although teachers do plan and project in a general way, they nevertheless must be responsive to the immediacy of the classroom and to the demand for on-the-spot decisions within the continuous flux of school life. Teaching and learning are typically characterized by emerging and unanticipated events, including changes in the moods and interests of students, student remarks or questions, difficulties or obstacles in learning tasks, sudden insights by students or teachers, and interference from outside sources. Moreover, even the more predictable elements—the elements that allow teachers to plan and project—by no means resemble lawlike regularities. Thus, rather than using terms such as "law," "prediction," and "control," with their connotations of science and technicality, it might be better to use looser and more modest terms, such as "routine," "order," "habit," "plan," "project," and "anticipate." The latter terms seem better suited to the usual settings of teaching and learning, which are more like the settings of ordinary life than the experimentally controlled ones of science.

Those who advocate following a model of natural science in studying education, or in the social-behavioral sciences, do have a ready reply to the charge that they have as yet been unable to produce laws, theories, or advances in knowledge anywhere near comparable to those that have been produced in the natural sciences. Their reply has been that human and social phenomena are very much more complex than physical phenomena. The implication is that, given more time, the complexities will eventually be unraveled and the advances in theory and knowledge will come forth. However, this reply self-servingly underestimates the complexity of the subject matter in the natural sciences; it underplays the fact that the model of natural science has had eighty years or more to demonstrate its effectiveness in the social sciences and in education; and it overlooks the fact that advocates of the model are unable to provide us with even a hint of what features of the social world are accessible to its program and aims. Thus, for teaching and learning, which are characterized by varying degrees of the planned and the spontaneous, the followers of natural science are unable to show us specifically where we might find lawlike regularities or the possibilities for prediction and control.

It is little wonder, then, that a notorious separation has arisen in education between the work of researchers and that of practitioners. Many educators are deeply concerned over how to get the research findings into the schools. They miss the point. Given the way in which the research data have been detached from their practical settings, it is not surprising that those data are not readily applicable to those settings.

There is a second, related problem with the way those who follow a model of natural science treat the object of their research as abstracted variables. Recent reconceptualizations of the social sciences have brought out a crucial distinction between the subject matters of the natural and the social sciences: physical reality can be objectified and conceptualized as independent of human interpretation in a way that social reality cannot be. Although both become the object of scientists' theoretical constructions and interpretations, the latter involves an additional level of interpretation. For, as social reality is itself a human construction, it is constituted by human interpretation.[4]

Suppose, for example, students in a particular class are writing short phrases on sheets of paper and then exchanging their writings, each commenting on the others'. What do we know of the meaning and significance of this activity from this description alone, or what would we know from simply observing this activity with no other information to go on? This activity could be a mere game, a recreation and a respite from the larger, more intense work routine of the class. Or it could be a challenging and motivating introduction to a new learning unit. Or it could be one step in a sequence of activities leading to a long-term educational goal. For us to know what it is, we would first have to know what the participants understand themselves to be doing. The activity *is* for them what they understand it to be. And it is possible that although to an observer each student might appear to be engaged in the same activity, there are significant differences among the students and the teacher in their interpretation of what is going on.

Thus, the behavioral and verbal actions that social or educational researchers study are constructed by the participants being studied and depend on the participants' interpretations. Before educational and social researchers can even claim to be studying reality, or before they can objectively observe and describe what they see, they must know the interpretive constructions of the participants being studied. However, as we have seen, variables are typically preselected and fixed. Thus, researchers are unable to account for the participants' interpretations, which constitute the reality of the settings.

To use the example of teacher praise again, various words and acts may satisfy a researcher's operational criteria for "teacher praise," yet they may vary greatly in their meanings in different situations. It is even possible for such words and acts to be interpreted by a particular teacher and classroom of students as ironical and as an oblique chastisement rather than as praise. A social scientist can never be sure in advance that others start from the same background assumptions and practices in constructing their interpretations. Yet the procedures of preselecting and fixing variables for study is a way of making just this kind of unwarranted, advanced assumption.

The third problem with the model of natural science lies in its adherence to the positivist ideal of knowledge. According to the positivist ideal, knowledge is only that which can be fully articulated and specified. This ideal has been at the root of the attempt to formulate a body of scientific principles, generalizations, and rules of teaching with which to advance the profession and train teachers. However, the positivist ideal has been criticized as much too narrow to account for the full range and variety of human knowing.[5] The broader conceptions of knowledge offered by Michael Oakeshott, Michael Polanyi, and Ludwig Wittgenstein appear to be particularly relevant to our discussion of educational and teaching practice because of their emphasis on practical knowing.[6] These three thinkers come remarkably close in their critiques and in the alternative view of knowing that they offer.

According to Oakeshott, every science, art, and practical activity—indeed, every human activity—always involves two inseparable sorts of knowledge: "technical" and "practical." Technical knowledge can be formulated as rules and maxims; it can be expressed, remembered, and put into practice; and it can be learned from books. The chief characteristic of technical knowledge is that it is susceptible of precise formulation. In contrast, practical knowledge is not reflective, cannot be formulated as rules, and exists only in use. Polanyi has also recognized that there are both "articulate" and "inarticulate" forms of knowledge. Any art, craft, or skill, including scientific skill, is achieved by the observance of a set of rules not known as such by the person following them. Although articulated rules and maxims can be useful, they do not determine practice and they cannot replace inarticulate, practical knowledge; on the contrary, they can serve as a guide only to those who can integrate them into their already existing practical knowledge. And, in a similar fashion, Wittgenstein attempted to overcome narrow positivist views of knowing by emphasizing the inarticulate elements in the acquisition and skilled use of language and other social practices. Moreover, these three thinkers have agreed that a skill or practice is passed on not by the deliberate teaching and learning of explicit rules, but rather, by use and practice, in the presence of a master who himself is unable to fully explicate what he knows and passes on to others. As Polanyi has said, an art that cannot be specified in detail cannot be transmitted by prescription, since no prescription for it exists.

Researchers following the model of natural science, then, attempt to separate the specifiable components of teaching from its inseparable unspecifiable, inarticulate components. This abstracting procedure results in distortion, the ultimate effects of which can be seen in the way the research findings become formulated as principles of teaching in textbooks and manuals. Typically, these principles are so abstractly and generally formulated that they strike teachers as too theoretical and impractical, as ambiguous in their meanings, and as unrelated to the concrete tasks and difficulties of teaching. When, on the other hand, the principles are specifically formulated, they appear trivial or mere truisms. Thus, the very research findings that are supposed to represent the achievements of the natural science model suggest instead serious inadequacies in its basic principles, assumptions, and aims.

The fourth and final problem with following a model of natural science is that it attempts to analyze education as if it were largely a technical practice, unencumbered by values, interests, and norms. Researchers following this model proceed as if the goals of education were given and unproblematic and as if the primary task were to identify technical means and methods that would most efficiently achieve those goals. Yet, in reality, education is through and through a value-based enterprise. Indeed, value components always take precedence over and determine the meaning and effects of the more technical components. Any technical method a particular teacher uses will have meaning and effects according to the values of the teacher and the students.

We can see the overriding importance of values if we briefly consider the teaching of any of the basic skills. Suppose, for example, that in teaching reading to young children a teacher is ignorant of or neglects broader educational purposes and values. If the teacher therefore narrowly focuses on the technical skills of beginning reading (e.g., word analysis, phonics, sight-word recognition, and phrasing), students may come to regard reading as primarily confined to school and unrelated to their larger goals in life. In this case the goal of genuine literacy is undermined. In contrast, a teacher who is aware of the broader purposes and values will strive to approach beginning reading in a way that encourages students to integrate reading into their lives and use it as a means of participating in our society's worthwhile projects in the arts, humanities, and sciences. The teacher might do this even while teaching the same basic skills as the first teacher. Thus, the effects will depend not so much on the technical aspects of teaching beginning reading as on the broader educational values brought to the task.

Thus, we encounter another reason for rejecting the assumption that in education variables can simply be abstracted and studied. We previously saw that this assumption is contradicted, first, by actions and events being interactive and open, second, by the reality of teaching and learning settings being constituted by the participants' interpretations, and third, by teaching practices having inarticulable and unspecifiable components that are inseparable from their articulable and specifiable components. Now we can add as a fourth contradiction to this assumption the fact that teaching and learning contexts are defined by values, norms, and interests.

The conflict between the perception of education as a technical versus value-based enterprise is also problematic at another level. To a significant extent, our educational values stem from our conception of what a person is. People should be educated so as to both carry on the culture and participate in its further development. People are not to be manipulated or controlled. Rather, they are to be regarded as capable of deliberation, judgment, discrimination, and choice with respect to life's projects and goals, as to a significant extent self-formative of personality and character, and as having absolute value. However, the perception of education as a technical enterprise suggests that its major task is to produce unproblematic educational results as efficiently as possible. In this way the natural science tradition promotes an instrumental view of students, a view that students should be manipulated and treated as mere means to achieving prescribed and externally imposed objectives. There is no place in the natural science tradition for the kind of study that will enlighten and enrich our understanding of the person and educational values. Even worse, the major tools of the tradition, such as the operational definition, objectification, standardization, experimental control, and statistical analysis, generally have reductive effects, so that value concepts are left to wither over time.

• • •

Let us now return to the difficulty that initiated our critique of the natural science model. As we saw, proponents of this model assert that teaching could become fully professionalized if it could claim a body of expert knowledge. Yet, despite their efforts, teaching has shown no signs of advancing in this way. Without a definitive body of knowledge there can be no general statements on the limits of teaching practice, there can be no prescriptions on what can and cannot be done, and there can be no general statements of impossibility. Of course, just because no definitive body of knowledge for teaching has as yet been achieved, this does not mean that it could not be achieved—even here we cannot presume to know an impossibility. However, we must question the reasonableness of such a goal in the light of the prolonged and persistent lack of progress or of any indication that the natural science program is even on the right track. Indeed, our analysis and evaluation of the natural science program for the study of education has been that it seriously misconceives and distorts educational practice.

Despite the apparent failure of some eighty years of effort in research, many educators still hope to place educational practice on a scientific basis. We may wonder at the power of the ideal to continue attracting supporters when it has produced no sign that it can become a reality. Much of the explanation lies in the fantastic educational future promised. The natural science ideal usually combines with a technical ideal, and so completely that in many educational practices the two become indistinguishable. Just what is the educational future promised by science and technology?

The promise is to transform education so that it would become progressive in the same way the sciences and technologies are commonly perceived to be progressive. Then the most recently created educational curricular methods and materials would not merely represent the latest in fads or fashions but would instead be objectively better than their predecessors. Moreover, being scientifically validated, these methods and materials would be free of personal and local limitations and idiosyncracies. And they could be made available to all our teachers, children, and schools across the nation.

Proponents of such scientific-technical standardization have thus far had most success in the area of standardized testing. Introduced into the schools early in this century, standardized tests soon became widely used. Today, such tests are considered an indispensable part of the educational process at every level. They are heavily relied on for evaluating schools and the progress of students; for comparing the effectiveness of varying programs, teaching methods, materials for learning, and learning systems; for diagnosing students' learning problems; for selecting and placing students into various programs, classes, and schools; and for educationally or vocationally guiding and counseling students. It is commonly believed that standardized tests contribute greatly to objectivity in making educational decisions.

There has been an attempt to extend this scientific-technical standardization to all aspects of educational practice. Thus, for example, we find at every level of education standard texts and workbooks for students, standard manuals of instruction for teachers, and standard curricular guides, all designed for use by different teachers and students working in different educational settings across the country. But, the first serious proposals to nationally integrate public school education as a scientific-technical system came in the late 1950s and early 1960s and centered on the use of teaching machines. These machines and their associated programmed learning materials were actually to teach students as well as to assess and evaluate them.

Specifically, a properly programmed unit or package would do the following: First, individually assess the students to determine whether each had the skills and knowledge needed to enter a unit. Second, present the unit in a carefully programmed way so that each step in the unit could be mastered by a student without help from the teacher and would as automatically as possible lead the student to the next step. Third, provide immediate feedback to students on how well they were doing in mastering the material. Fourth, for a student who failed to respond adequately or master a step, provide corrective feedback or an alternative keyed branched sequence. Fifth, test the student on overall mastery upon completion of the programmed unit. Finally, provide a complete record of each student's responses and performance in all of the foregoing. In short, the functions of assessing, teaching, and evaluating students were to be fully integrated into a system that could be regarded as objective, standardized, and independent of any teacher's personal biases or limitations.

As might be expected, educators began to fear that teaching machines and programmed materials would displace teachers and make them obsolete, just as technical systems have made many in our economy obsolete during the last two centuries. True, advocates offered public assurances that the new technology would only free teachers from their more routine tasks so that they might devote their time to more creative teaching and to interactions with individual students. But then they would by implication contradict these assurances by claiming that programming was not limited to routine tasks or to drilling students but could be extended to teaching problem solving and creative thought—that there was in principle no limit to what could be taught in this way. The expectations and fears that accompanied the introduction of teaching machines and programmed materials may seem naive today, but the recent introduction of computer-assisted systems of instruction has produced similar reactions.

Thus, in the same way that the glowing future promised by science and technology can beguile and attract, so can it frighten and repel. Both the attraction and the repulsion are based on a vision of machines displacing people. For those who are attracted, science and technology hold out the promise of replacing the personal, local, and limited with the standard and objective, thereby insuring that the very best in teaching and curricula are available to all students across the nation. For others, they threaten to so reduce the need for personal interaction that teachers would become, at best, peripheral to the education of students.

Ultimately, however, both sets of feelings are based on exaggerated notions of what science and technology can do, either for education or to it. Ignored are the inherent limits in the use of impersonal systems and material products. One way of seeing these limits is to return to our earlier discussion of the two inseparable components of all knowledge and skills. If there is always an unspecifiable component, then it is not possible to rely entirely, or even primarily, on impersonal systems and material products, as these can only contain the component of knowledge we can build into them, the specifiable component.

Another way to see the inherent limits in the use of systems and products is to consider their dependence on the meanings that people must bring to them if they are to achieve their intended purposes. Not only are they created by people whose meanings, values, and purposes are represented in them, but those who would learn and profit from them must rely on their own histories of personal interaction and socialization to understand the representations. The young become inducted into a culture and committed to its values and traditions through their contacts with mature adults who they find inspirational, admirable, and worthy of emulation. Impersonal systems and material products can also teach, educate, and inspire, but only if previous personal interaction and socialization have prepared the way and can bring to life their representations. The young and the uninitiated can be inspired to commitment and long-term effort by the mature and accomplished, who represent to them the kinds of people they might become and the kinds of lives they might create. A heroic life portrayed on film or in a written biography might do the same, but only for those young people whose personal and social experiences have already prepared them to find meaning in these representations. Audiences and readers, to fully respond to films or written texts, must, in a sense, be able to cooperatively construct with the absent authors a meaningful experience; they must enter into various kinds of dialogues with authors. Such creative constructions are built on personal and social interactions.

To turn our discussion to the context of schooling, the initial stages of reading and writing instruction may appear to be primarily a technical task of efficiently transmitting certain skills. What is overlooked, however, is that the efficient transmission of skills through workbooks, exercise sheets, and programmed materials can lead to genuine literacy only if the students are already prepared to see that their engagement with the material has meaning, that reading and writing have significance and value for their lives beyond the tasks of schooling. Teachers are crucial in transmitting such insights. Especially at the beginning of any educational journey, students' firsthand interactions with educated and accomplished teachers are essential. Teachers can inspire, exemplify, and point the way; they can call out from students those latent potentialities that can so easily remain unrealized. And, far from being confined to the early years of schooling, educational journeys are initiated at various stages of life. The professions and the disciplines of the arts and sciences ordinarily require that initiates come into personal contact with masters. It is through contact with living examples that beginning students obtain their clearest images of what mastery can mean and of what they themselves might someday become.

In short, once the education of students has been successfully initiated and as long as it is firmly supported by living teachers who guide and inspire, then systems and products can play an important ancillary role. A proper understanding of this relationship can protect us from being seduced by idealized visions of a scientific-technical education. Alternatively, it can protect us from being overcome by dark visions of an educational future in which machines have replaced teachers. Most important, perhaps, such understanding can make it possible for us to use machines wisely in serving our educational values.

• • •

Our examination of whether we might claim to be able to identify impossibilities in education has suggested that there is something amiss in attempts to place educational practice on a scientific or technical basis. The discussion has repeatedly drawn us back to larger educational contexts and values. We have found that these override the narrower, more technical and instrumental aspects of teaching and learning. Moreover, if we include the goals of developing good persons and a good society among our educational aims, then such a broad, value-based and moral enterprise does not seem at all congruent with the image of a technical practice or of a definitive body of knowledge. It is not just the usually recognized difficulty that there are varying and even conflicting values; it is more the difficulty that such fundamental values and moral views are of necessity global and open in meaning. Even if we could come to a fair degree of consensus on educational or social goals, it is not in the nature of such goals to be precisely defined. Rather, they serve as regulating ideals, as generalized standards that help us to select and discriminate among our daily activities, and as guidelines requiring constant creative interpretation. Furthermore, the act of moving toward and achieving our ultimate goals tends to increase our understanding of them and to modify them in various ways.

For example, let us suppose we were able to achieve consensus not only on fundamental goals and values but even on an educational program. Experience tells us that as soon as we began to implement the program, our understanding of the program and its goals would change in significant ways. And accomplishment of the program goals would affect our understanding of what it was we had accomplished and our understanding of our educational ideals. All of this suggests an image of educational theory and practice very different from the one that has motivated attempts to develop a definitive body of professional knowledge for education.

Conceived of most broadly and fundamentally, the educational task is to transmit our most valued cultural ideals and traditions, and thereby to make people better, a decidedly nontechnical task. Cultural ideals are inherently regulative and inspirational rather than prescriptive. And although cultural traditions, projects, and achievements are in one sense established and there for us, they are also open and developmental. A genuinely participating member of the culture must know and want to know something more than the settled and the definitive, something more than merely what has been done and accomplished—that alone would be static knowledge, and it would mean the demise of the culture. One who genuinely participates must engage in and carry on traditions and ideals, a task combining established knowledge and creative interpretation. In the same way, the educational transmission of cultural ideals and traditions cannot be accomplished by following a body of rules. Instead, the educational institutions must create environments generally supporting valued ideals and traditions, and the teachers in those institutions must embody and exemplify them.

Thus, educational development, like overall cultural development, is constantly self-transforming and creative. As we educate, we deepen our understanding of what it means to educate; as we both fail and succeed in achieving objectives, we better understand those objectives and new ones emerge; as we complete projects and accomplish aims, ever new projects and aims are in the making. Rather than a definitive body of knowledge, or a set of prescriptive rules of operations, or even a set of statements of impossibilities, it would seem that educators need models and examples of educational ideals that would not only enrich their understanding, but that would inspire them and reveal possibilities for human and social development.

Notes

1. See, for example, Fred R. Dallmayer and Thomas A. McCarthy (eds.), *Understanding and Social Inquiry*, University of Notre Dame Press, Notre Dame, Ind., 1977; Kenneth J. Gergen, *Toward Transformation in Social Knowledge*, Springer-Verlag, New York, 1982; Donald Polkinghorne, *Methodology for the Social Sciences: Systems of Inquiry*, State University of New York Press, Albany, 1983; Calvin O. Schrag, *Radical Reflection and the Origin of the Human Sciences*, Purdue University Press, West Lafayette, Ind., 1980; T. W. Wann (ed.), *Behaviorism and Phenomenology: Contrasting Bases for Modern Psychology*, University of Chicago Press, Chicago, 1964.

2. A. J. Ayer (ed.), *Logical Positivism*, Free Press, Glencoe, Ill., 1959; Brand Blanshard, *Reason and Analysis*, Open Court, LaSalle, Ill., 1973; Lezak Kolakowski, *The Alienation of Reason:*

A History of Positivist Thought, Doubleday, Garden City, New York, 1969; Gerard Radnitzky, *Contemporary Schools of Metascience,* 3rd ed., Henry Regnery, Chicago, 1973.

3. Philip W. Jackson, *Life in Classrooms,* Holt, Rinehart and Winston, New York, 1968; John Eggleston (ed.), *Teacher Decision-Making in the Classroom,* Routledge & Kegan Paul, Boston, 1979; Peter Woods (ed.), *Teacher Strategies: Explorations in the Sociology of the School,* Croom Helm, London, 1980.

4. Charles Taylor, "Interpretation and the Science of Man," *Review of Metaphysics,* 25: 3–34 (1971) (reprinted in Dallmayer and McCarthy, eds., *Understanding and Social Inquiry*).

5. Richard J. Bernstein, *Beyond Objectivism and Relativism: Science, Hermeneutics, and Praxis,* University of Pennsylvania Press, Philadelphia, 1983; Brand Blanshard, *Reason and Analysis,* Open Court, LaSalle, Ill., 1962; Stanley L. Jaki, *The Road of Science and the Ways to God,* University of Chicago Press, Chicago, 1978; Maurice Mandelbaum, *History, Man and Reason,* Johns Hopkins University Press, Baltimore, 1971; Thomas McCarthy, *The Critical Theory of Jurgen Habermas,* MIT Press, Cambridge, Mass., 1978.

6. See Michael Oakeshott, *Rationalism in Politics,* Methuen, London, 1962; Michael Polanyi, *Personal Knowledge,* University of Chicago Press, Chicago, 1962; and on Wittgenstein's views, see Sabina Lovibond, *Realism and Imagination in Ethics,* University of Minnesota Press, Minneapolis, 1983, pp. 27–31.

POETRY AND THE IMPOSSIBLE

People use words to communicate with one another. In many kinds of discourse—certainly in scientific discourse—it is desirable that words and phrases be used with as little ambiguity as possible. Similarly, dictionary writers attempt precise, delimiting definitions of words. Here is *Webster's* primary definition for the word "rose":

> 1 a: any of a genus (*Rosa* of the family Rosaceae, the rose family) of usu. prickly shrubs with pinnate leaves and showy flowers having five petals in the wild state but being often double or semidouble under cultivation

Additional meanings include "a color averaging a moderate purplish red," "a gem with a rose cut," and the past tense of the verb "rise".

The Poet's Words

The agenda for poets is somewhat different. Words are not only tools of communication, they are also the medium in which poets work, just as paint is the medium in which painters work. Words have a texture. They possess associative, suggestive qualities; what they connote is as important as what they denote. So that "rose" may encompass any or all of its dictionary meanings—and more. A rose has links both to the history of the world (e.g., the horticulture of roses, England's War of the Roses) and also to the specific literary history of the word. It is connected to Shakespeare's rose that by any name would smell as sweet, to Yeats' Rose of the World, to Abie's Irish Rose, to Gertrude Stein's "rose is a rose is a rose is a rose," and so on. In some of these, the word "rose" takes on symbolic meaning. Stein, on the other hand, hoped for a fresh sense of the flower for which "rose" is the name: In explaining her famous repetition, she is cited as telling a university audience: "I know that in daily life we don't go around saying [that], but I think that in that line the rose is red for the first time in English poetry for a hundred years."[1]

A poet may also be tuned to a word's etymology or to other of its linguistic aspects. "Rose" is a four-letter word. It is a homophone for "rows," "rhos," "roes," and "Rowe's." Visually, in its lower-case form, all of the letters are small, with no above-or-below-the-line loops (notice the egalitarian effect of the Gertrude Stein line: "rose is a rose is a rose is a rose."). "Rose" has a long "o" sound. It rhymes easily with both nouns and conjugated verbs: "toes," "hose"; "froze," "goes." The "r" can cluster alliteratively with other "r" words. The particular tilt of the word's meaning will depend on the words that surround it.

Although poetry and prose share language as their medium, it is poetry that has since antiquity been considered one of the arts. In considering the impossibilities that may be inherent in poetry, it is important to bear in mind that this art form, to which the Greeks assigned three Muses (Erato—love poetry, Euterpe—lyric poetry, Calliope—epic poetry), is more closely allied with dance, music, and drama than it is with ordinary discourse.

By its very nature, the world of poetry, like that of dreams, makes possible the apparently impossible. It lives companionably with paradox and ambiguity. It is at home with contradictions. John Keats gave a name to this unique quality:

It struck me what quality went to form a man of achievement
especially in literature, and which Shakespeare possessed so
enormously—I mean *Negative Capability,* that is, when a man is
capable of being in uncertainties, mysteries, doubts without any
irritable reaching after fact and reason.[2]

"Do I contradict myself?" asks Walt Whitman in "Song of Myself."
"Very well, then, I contradict myself. / (I am large, I contain mul-
titudes)."

Ambiguity can be a creative force in poetry. If a single word may
have multiple meanings, then so, of course, may clusters of words.
Ambiguity, as defined by William Empson in his seminal book,
Seven Types of Ambiguity, is "any verbal nuance, however slight,
which gives room for alternative reactions to the same piece of
language."[3] Poetry tends to be particularly rich in such nuances.
Consider this stanza from William Butler Yeats' poem, "The Circus
Animals' Desertion," written in his old age:

> *Those masterful images because complete*
> *Grew in pure mind, but out of what began?*
> *A mound of refuse or the sweepings of a street,*
> *Old kettles, old bones, old rags, that raving slut*
> *Who keeps the till. Now that my ladder's gone*
> *I must lie down where all the ladders start,*
> *In the foul rag-and-bone shop of the heart.*[4]

This single stanza is the last of three sections in the poem, so that
some of its words may refer back to earlier sections. Who, we ask, is
"that raving slut / Who keeps the till," and what "ladder" is Yeats
referring to? Perhaps these are simply props for scene setting, like
the sweepings of the street and the old kettles, introduced to help
produce a mood for the poem's conclusion. "That raving slut" could
be a barmaid in a pub in a broken-down neighborhood. But she
might also be the "pity-crazed" Countess Cathleen, who is described
in a earlier stanza as being enslaved to fanaticism and hate, and who,
we are told (in footnotes about Yeats' life), is an idealized version of
Yeats' lifelong love, Maude Gonne—she who "keeps the till," that
is, who is the keeper of his love-filled heart.

The ladder evokes, as a first image, an actual ladder, one among
"all the ladders" lying stacked in a shop. It may also be a symbolic
ladder designed to lift the poet out of the muck, out of the "foul

rag-and-bone shop of the heart." But in addition, and more clearly, it is metaphor: "now that my ladder's gone" refers to the speaker's impotence in old age. "Gone" is too much like "Gonne" for the poet not to have been clear about the connection, and perhaps there are echoes of the youthful "lad" in "ladder." The shop, Yeats says, is the heart; it is the life force. Thus the stanza lends itself to a number of interpretations, all of which enrich a reading of the poem.

Theoretical Impossibilities

Like the White Queen in *Alice Through the Looking Glass*, poets are capable of believing six impossible things before breakfast. Here is my own list of the kinds of theoretical impossibilities that poetry makes possible: (1) the literally impossible; (2) the impossibility of being someone other than oneself; (3) the impossibility of doing that which has never been done; (4) the impossibility of changing the unchangeable; (5) the impossibility of equating opposites; and (6) the impossibility of adequate translation. Poetry make these possible by a number of devices, including metaphor and associative leaps of the imagination. After considering these impossibilities-made-possible, I will turn to the few rock-bottom impossibilities that do, I believe, exist in poetry.

The Literally Impossible

A specific instance of the literally impossible occurs in Wilfred Owen's moving World War I poem, "Strange Meeting." The poet meets—"down some profound dull tunnel"—the enemy he killed. They speak. While on a literal level this is impossible, in the realm of dream or hallucination it has great validity. (It is made all the more poignant by the fact that Owen, who served as a British soldier, was killed at age 25 one week before the armistice of 1918.) His recurrent theme in this and other poems is "the pity of war," its waste. The enemy identifies himself fraternally: "I am the enemy you killed, my friend."

In the final stanza of "Sailing to Byzantium," Yeats alters the natural law by which life is a finite time-line from birth to death:

> *Once out of nature I shall never take*
> *My bodily form from any natural thing*
> *But such a form as Grecian goldsmiths make*

> *Of hammered gold and gold enamelling*
> *To keep a drowsy Emperor awake;*
> *Or set upon a golden bough to sing*
> *To lords and ladies of Byzantium*
> *Of what is past, or passing, or to come.*[5]

Upon his death, Yeats proposes to become, not dust and ashes but a bird of hammered gold, an immortal poet-bird. He will do the impossible, he will conquer time.

Impossible, too, on the literal level, is the imagined world of the surrealist poets, with its taut interaction between objective fact and subjective fantasy. In his poem "Unchopping a Tree," W. S. Merwin runs time backward, meticulously reattaching the parts of a tree in the order in which they were chopped off. Then he reenters real time: "There is nothing more you can do. / Others are waiting. / Everything is going to have to be put back."[6]

Marianne Moore, hardly a surrealist herself, speaks of poets (in her poem "Poetry") as "literalists of the imagination," and says of poetry: "not till the poets among us can ... present for inspection 'imaginary gardens with real toads in them' shall we have it."

More generally, metaphor—one of poetry's central elements—presents another apparent literal impossibility. Both metaphor and simile work by analogy. Simile says, this is *like* that; metaphor says, this *is* that. We have no problem of logic with Robert Burns' "my luve is like a red, red rose." Robert Frost's statement to his beloved—"You, of course, are a rose— / But were always a rose"—is metaphor, literally false but emotionally/imaginatively true. We understand it intuitively; we place the two parts of the unstated analogy side by side and they meld.

The Impossibility of Being Someone Other Than Oneself

The device of taking on a persona is so familiar to us that we are apt to forget that it is only a device—that it is, in fact, fantasy, a special kind of literal impossibility. One can in a poem, as in other forms of creative writing, assume the voice of another—whether living or dead, male or female, young or old, and whether human, animal, vegetable, or mineral. On a literal level, this can only be understood as a putting on of a mask.

A well-known example of the persona appears in Browning's "My Last Duchess," in which the speaker of the poem is the Duke of

Ferrara. In "Crusoe in England," Elizabeth Bishop speaks in the voice of a storybook character, Robinson Crusoe—a figure of the opposite sex and from another era. The speakers in Sylvia Plath's "Mushrooms" are—mushrooms. Emily Dickinson often writes in the voice of someone who is dead: "I heard a fly buzz when I died." In John Berryman's "Homage to Mistress Bradstreet," the speaker in many of the poems is Anne Bradstreet, America's first (seventeenth-century) woman poet.

The Impossibility of Doing That Which Has Never Been Done

Dream, fantasy, imagination—these are some of the most impelling motives for the poet. Thus, poems will often leave the familiar, known world behind. A case in point is Alfred Lord Tennyson's "Locksley Hall," written in 1842, when the poet was a young man (it is from this poem that the line "In the spring a young man's fancy lightly turns to thoughts of love" entered our repertoire). Long before the advent of airplanes, global wars, or the United Nations, Tennyson wrote:

For I dipt into the future, far as human eye could see,
Saw the Vision of the world, and all the wonder that would be;

Saw the heavens fill with commerce, argosies of magic sails,
Pilots of the purple twilight, dropping down with costly bales;

Heard the heavens fill with shouting, and there rain'd a ghastly dew
From the nations' airy navies grappling in the central blue;

Far along the world-wide whisper of the southwind rushing warm,
With the standards of the peoples plunging thro' the thunder-storm;

Till the war-drums throbbed no longer, and the battle-flags were furl'd
In the Parliament of man, the Federation of the world.

This impossibility may also be viewed within the historic context of poetry itself; that is, a poem may—in terms of its form or content—do what has previously been "impossible" in poetry. Like other arts, poetry has a long history of shifting tastes, borrowings from other cultures, and experimentation. One generation of artists learns from, responds to, and changes that which previous generations have done. Sometimes the older work is rejected out of hand by the avant garde. Often, the tastes of a number of generations exist side by side.

As examples of shifting tastes, I offer the twentieth century's response to two earlier "impossibilities": (1) there can be no poetry without rhyme or meter; (2) it is impossible for poetry to be prose.

For many centuries, poetry depended heavily on rhyme and meter. Before Gutenberg and the invention of the printing press, poems were, in large part, transmitted orally by bards and troubadours. Rhyme and meter were important mnemonic devices; they helped to jog the memory. Gradually, the boundaries of poetry were pushed back. And since Whitman's arrival on the scene of English-American poetry, free verse has come into its own. Free verse has its own subtle prosody—it is often, for example, cadenced and full of sound—but regular rhyme and set meters are no longer requisites.

As for the poetry-prose issue, it would seem almost by definition that poetry cannot be prose. There exists, however, an entire genre of contemporary poems, originating with Baudelaire, known as "prose poems." Prose poems look like regular paragraphs; visually, they do not resemble stanzas. These poems, too, have their special attributes—an intensity and economy of words, a surreal quality, often a tough-mindedness, wit, and humor. Conversely, we can think of prose passages from novels that differ from poetry only by the absence of formal line breaks. Portions of *Moby Dick* come immediately to mind. As is the case with other media, the edge between poetry and prose has softened.

The Impossibility of Changing the Unchangeable

If it seems impossible to beat the system, you can outwit it by imaginative efforts. In George Orwell's novel *1984*, prisoners were locked in the infamous Room 101 and confronted with their own worst fears (rats, wild beasts, burial alive, whatever was "worst") in order to brainwash them into loving Big Brother. In my poem "Resisting Big Brother: An Exercise for 1984," an obsessive fear of insects is overcome, thereby making it possible to change the circumstances under which Big Brother exercises control:

> *A room, the Ministry of Love's Room 101,*
> *all plumbing and no windows.*
> *Grubs seethe in the drainpipes,*
> *spiders mass on the ceiling.*
> *At my feet, flies with torn-off wings*
> *begin their slow climb.*

I'm tied to the seat.
The Marsh King waits
to suck me down with sewer beetles.
Big Brother knows—
he rigged this room for me.
He knows what's worst, he's watching.

I will not love him!
(The floor heaves, the ceiling tightens).
My handcuffed mind slips sideways,
conjuring libraries:
Charlotte's Web, The First Book of Insects,
Darwin and the Beagle.
Survival hangs on such small changes.

The room subsides.
Only the spiders stay, as they must,
in their natural corners.
I watch the one who squats above me.
She spins no words for me
but she's making something:
a line to reel herself back up on.
I watch her drop—
that hairline plunge,
the light, retrievable body.

The Impossibility of Equating Opposites

For the poet, paradox and self-contradiction can be accepted conditions of life, as they are in the Walt Whitman lines quoted earlier. In Theodore Roethke's villanelle "The Waking," the poet equates a number of seeming opposites: waking and sleeping, thinking and feeling, falling away and permanence, shaking and steadiness. Consider the final stanza:

This shaking keeps me steady. I should know.
What falls away is always. And is near.
I wake to sleep, and take my waking slow.
I learn by going where I have to go.

Perhaps the greatest paradox in this poem is the fact that so antirational a stance should be presented within the rigid, patterned framework of the villanelle. (This old French verse form uses only two rhymes in its six stanzas and has a fixed pattern in which the first and third lines of the opening tercet recur alternately as the closing line of the following four tercets, with both lines repeated at the end of the final quatrain.)

The Impossibility of Adequate Translation

The question of adequate translation will serve as a bridge between this list of theoretical impossibilities and the few hardcore impossibilities for poetry that do exist. The nature of language is such that one cannot convey totally into another language the particular combination of a poem's words, word order, tonal qualities and other prosodic elements that makes the poem a unique construct, not to mention the cultural implications for a reader of the original. "The best translation," says Robert Bly, "resembles a Persian rug seen from the back—the pattern is apparent but not much more."[7] Additional problems for the translator arise when the structure of the two languages is widely disparate. Richmond Lattimore notes that Greek "welds words where English has to string them."[8]

A good verse translation must itself be an act of poetry. It offers us a poem in English, and we tend to judge the quality of the original, foreign poem by the quality of the English poem we read. There are verse translations that have entered into our language as superb English poems—the King James version of the Psalms, for example.

Such a happy correspondence between the original and the English version is rare. This came home forcibly to me when I first tried to read Boris Pasternak's poems. All contemporary Russian writers speak glowingly of Pasternak. Since I cannot read Russian, I turned to a book of translations and was dismayed—the poems seemed so flat and banal, so singsongy and rhymy. I looked at every book of Pasternak translations that I could find. Only when I came upon a transliteration-plus-translation of a single Pasternak poem by Babette Deutsch[9] did I finally discover Pasternak's wonderfully modulated percussive beat; the poem looked and sounded marvelous.

This leads me, as an aside, to the efforts of contemporary poets to solve some of the problems of translation. A genuinely new approach, like that in Burnshaw's *The Poem Itself*,[10] goes a long way toward showing a reader what is happening in the original poem. Burnshaw does not translate the original poem into an English poem; rather, his device is to place the original poem side by side with an extensive English prose commentary/translation of words and phrases, clarifying different shades of meaning where appropriate. What his book does for poetry in the Romance languages, *The Modern Hebrew Poem Itself*[11] does for Hebrew poetry, adding an English transliteration to the original poem and the prose commentary/translation. Such an approach helps the reader to absorb the flavor of the original and to enter the poem itself. But while a poem may be translated with varying degrees of success, no translator can hope to transpose the original poem into a perfect English counterpart.

A Logical Impossibility

Given the basic protoplasmic soup from which poems emerge and Keats' "negative capability," is there anything inherently impossible to poetry? The answer is yes. Poetry is an art form whose medium is words; therefore, it is impossible for there to be a poem without words.

When Sibelius called a musical piece a "tone poem," he was using figurative language: this orchestral composition, based on a literary subject and suggestive of poetic sentiments and images, is *like* a poem. When pop poet Rod McKuen tells us (in words) that a poem need not be written to be a poem, that feelings alone can be poems, he, too, is speaking figuratively. The same is true of a dance critic who says of a performance that it was "sheer poetry." They are exercising their prerogatives to expand the sense of a word, "poetry." For poets themselves, however, a minimal definition of poetry would have to be *poetry is an art form whose medium is words*.

What kinds of words? Are there words that are not "poetic"? How many words? In what order? Can there be a one-word poem? A one-line poem?

What kind of words does poetry use? This chapter began with a general discussion of the poet's words. The range is at least from skylarks and roses to excrement and fleas (as in John Donne's "The Flea" and Robert Burns' "To A Louse"). The range is from abstract language to the most concrete of nouns and verbs to an emphasis on other parts of speech, as in William Carlos Williams' poem

THE LOCUST TREE IN FLOWER

> *Among*
> *of*
> *green*
>
> *stiff*
> *old*
> *bright*
>
> *broken*
> *branch*
> *come*
>
> *white*
> *sweet*
> *May*
>
> *again*

Under the umbrella of its informative title, the disjunctive form of this poem—its isolated words—demonstrates its meaning. Just as spring brings the disparate parts of the wintered-over locust tree into renewed blossoming, so the poet brings selected single prepositions, adjectives, and nouns together as a living unit; syntax emerges with the interjection of the evocative verb "come." We can almost sense the sap rising upward from the word "again."

How many words constitute a poem? Can a poem consist of the single word "rose"? "Rose" could, perhaps, be used as a mantra for meditation, repeated to oneself. But a mantra is not a poem. If a single word is repeated on paper, as Aram Saroyan repeats the word "crickets" down the right-hand side of an entire page, does that constitute a poem? Here we enter the realm of "concrete poetry," where the medium—the visual appearance of the poem on the page—is the message. Concrete poems exist on the cusp of graphic art, just as prose poems exist on the cusp of prose.

Can there be poems of just one line? Although I have seen a number of one-liners cited in textbooks (including aphorisms), for me they lack sufficient resonance to function as poetry. If one could quantify poetry by determining how few words can make a poem, I believe the magic of poetry would only begin to appear with the couplet, as in Robert Frost's

THE SECRET SITS

We dance around in a ring and suppose,
But the Secret sits in the middle and knows.

and in Louise Bogan's epigrammatic

SOLITARY OBSERVATION BROUGHT BACK
FROM A SOJOURN IN HELL

At midnight tears
Run into your ears.

And then there is that shortest verse in the English language, by
"Anon.":

FLEAS

Adam
Had 'em.

At the other end of this countdown, a single poem may be an epic, a
long narrative; it may fill an entire book.

The Impossibility of Transmitting the Creative Process

It is in relationship to one another that words form poems. But
the minimal definition proposed earlier—that poetry is an art form
whose medium is words—is too broad—it does not differentiate between poetry and other forms of creative writing. Coleridge characterized prose as "words in their best order" and poetry as "the best
words in their best order." This begs the question. What does "best"
mean, and how is it arrived at?

We are now in the presence of a second impossibility, that of explaining the mystery of the creative process in poetry. Poets and critics have, nevertheless, tried to provide us with some clues.

- A. E. Housman: "If I were obliged not to define poetry, but to
  name the class of things to which it belongs, I should call it a
  secretion; whether a natural secretion like turpentine in the fir, or
  a morbid secretion, like the pearl in the oyster."[12]

- Carl Sandburg: "Poetry is the tracing of the trajectories of a finite sound to the infinite points of its echoes. . . . is a search for syllables to shoot at the barriers of the unknown and the unknowable. . . . is the achievement of the synthesis of hyacinths and biscuits."[13]

- Christopher Fry: "Poetry is the language in which man explores his own amazement."[14]

- And, in her book *Iconographs,* May Swenson: "Poetry is made with words of a language. And we say, 'But, of course.' It is just this 'matter of course' that poetry holds to the nostrils, sticks into the ears, puts on the tongue, flashes into the eyes of anyone who comes to meet it. It is done with words; with their combination—sometimes with their unstringing. If so, it is in order to make the mind re-member (by dismemberment) the elements, the smallest particles, ventricles, radicals, down to, or into, the Grain—the buried grain of language on which depends the transfer and expansion of consciousness—of Sense. And no grain, of sense, without sensation. To *sense* becomes then to *make sense.*"[15]

From these efforts to provide a definition, we can extract a few of poetry's special qualities: its grounding in the physical senses and in experience, its echoing sounds, its leaps of imagination, its capacity for amazement, its immersion in the elemental stuff of words.

Three lines from Yeats may serve to demonstrate how this combination of elements invests the best poems with a kind of aura and enables them to vault the barriers of the impossible.

In the Yeats stanza previously cited, the image of old rags sets up reverberations with other Yeats images of old age, such as the one in the second stanza of "Sailing to Byzantium":

> *An aged man is but a paltry thing,*
> *A tattered coat upon a stick, unless*
> *Soul clap its hands and sing . . .*

There is an astonishing leap in this poem, from the image of an old man as a scarecrow to the sudden vision of Soul clapping its hands and singing. This is not a mere fantastical image—it is inspired metaphor, an essential truth for the poet. The unstated analogy works like this: the human soul is a reality, like an inner man dwelling within the body. The outer man may be falling apart, but the inner man can continue to perform acts of ecstasy.

How does a leap such as this occur, from scarecrow to handclapping soul? While I cannot know how Yeats actually got there, through what series of associations, a close reading of the lines suggests one possible route—through the image, via the words and their sounds. First, the image: old man as scarecrow with arms stuck stiffly out, unable to close or to embrace. The only thing left untouched by the aging, weathering process is the inner man, the soul. And the soul, being incorporeal, has the option to be limber and young, relieved to bring those stiff arms together, bend the elbows, and clap hands as it sings praises.

Second, the words and sounds of the first line—"An aged man is but a paltry thing"—keep reverberating. The "a" of "man" is echoed in "tattered," "clap," and "hands"; the "t" of "but" reiterated in "paltry," "tattered," "coat," "stick." With the appearance of "stick," a shift of sound occurs; the "s" words begin: "unless," "soul," "hands," "sing." The unusual adjective "paltry" asks for some kind of resolution in sound as well as in meaning. The "awl" sound carries over into "soul," the "p" finds its echo in "clap"—and, of course, "sing" rhymes with "thing."

In three short lines, the magical properties that inhere in a poem's words become apparent. The words move, as it were, by handholds from sound to sound until the image makes its great leap, arcing like an electric spark across space.

To trace the visible signs of the creative process is not to explain how it leaps inside the creator. One can practise the many intricate aspects of the craft of poetry, write "in the voice of" admired poets, point to the art in great poems, do exercises to strengthen the imagination, and even attempt to coax intuition out of hiding. Still, the mystery of the creative process remains. It is, so far, unknowable and, therefore, unteachable. Transmitting the creative process is one of the few genuine impossibilities in an art which makes so many things possible.

Notes

1. *The Yale Gertrude Stein,* Yale University Press, New Haven, 1980, p. xvii.

2. *Letters of John Keats,* Oxford University Press, London, 1952, p. 69. From a letter to George and Thomas Keats dated December 22, 1817.

3. William Empson, *Seven Types of Ambiguity*, New Directions, New York, 1966, p. 1.

4. *Selected Poems and Two Plays of William Butler Yeats*, M. L. Rosenthal (ed.), Collier Books, Macmillan, New York, 1966, p. 185.

5. Ibid., p. 96.

6. *The Prose Poem*, Michael Benedikt (ed.), Laurel Editions, Dell, New York, 1976, pp. 511–14.

7. Robert Bly, *Eight Stages of Translation*, Rowan Tree Press, Boston, 1983, p. 48.

8. Richmond Lattimore, "Practical Notes on Translating Greek Poetry," in Reuben A. Brower (ed.), *On Translation*, Oxford University Press, New York, 1966, p. 50.

9. In Josephine Miles, *The Ways of the Poem*, Prentice-Hall, Englewood Cliffs, N.J., 1961, pp. 22–25.

10. Stanley Burnshaw (ed.), *The Poem Itself*, World Publishing Co., Cleveland, 1960.

11. Stanley Burnshaw, T. Carmi, and Ezra Spicehandler (eds.), *The Modern Hebrew Poem Itself*, Holt, Rinehart and Winston, New York, 1965.

12. A. E. Housman, "The Name and Nature of Poetry," in Brewster Ghiselin (ed.), *The Creative Process*, Mentor Book, 1964, p. 91.

13. *Complete Poems of Carl Sandburg*, Harcourt, Brace, New York, 1950, p. 317. From "Tentative (First Model) Definitions of Poetry."

14. Robert Skelton, *Poetry*, English Universities Press, London, 1963, p. 5.

15. May Swenson, *Iconographs*, Scribner's, New York, 1970, p. 87.

CHAPTER SEVENTEEN • EVERETT HAFNER

LARGO PRESTISSIMO ASSAI: THE OUTER EDGES OF MUSIC

The end of our foundation is the knowledge of causes and secret motions of things, and the enlarging of human empire to the effecting of all things possible.

Francis Bacon, *New Atlantis* (1624)

Throughout most of its long history, Western music has moved its frontiers steadily forward while launching a variety of experimental probes. The twentieth century, with its rapid succession of social and technological upheavals, has witnessed an extraordinary acceleration of new ideas in the arts, and the parade of movements in music has been especially swift and boisterous. The passing stream of impressionism, atonality, neotonality, expressionism, neoclassicism, serialism, polytonality, ultrarationality, aleatorism, neovirtuosity, postserialism, third stream, minimalism, mixed media, and a rising staccato of movements in pop—all of this bespeaks a century of extreme eclecticism in which each composer, if not each composition, attempts to set forth a new style. Like every age, this century has yielded its share of masterpieces along with an abundance of music easily forgotten. It is the enormous range of styles and aesthetic views that sets our century apart. Like the art of every age, twentieth-century music embodies the endless struggle between loyalty to tradition and rebellion against it. But again there is a difference: the hostilities have grown to new proportions, with big guns in the hands of composers, performers, critics, and the public. Finally, in the twentieth century we witness the continuing evolution of the technology that provides us with new ways of making and hearing music. But what was once a relatively slow and easily assimilable development of instruments has become an explosion of technique, growing so rapidly that we have not yet had the time to explore it to the full, much less to master it and put it to good use. Of the three themes so far discernible in the story of our time, it may well be the technical revolution that will have the greatest effect on the future of music. Under that assumption, despite the usual hazards of speculation, we should now begin to explore its more obvious implications.

We can approach the problem in a fruitful way by dealing with the notions of possibility and impossibility in the production and perception of musical sound. Three questions immediately suggest themselves, all concerned with limits of possibility and all having to do with rates at which we handle the flow of sound in music. The first, put simply, asks how fast we can play. (There is, of course, no lower limit; one might hold a single organ tone for a lifetime.) Let's begin with the instrument we all possess: the human voice raised in song. How can we give a measure of the rate at which fundamental elements of song are sent forth and received? The problem can be broken down into a few steps.

By manipulation of the vocal tract we are capable of producing about a hundred different phonetic elements, of which five or so make up the average word. Now there are ten billion ways of choosing five things in sequence out of a hundred; thus we have a rough estimate of the largest possible human vocabulary. Next, in singing the word we choose one out of a few dozen possible pitches, as well as one of several distinguishable levels of loudness. The vocabulary of song has thus risen to about a trillion.

At this point we take advantage of an idea given us by the mathematical treatment of communication, known as information theory, developed by Claude Shannon and his collaborators at the Bell Telephone Laboratories. The idea, in its simplest form, is to define the information content of an event as the length of the binary number of possibilities from which the event was chosen. Thus, when we choose one event out of a possible fifty-two, as when we draw a playing card from the deck, we are selecting a binary number between 00000 and 11011; the event contains five bits (binary digits) of information. In the case of the largest possible vocabulary of song, with its trillion or so choices, the binary numbers are about forty digits long; the event contains forty bits of information. Finally, to arrive at a limiting *rate* of production, we merely multiply the information measure of an event by the number of events per second of time. If our singing capacity is limited to, say, five words per second, we have a measure of our first musical impossibility: song cannot be produced at rates greater than about two hundred bits per second.

We can come to this answer by an entirely different route, using our experience with speech synthesis. We now have instruments that generate vocal sound electronically, using the "vocoder" principle, which was also developed at Bell Labs. The vocoder analyzes a voice signal at its input with a set of filters, information from which is sent to an identical set of filters at the output. An electronic oscillator is fed to the output filters, which manipulate the signal to produce a replica of the original voice at a pitch determined by the oscillator. The purpose of the research was to discover, by experiment, the rate at which information had to be sent from one end of the system to the other in order to reproduce fast speech intelligibly. The results have a direct bearing on the question we are raising here. It was found that five filters, each delivering four bits of information, are just sufficient to do the job. Thus, when phonetic events are passing through the system at a speed of ten per second, the measure of information flow agrees with our rough estimate. We must, of course, add a few more bits of information to reproduce the pitch changes in song.

Similar calculations and experiments divulge limits of performance on our musical artifacts—the keyboards, winds, strings, and drums of long tradition. We find, without surprise, that the solo performer easily passes beyond the vocalizing limit, but not by far. The pianoforte, with its rich dynamic and polyphonic capabilities, is at the head of the list, but its limit remains in the region of a few hundred bits per second. Obviously we take a large step when we progress to the musical ensemble. A large orchestra with chorus, all performing at full tilt, can send us acoustic information at the rate of a few thousand bits per second; we can accept this as the limit achievable by human muscular effort—what might be called the "calisthenic" limit.

Before proceeding, it is important to remind ourselves that it is not the sole aim of performers to play as fast as possible. Our intent in raising this question is to get more generally at the limits placed by our bodies and our instruments on the possible *variety* of musical experience; we must consider not only tempo, but also such essential matters as dynamic level, pitch nuance, ornamentation, glissando, portamento, sostenuto, articulation, and above all, the timbre of musical sound. Increased capability in any of these respects expands the vocabulary of music and hence the richness of information that it sends to us. Most of the subtlety of music is difficult to quantify and therefore has no easy place in the calculations we have been reviewing. Thus, for example, the variety of sound in the human voice is surely far greater than our simple model would suggest. The piano, on the other hand, presents relatively little opportunity for varying the quality of sound. Its pitches are strictly predetermined, it has very little timbral range, and the percussive attack and slow decay of its tones are fixed characteristics of the instrument. It therefore fits well into our stripped-down model of information flow.

Our next question deals with the capacity of the human auditory system for perceiving sound. What is the highest possible bit rate at which we can process music? Here we can begin by looking at the structure that produces raw data: the cochlea of the inner ear. It contains thirty thousand hairlike nerve endings coiled in liquid and set into vibration by motion of the eardrum. Each nerve responds by sending electric impulses to the brain, where the entire set of data can be interpreted on the basis of times at which impulses arrive and patterns of distribution across the cochlea. The result is our sensation of sound in its three basic characteristics: pitch, timbre, and loudness. The rate at which the brain swallows data in this process is enormous and difficult to estimate with precision, but it may well lie in the neighborhood of a hundred thousand bits per second. Fortunately, as before, there is a direct experimental approach to the question. We appeal to recent developments in digital storage and reproduction of music. This technique works by sampling patterns of sound at very short time intervals and storing the magnitude of each sample as a binary number. We find that good fidelity of reproduction requires sampling rates of at least forty thousand per second and precisions of at least ten bits per sample. Thus the process involves information flow at the rate of a few hundred thousand bits per second, not significantly different from crude estimates of what our auditory system can handle. And so we have our second musical impossibility: music at higher rates than this would be imperceptible.

Suddenly we seem to have uncovered a paradox. There is a huge gap—a factor of several hundred—between the calisthenic limit set by our mechanical instruments and the limit at which perception stops. How, then, can it be that the recording process requires its very high rate when it only has to deal with the sounds of an orchestra? The answer lies in a property of the ear not yet mentioned: its sensitivity to high frequencies. Human hearing covers the range from twenty to twenty thousand vibrations per second, ten octaves of musical sound. The fundamental frequencies of instrumental tones, represented by notes on the musical staff, end at about five thousand, but the richness of their sounds comes from harmonics that rise to the limit of hearing. Imagine now a single tone vibrating twenty thousand times per second. The recording process needs at least two samples for each vibration (one for its peak and one for its valley) and ten bits to measure its amplitude, leading us once again to a bit rate of a few hundred thousand per second. But the information measure of a pure sustained tone is actually quite small; we need only ten bits or so to set its frequency and ten more for its amplitude. What we learn from this is that high fidelity recording, like the brain, has a far greater capacity for processing sound than is necessary for the richest possible orchestral music. The great untapped resource stands open before us, a vast continent of sound waiting to be explored.

We come to the third question, following naturally from what has gone before. Somewhere between the upper limit of performance and the limit of perception is the point beyond which we cannot *comprehend* music. Where? It is a tantalizing question; at the moment, we have neither a theoretical model nor a body of experience to answer it. Some tentative clues, perhaps, are to be found in our response to the twelve-tone technique of composition devised by Arnold Schoenberg and pursued by many followers during the middle decades of this century. It is a deeply intellectual music that makes a sharp iconoclastic break with the past, and in particular with the baroque, classical, and romantic styles that are still most comfortable to Western ears. Thus it studiously avoids all the melodic and harmonic conventions that have accumulated over the ages. Instead, the composer invents a "row" of twelve different tones using the notes of the chromatic scale without repetition. His composition states the row and a sequence of variations using inversion, retrogression, transposition, and counterpoint. Most of this music is difficult to memorize and perform, and intensely puzzling to audiences even after many hearings. (It has nevertheless contributed briefly to at least one masterpiece—the powerful opera *Wozzeck*, where Alban Berg's lyric and dramatic gifts brought the twelve-tone method into human focus.) The movement has lost its momentum and is likely to evaporate.

What may have been missing from this music is the happy combination of spontaneity and inevitability that we appreciate in earlier works. Bach wrote a cantata every week the way you or I would write a letter; Mozart wrote scores while at billiards; and although Beethoven labored over each note, we hear it with the feeling that it is the only note possible. Not so with twelve-tone music. There are almost five hundred million possible tone rows, and most of them are fair game. The composer, sitting with his charts and calculations, tends to produce a work in which the agony of labor is audible and yet *no* note seems irreplaceable. Thus the structure of the row easily escapes us. Music that is memorable and comprehensible has a strong element of redundancy; we develop an appreciation of its style to the point where the ear could replace a note if it were taken away. By following up this idea in theory and experiment, we may be able to take one of the many necessary steps toward dividing the possible from the impossible in comprehension of music.

The electronic machines of our time have abruptly erased the calisthenic performance limits of old. They have also expanded the vocabulary of sonic elements and the rate at which they can be presented to our ears. We can form every timbre, sound any pitch, build any chord, create bizarre scales, manipulate sounds of nature, transform the human voice, run the gamut of dynamic levels, stretch and shrink the attacks and decays of articulated tones, and deliver our acoustic events at all tempi from the slowest *largo* to the fastest perceptible *prestissimo assai*. Music that would have been deemed impossible from antiquity to the near past is suddenly accessible to every composer who takes the pains to master new technique. The theme of shifting possibility has run through all the centuries of Western philosophy; as Pliny the Elder wondered long ago, how many things are looked upon as quite impossible until they have been actually effected? The composer of today and tomorrow need no longer be concerned with music that is exclusively handmade, nor need he depend on secondhand performances in the concert hall. Working at his own pace in the studio, the composer constructs his sounds, assembles them into musical structures, stores the result on tape or computer disk, and *hears* his piece at every stage of its construction. Disappearing are the days when he worked out orchestral parts at the piano, wrote the score on conventional staves, and finally sought out an ensemble to produce the actual sound of the piece. He is his own performer, reviving a stance long neglected since Paganini, Liszt, Chopin, and Rachmaninoff left the recital halls.

Thus, with instruments of our own time, we are beginning to explore regions of sound hitherto inaccessible, someday to understand where the frontiers of comprehensible music actually lie. It is to be a qualitatively new era in the history, for until now our fingers have been in the way of our imaginations. There is a profound remark by Alfred Whitehead that describes our condition: "Our minds are finite, and yet even in these circumstances of finitude we are surrounded by possibilities that are infinite, and the purpose of human life is to grasp as much as we can out of that infinitude." Whitehead was speaking in general terms about the human intellect, but the special case of contemporary music is strikingly germane.

The creeping tide of human evolution is as slow as the flood of new technology is swift. Our limits of sonic perception may eventually move forward, but the time for that is surely very far away. Let us instead, as a matter of interest, look backward in time, wondering how our remarkable sense of hearing may have evolved. And let us focus on one especially acute aspect of human hearing: the ability to distinguish between two closely spaced pitches. Many tests reveal that we can detect changes of one-tenth of a semitone, which is a precision of about one-half of one percent. This ability has no strong connection with musical talent or training; it is a gift given to all of us at birth. We are naturally inclined to ask how such an extraordinary capability could have evolved. Why has nature put together the particular collection of membrane, bone, liquid, and neuron we find in our ears? Keen hearing is crucial for survival. But how to account for an acuity of such high degree that the human ear can distinguish pitches less than a tenth of a semitone apart? Such skill can only exercise itself in the presence of sound that is precisely organized and nicely sustained. Those are not properties easily found in the cries and calls of most species; intricate bird song provides the closest example. It was most probably the human voice itself that produced the appropriate stimulus for pitch discrimination, and hence the condition for success in natural selection. Going slightly further, we might suppose that human song and human ear evolved in partnership, not merely for communication of need and desire, but for the joy of the measured sound itself—that is, for the joy of music. We are still only separated by a stone's throw in time from those beginnings; music in itself, abstract and stretched toward its limits, is still the kindest elixir for prolongation of our lives and the life of our species. Its disappearance, perhaps even its diminution, would be dangerous. Henry Seidel Canby said of poetry, and it can be said with greater force of music, that it "remembers things impossible for us, impossible but intelligible, and which will become unintelligible at our peril."

WHAT CAN BE KNOWN?

S cience has often demonstrated that things widely held to be impossible can in fact be done; philosophy, in contrast, has often sought to demonstrate that things widely regarded as perfectly feasible are in fact impossible. From the days when the pre-Socratic Greeks—by arguments subtle enough to remain intriguing even today—tried to show that motion, or indeed change of any sort, is impossible, or alternatively that change is so all-pervasive that it is impossible to step into the same river twice, such attempts have been a recurrent feature of Western philosophy. This chapter looks at some examples, drawn mainly from more recent philosophy, of arguments that purport to establish certain intellectual impossibilities, to prove to us that we cannot even in principle know some of the things we have always supposed we knew. The first section outlines these skeptical arguments; the second section considers some counterarguments; the third and final section tries to show that, while the counterarguments may be in the end the more effective, we have still something important to learn from the skeptics about the extent and the nature of human knowledge.

The Skeptic's Case

All of us, every day, by implication at least, make a great many claims to knowledge about ourselves and our world. And we may well pride ourselves on not making such claims recklessly or at random; we make them only where we have grounds for doing so. The trouble is that what we are accustomed to call "grounds," or even "good grounds," for claiming to know that S (where S is some statement) often prove on examination to be *logically inadequate* (i.e., it is logically quite possible that the grounds in question should be realized and S still be false). There is thus a kind of logical gap between our knowledge-claims and the grounds on which we make them, and it is in this gap that philosophical skepticism characteristically takes root.

Most of us, for example, would claim to know a good deal about the familiar objects around us, about the properties of iron and mercury, of water and electricity, about the life cycles of common plants and the habits of domestic animals. And in countless circumstances we act without hesitation on the assumption that we have such knowledge. But what grounds do we have for such knowledge-claims? The obvious answer is that we have long familiarity with the objects in question, that we have encountered or heard or read of many examples thereof; and, for the most part, we are happy to accept such familiarity as sufficient grounds for generalizing about their properties. And yet, as a matter of elementary logic, from the premise that all observed, or noted, members of a class or species X have the feature Y, we cannot validly infer that all members of X, without qualification, have Y. It is always logically possible that all the members we have taken account of belong to a subclass of X, which is indeed characterized by Y, but that there are other subclasses, hitherto unnoted, which are not.

Here we have the time-honored "problem of induction": if our only data concern specific members of an unrestricted class, how can we establish the truth of generalizations about all its members? And, despite a lot of time and ingenuity expended on the problem, the answer seems to remain obstinately that we cannot, that there is no logically valid way of doing it. The logical gap between premises and conclusion is theoretically impassable. This is a startling conclusion, especially if—as has been widely supposed—the purpose of natural science is precisely to arrive at a knowledge of general laws about the workings of nature on the basis of observations of particular elements thereof. Manifestly, to find that a given law holds in one instance, or even in a thousand instances, (and to find no instances of its failure despite extensive search) is not sufficient to establish that it holds universally. Thus, the skeptic's argument goes, there is an elementary logical fallacy at the heart of our purported scientific methods. And it would seem we can avoid this fallacy only if, following the example of Sir Karl Popper, we abandon our claims to knowledge, properly so called, of any general "laws of nature," even those most widely accepted and well corroborated, and regard all attempted formulations as nothing more than conjectures, permanently open to the possibility of refutation.

Once we start thinking along these lines, skepticism is liable to spread to other knowledge-claims as well, with even more disquieting results. What makes all, or almost all, such claims vulnerable is, in essence, the smallness of the base on which we are constrained to rest them. We may talk grandly of the order and pattern of nature, of the whole scheme of things—but does it not seem presumptuous, even pathetic, to do so, when we recall how little of it we have experienced, and for how short a span of time? The magnitude of the claims seem irrevocably at odds with the finitude of the claimants. And, the skeptical argument goes on, we are not even justified in supposing that we have as our base what *we* (humanity at large) have discovered in the way of objective, mind-independent facts about how things actually are, even in our own corner of the universe. Strictly, *I* have to start from the base of my own individual experience (including, of course, what I ordinarily take to be experience of the speech and writings of others). And, strictly, I can only say how things appear to me, not how they actually are. Again, an impassable logical gap seems to open up before us—from no statement of the form "It appears to me that S" can we validly infer S; for it is always possible that things are in actuality different from the way they appear to me. "Each in his narrow cell forever laid" wrote Gray of the village dead; and we seem now to be obliged to say something similar of the living—each is forever shut away from the world as it is in itself, in the narrow cell of his or her own experience. I can say, with Descartes, "I think . . . " and go on to say what I think, but never, with an altogether clear intellectual conscience, can I abandon this autobiographical preface.

Even disciplines like pure mathematics or logic are vulnerable to the skeptic's critique. They have often been presented as paradigms of objectivity and certainty—and we can, indeed, appreciate the reasons for this. Euclid's geometry and Aristotle's logic, for example, survived for centuries, intact in all essentials, apparently commending themselves simply by their inherent rightness to anyone capable of understanding them, regardless of any differences of individual constitution or cultural background. So, understandably enough, they came to be treated as ideals to be followed so far as possible in other fields of research; the dream of a universal mathematics has recurred throughout the history of Western thought. Clearly, as nonempirical or nonexperimental studies, they are exempt from some possibilities of error or uncertainty; our problem of induction cannot trouble us here insofar as no observation can possibly refute a thesis in pure mathematics or logic. But they are by no means exempt from all such possibilities. Thus, however rigorous the rules of, say, a calculus, they do not apply themselves; they do not *compel* me, in any literal sense, to make certain moves. *I* have to apply them, to decide what they require of me in this or that particular case, whether this does or does not follow from that. I may, of course, very often feel that there is only one possible way of doing it and hence no need or room for decision; but couldn't such a feeling simply be a result of my lack of imagination or my orthodox training or some arbitrary, unrecognized assumption on my part that some genius will eventually expose? And in mathematics and logic, as in natural science, recent history can be invoked to reinforce the theoretical argument. Things long accepted as settled and unassailable have been shown to be less than totally rigorous or complete, and in need of amendment. Even here, it would seem, "This must be so" is reduced to "*I* cannot think otherwise." Thus conscience makes relativists of us all.

We might well wish for a discipline so strict as to leave no room for any personal or subjective element, a discipline that would, as it were, make the decisions for us and use our services merely to record them. But we seem always, in Sartre's famous phrase, condemned to be free; and nothing can take the responsibility away from us. Even if we postulate divine revelations of truth, don't we still have to decide which of our experiences are genuinely revelatory and which mere self-delusion, or which professed prophets are indeed what they claim to be? In essence, then, we have a variety of experiences; for example, we see the arrangement of colors and shapes in the room or landscape around us, and, in less literal senses, we see that certain principles have to be true, or, in a religious context, we see the light. And on the basis of such experiences, we may build up a picture of a solid, mind-independent world about us, of an order to which it must conform, of a deity who controls it. Doubtless such projections from, or beyond, our experiences are understandable, and any recognizably human life involves making them. What is impossible, according to the skeptic, is to show that any of our projections are logically required or justified by the initial experiences.

We may note briefly two further examples. First, consider Descartes' famous speculations, in his first *Meditation*, as to whether all the experiences of his life might consist merely of dreams—determined by nothing, and representing nothing, independent of his own mind. The essential point was that this possibility remained no matter what qualities these experiences exhibited, however vivid and coherent they might be, and however free they might be, in most instances, from his own control. Or even if they were not generated by his own mind in the way dream-images are, there were other possible explanations for their origin (e.g., that they were fed into his mind by God or by a "malignant demon") in addition to the explanation he had hitherto accepted, namely, that they were, for the most part, determined by a mind-independent material world whose features they represented with at least a substantial measure of accuracy. And he found it was impossible to tell, however meticulously he examined the content of his experiences, which of these explanatory hypotheses was the right one.

Second, there is the long-standing "problem of other minds." Even if it is granted that my experiences, or some of them, *are* experiences of a mind-independent physical world, and that I observe in this world bodies closely similar in structure and function to my own, isn't there a special difficulty in establishing that there are also other minds and that these have experiences in any way similar to mine? I may notice that when these other bodies are injured they wince and emit cries, and on the basis of my own experience in similar circumstances, I may assume that the wincing and crying is accompanied by a sensation of pain. But, clearly, in doing so I am relying on an inductive argument, which is of course open to our objections to induction in general. Further, this has to be a particularly weak inductive argument, since in only one case (i.e., my own) out of many millions do I have actual evidence that the physical injury and the physical reaction are accompanied by a distinctive sensation. In no other case can I possibly check that the accompanying experience resembles mine or, indeed, that there is any experience at all. A world of beings similar in physical appearance and behavior but radically different in experience, or in which all but one are automata and wholly insentient, is certainly a possibility. Psychologically, it may be very difficult for us to take such a possibility seriously; but, again, the point to be made is the logical one, that our claims to knowledge of other minds do not, and cannot, have any logically sufficient basis in our experience.

So—granted that knowledge that S, properly so called, entails having logically sufficient grounds for thinking that S—it would appear that it is strictly impossible to know that my neighbor has any specific thoughts or feelings or indeed any thoughts or feelings at all; or that he has any physical existence in a world independent of my experience; or that there is such a world; or, if there is, that it is subject to any fixed and permanent order or design.

Starting from the obvious and apparently innocuous point that I can seek knowledge of the world only by observing it and thinking about it, the skeptic undertakes to show, by arguments at least prima facie effective, that I can best arrive, by such means, at knowledge of how *I* see the world or of what *I* think about it. The objective, impersonal knowledge that I set out to achieve is impossible. Common sense rebels and insists that it is impossible that such knowledge is impossible, that somewhere in the skeptic's case there must be a fallacy. Perhaps so, but where exactly does it lie?

In Defense of Common Sense

An obvious and often quite effective countermove to the skeptic's arguments is to point out to him that, for a professed skeptic, he is being surprisingly dogmatic. Once this countermove is made, his arguments are always liable to turn back on themselves and become self-destructive. Can we *prove* that the range of our knowledge is as limited as skepticism would have it, without being obliged to admit that we do not know that the premises of our proof are true or the steps of the argument valid? If not, our dramatic statements of purportedly inexorable principles "We cannot know . . . " degenerate into "I do not think we can know . . . " Thus, following Descartes, I may say that, despite what I now see and feel, I do not know that there is a table before me, and give as a reason that I have often had equally vivid and convincing experiences that turned out to be dreams. But is the statement "I have dreamt of tables" in any way more manifestly true or worthy of acceptance than the statement "Here is a table," so that we should take the one uncritically as a premise and treat the other as open to doubt? If not, then we cannot prove our skeptical conclusions ... and of course cannot prove that we cannot prove them ... and so on.

More constructively, we may turn our attention to the words the skeptic uses in presenting his characteristic theses. Much of twentieth-century philosophy, especially in the English-speaking world, has been characterized by the development of self-awareness about our role, not just as thinkers but as *speakers*—and about the obligations and constraints the use of a language imposes on us, especially when we use it to discuss philosophy. And, in important respects, this development has reversed the tendency toward the extremes of skepticism that we noted in the previous section. Whereas reflection on our role as thinkers reminds us of the extent to which each of us is on his or her own, shut up with an inescapably private vision of the world, reflection on our speech focuses attention on something essentially shared or public, our medium of communication. And when we begin to work out the conditions of acquiring and using such a medium, it seems that the insistence on the privacy of experience has to be modified; if we are to talk to each other meaningfully about anything, even about mental isolation, we must in some measure inhabit and experience the same world, and respond to it in the same way.

To start from a very obvious point, for any word properly so called (as opposed to a mere random sound or mark), it must be possible to distinguish between correct and incorrect uses thereof. But what determines what are the correct—and hence the incorrect—uses of any given word? According to Wittgenstein's famous dictum "the meaning of a word is its use in the language,"[2] such a determination depends simply on what is conventionally accepted, or done, by native speakers of the language in which the word occurs. And there is nothing else that determines what it is to use a word correctly (i.e., in accordance with its proper meaning); to master a language is to learn to conform to the accepted usages of that language. The philosopher, then, like any other language-user must, to avoid being misleading or unintelligible, beware of misusing words or taking liberties with their accepted usage.

Suppose, then, we say that we do not know the sun will rise tomorrow, that this is, in Popper's terms, a well-corroborated conjecture rather than a piece of knowledge. Whatever the value of the arguments that lead us to this conclusion, must we not admit that in so saying we are misusing the word "know"—as this is precisely the kind of example from which we learn, and teach, the correct (convention-sanctioned) use of "know" and its derivatives, a paradigm example of what is ordinarily meant by "knowledge"? If we complain that we are dissatisfied with the grounds on which things are said to be known, it can be answered: But nonetheless, this is how the word "know," which is public property, is actually used; this is the sort of situation in which we are, by convention, entitled to say "I know . . ." If you want to apply criteria more stringent than the accepted ones for knowledge, then you ought, in the interests of clarity, to introduce some new word. You may, of course, quite properly point out, *in a particular case,* that someone is misusing a word—that the accepted criteria for its use are not met. What you may not say is that a word is *ordinarily or systematically* misused by a whole community of language-users—simply because whatever they do is, ipso facto, correct usage. Hence to say, on whatever grounds, that contrary to what is generally believed or stated, there is no such thing as, for example, scientific or historical knowledge, has to be wrong; to say so is simply to misuse the word "knowledge" or at least to propose some new and misleading use thereof.

Or, again, are there not well-understood, even if rarely explicated, uses for terms like "illusion" and "dream," and for "real" and "veridical," and criteria for distinguishing them, which we master early in life? Of course, as with most other words, the criteria for their application are not ideally precise or foolproof, and we may on occasion be uncertain or mistaken. But if, for example, we are looking at the books and papers on the table before us, under standard conditions of light and eyesight, and someone says "But perhaps even this is an illusion," are we not entitled to reply, quite literally, "Well if this is, or even could be, illusion rather than reality, then we simply do not know what these terms mean"? For by the rules of ordinary usage, how we see things under these conditions *is* how they really are; and what do we achieve, except confusion, by keeping the words and rejecting the rules? Or consider Descartes' claim that "there exist no certain marks by which the state of waking can ever be distinguished from sleep."[2] But, if so, then how do we learn or teach the uses of the appropriate terms? How does a child learn when it is correct to say "I dreamt I saw . . ." and when "I really did see . . . ," unless we can point out to the child the sort of situation in which the one is appropriate and the *different* sort in which the other is? Unless we have some way of teaching and learning how to distinguish dreaming from waking, we cannot meaningfully ask, Are we dreaming or awake? If we can even wonder which state we are in, then ipso facto we have some means of telling the difference. Either the problem cannot be raised at all or it can in principle be solved.

Thus the skeptic appears to be in permanent danger of being outflanked, of advancing so far or so rashly that his lines of communication with his linguistic base are liable to be cut. To set up his problems, to get us worried, for example, over whether we really see what we think we see before us or whether it might all be an illusion or a dream, he has perforce to draw on our common conceptual and linguistic store for the appropriate concepts and the terminology in which they are embodied. But then, in order to give his characteristic demonstration that the problems can never be solved, he has at some point to discard, in effect, the commonly accepted rules for using such equipment and introduce new ones. Under the old rules the problems can be raised and they can in principle be solved; under the new ones they cannot be solved, but then neither can they meaningfully be raised. As Sir Peter Strawson once put it, the skeptic "pretends to accept a conceptual scheme, but at the same time quietly rejects one of the conditions of its employment. Thus his doubts are unreal, not simply because they are logically irresoluble doubts, but because they amount to the rejection of the whole conceptual scheme within which alone such doubts make sense."[3]

Further, if Wittgenstein's famous critique of the idea of a "private language"[4] is successful, some of our more extreme manifestations of skepticism can be countered by an appeal, not to the conventions governing the appropriate elements in our language, but to the mere fact that we have any language at all. Briefly, a private language is not merely some kind of code (say, for writing a secret diary) that is contingently private, in that its inventor *could* teach it to others, although as it happens he doesn't want to. Rather, it must be essentially or necessarily private, that is, theoretically unteachable to anyone other than its inventor. Suppose, for example, I decide to invent names for various sensations that I have from time to time. I focus on a given sensation and elect to call it S_1, then on another and call that S_2, and so forth. I then use my newly coined vocabulary to record such things as "I had S_1 again today," "S_2 was very troublesome this morning," ... Given that the sensations are private—insofar as I cannot produce them to show them to or share them with anyone else—and that the function of S_1, S_2, S_n is to name them, then clearly I cannot teach you what they mean, in the way that I might teach a child, say, the meaning of flower names. There is no conceivable situation in which I might say "Look, there's an S_1," as I might say, "Look, there's a primrose." Thus, if the function of S_1 is to name something that I alone can experience, I alone can know what "I had S_1 again this morning" means and, a fortiori, whether it is true or not.

Still, it may be said, even if such a vocabulary has a very limited use, being restricted of necessity to a single user, why should I not develop it as a means of keeping private records of my experience, if I so desire? Wittgenstein's answer derives from his analysis of what is entailed in obeying rules of any kind. The use of a language is taken as a particular example of a rule-governed activity, and the critique of private language is a particular application of the critique of private rules. Suppose I make for myself a rule that is private in this strict sense, such that it is theoretically impossible for anyone else to tell whether I am obeying it or not. What does obedience amount to here? Presumably, it is simply doing whatever it *seems to me,* or whatever *I think,* the rules require in each novel situation. But according to Wittgenstein, "to *think* one is obeying a rule is not to obey a rule. Hence it is not possible to obey a rule 'privately': otherwise thinking one was obeying a rule would be the same thing as obeying it."[5] Unless there is the possibility of an independent check, of circumstances in which I should be constrained to say "I thought I was applying the rule correctly but I was wrong," there is simply no rule properly so called. A rule as such requires discipline, placing oneself under authority; and a purported "rule" that can never, in principle, stop me from doing what I think fit is simply not the genuine article.

It may be objected that, ordinarily at least, what a given rule requires of us is so transparent as to leave no need or room for any process of interpretation. But, according to Wittgenstein, this is because we have been trained, through a long, usually unsystematic, process of observing the practice of others and experimenting for ourselves, to a point where doubts or alternative interpretations simply do not occur to us. Any rule, however formulated, leaves open the logical possibility of different interpretations; as we noted in the previous section, a rule does not and cannot anticipate every particular situation to which it applies and give foolproof specifications as to what is to be done in that situation. Even if such things rarely happen outside teachers' nightmares, it is always conceivable that pupils, however willing they may be to follow a rule we have given them (say, for constructing an arithmetical series) and however convinced they may be that they *are* following it, may still keep applying it in ways at variance with our own—and each time be as confident that the rule requires X as we are that it requires Y. And, in this situation, what could we do for them? Apart from the statement of the rule itself, we could only offer them examples of how *we* apply it; and it is, of course, possible to stray from the common path in trying to follow an example, just as it is in trying to follow a general rule. All we can do is hope that the cumulative effect of our examples will, in time, cure them of their eccentricity and persuade them to see things our way; and no doubt this is what usually happens. (General education would be impossible if it did not.) We may compare the way in which, for most of us, long familiarity with naturalistic drawing and perspective makes it seem natural and inevitable to interpret a certain combination of lines on paper as, say, a representation of a house or a landscape—and there seems to be simply no other way of taking it. But then we show it to someone with a very different background and training, perhaps someone from a culture in which representational art is forbidden on religious grounds, and he or she can see nothing on the paper but a two-dimensional pattern of shapes. Are we not thereupon obliged to admit that there are different possible interpretations and that ours is determined, not just by the drawing itself, but by what we have become *accustomed* to make of such drawings?

We cannot, then, in any activity that professes to be disciplined or rule governed, dispense with the role of custom, of a common practice. "To obey a rule, to make a report, to give an order, to play a game of chess, are *customs* (uses, institutions)."[6] Since we have never, or very rarely, had to work outside such a framework of custom, etcetera, it is easy to overlook its importance, but without it there would be no standard or criterion, independent of our subjective impressions, to distinguish permissible from impermissible, right from wrong. And the enforced absence of such a standard is the crucial objection to the idea of a private language. Wittgenstein's point is not merely that, since all memory is fallible, when I think my present sensation is an S_1 in the sense I have given that term, I may be mistaken. Rather, it is that we have left no space, as it were, in which the concepts of error—and hence of rightness also—are free to operate. And without such space we can have no genuinely rule-governed activity and hence no genuine language.

If Wittgenstein's critique is successful—a point still debated among philosophers—the philosophical consequences are important. Skepticism, as we have seen, opens up the possibility that all our experiences, including those that we are wont to call experiences of the speech and writings of other rational beings, are private to ourselves and are not representations or revelations of any world outside. Thus, for example, Descartes in his *Meditations* feels constrained to take seriously—and try to disprove—the possibility that he is "alone in the world," that nothing exists except himself, the thinker, and the various contents of his consciousness. But if Wittgenstein is right, the mere existence of a language in which to say "Perhaps only I exist," or indeed anything else whatsoever, is sufficient to rule out such possibilities. For if all the contents of my experience were private and unshareable in the way that dream-images or hallucinations are, then my whole language would perforce be private in Wittgenstein's sense. All my words would have the function of indicating elements and aspects of this private world, and hence there is no way in which their use could be taught (even if there were a potential learner) and no way in which rules, properly so called, could be created for their use. Language requires a shared or shareable world in which rules can be developed and transmitted. It is tempting to say that it requires also the actual existence of a plurality of language-users—and thus, in effect, to supplement Descartes' famous "I think, therefore I am" with "I speak, therefore we are." But it would seem that, strictly, all that is required is the *possibility* of being taught to others, not the actuality (hence our proviso "shared *or* shareable"). If the last person left alive invented words for new, postholocaust phenomena, these words would not be elements of a private language in the relevant sense, since they would, in principle, be teachable, even though, as a matter of fact, there was no one left to learn them. But teachability or learnability *does* require a shareable world, that is, one that exists independently of any individual consciousness. Hence "Perhaps it is all a dream" is self-refuting; if it is meaningful (i.e., an exercise in the use of language as opposed to mere pointless sound or mark making), then it cannot be true.

Wittgenstein in fact goes on to devote a good deal of attention to the ways in which we actually use our shared or public world in developing a vocabulary for talking about out sensations, dreams, fantasies, and so forth. Manifestly, it *is* possible to teach a child the proper use of words like "pain," "joy," "dream," "want," "think," without being able to point and say "Look, there's a pain" (or whatever) as we say "Look, there's a penny." And it is easy enough to recall or envisage the sort of situation in which such words are learnt. A child scrapes his or her knee, or gets scalded with hot water, and cries; people talk to the child sympathetically about the pain, how it hurts, and so forth. Thus, children acquire a pain vocabulary, by learning that pains, hurts, and so forth are what they experience in certain kinds of situation. We should notice that Wittgenstein is not offering us behaviorism in the sense of identifying pain *with* physical injury or with our physical reactions thereto. Rather, he is identifying it *by means of* such physical conditions, so that pain is, in effect, by definition what is experienced (by anyone) under these conditions; that is, there is a logical and not merely an empirical link between pain, as such, and its physical conditions. Hence, a pain vocabulary is teachable; and hence also we can tell, in suitable circumstances, without having to rely on a notoriously weak induction from our own case, that someone else is in pain. If a man has been knocked down and injured in a street accident and is writhing and groaning on the ground, this is a paradigm example of the kind of situation in which pain is properly ascribed; and to question its ascription, on the grounds that we cannot introspect the feelings of the injured man, is merely a willful refusal to accept the rules of the language we purport to use. "Just try—in a real case—to doubt someone else's fear or pain," says Wittgenstein;[7] and his point is a logical rather than a psychological one.

We may still, perhaps, be bothered by the skeptic's questions: But couldn't he be just pretending to be in pain? Or feeling something quite different from what I should feel under similar circumstances? Or even making these sounds and movements without feeling anything at all? And, of course, in particular cases we might find it difficult or impossible to answer such questions—for example, if we have not been able to observe the physical situation closely enough. But again, the Wittgensteinian argument goes, they cannot be unanswerable in principle, for to raise them at all we must have learnt by what criteria it is correct (convention sanctioned) to distinguish between being in pain and pretending to be in pain, feeling the same and feeling differently, feeling something and feeling nothing. We can, obviously, be fooled on occasion—say, by a skillful actor; but it simply does not make sense to suggest that, even possibly, we always are. As J. L. Austin once remarked, that you cannot fool all the people all the time is an analytic truth.[8]

The Lessons of Skepticism

So it would seem that the current of language draws us away from the wilder shores of skepticism and we cannot sail against it. The rules for the correct and coherent use of our language—or the very fact of our having any language at all—determine to an important degree the world views we can consistently hold. The effect on philosophy of Wittgenstein's work—and of the whole "ordinary language" approach in general—has thus been conservative; it inhibits the kind of free-ranging speculation that characterized much of philosophy in the past. That space and time are unreal, that matter does not exist, that we live in a world of appearances and can never know the reality of things—on a variety of grounds thinkers over many centuries have taken such ideas seriously. But if we can dispose of them simply by pointing out that there are plenty of well-understood circumstances in everyday life in which it is quite correct to say that a body really has certain spatial characteristics or that events really occupy a certain span of time, that there are lots of examples of pieces of matter all around us, that we are fully entitled, in many situations, to pronounce on how things are in reality as well as how they appear, and that to suggest otherwise is only to misuse language, then the speculation—and with it, some might say, much of the interest and fun of philosophy—has to come to an end.

Yet, though undoubtedly the ordinary language philosophers have a telling point to make, this insistence on conservatism, on a philosophy that of necessity "leaves everything as it is"[9] as Wittgenstein put it, may itself be in some measure misleading. Consider the favorite Wittgensteinian analogy between using a language and playing a game. We are invited to compare our linguistic equipment with, for example, a set of chessmen plus rules setting out the objectives and the permissible moves of chess. And doubtless the analogy is, in important respects, illuminating. But as the point of drawing an analogy—of saying, in effect, think of X as being like Y—is that Y is simpler and easier to understand than X and hence, in all likelihood, less subtle, we must expect the analogy to break down at some point, to distort or obscure some feature of X.

Thus, the rules of chess impose strict and well-defined limitations on the originality of the chess player (which is not, of course, to say that they stifle it altogether). As long as the chess player remains a chess player, rather than the inventor of some new game with chessmen, his or her imagination is perforce disciplined by the existing rules. But to what extent are we similarly restricted in speaking or writing a language? Do the rules of our language make it not merely difficult but literally impossible to give a coherent statement within it of ideas like those mentioned—so that originality along these lines carries us inevitably into the realm of the inexpressible?

It is perhaps well to remember that fighting against the current of language is by no means an experience peculiar to the more radical, or more eccentric, metaphysicians. Sir Karl Popper recalls, in this connection, how difficult it was to find a self-consistent and unparadoxical way of presenting differential and integral calculus and speculates that "had there been a Wittgenstein to use his weapons against the pioneers of the calculus, and had he succeeded in eliminating their nonsense . . . he would have strangled one of the most fascinating and philosophically important developments in the history of thought."[10] In the field of physics, there have been similar problems over putting into words the essentials of relativity and quantum theory. And we may even imagine some seventeenth-century precursor of Wittgenstein gently pointing out to Galileo that "the earth" was simply not a permissible subject for verbs of motion. One could speak of things moving over, or in relation to, the surface of the earth or landmarks thereon but not of the earth itself as moving. Yet, while doubtless some such rule was observed in contemporary speech and any breach of it was liable to create some initial confusion, it is evident that many people found it possible to adjust themselves to a revision of the rules governing their use of verbs of motion and accept sentences like "The earth moves" as significant. And had they been too respectful of tradition and linguistic etiquette to do so, a major scientific advance would have been effectively blocked. As Popper says (with some pardonable exaggeration), "there is not a classic of science, or of mathematics, or indeed a book worth reading that could not be shown, by a skillful application of the technique of language analysis, to contain many meaningless pseudo-propositions."[11]

While the use of language is undeniably a disciplined activity, and it may appear merely an innocuous variation of this to call it rule governed, it is well to be wary of such terms and their associations. It is doubtful if any of us could, on demand, formulate a set of rules delimiting all the permissible uses even of commonplace words like "white" or "round." And is there not something strange, and suspect, about the suggestion that the transmission of language consists in the teaching and learning of sets of rules that neither mentors nor pupils are ever able to specify—and which, apparently, they never need to specify? It is perhaps less misleading to think of preexisting linguistic usage as providing learners not so much with a set of rules, like those of a game, but rather with a set of *precedents*, which they are then in effect invited to adapt to novel situations (cf. the lawyer's distinction between statute law and case law). Thus, the permissible uses of a word are not permanently fixed by a set of rules; meaning, like freedom, broadens out from precedent to precedent. And when a philosopher or, indeed, a poet—Whitehead or Heidegger, say, or Hopkins or Dylan Thomas—takes liberties with common usage and combines words in unexpected ways in an effort to put across an unusual view of things, we cannot, simply on the basis of preset rules, say "Nonsense, you cannot meanfully use words like this; it is just not permitted." The only thing barred is stretching or bending the precedents furnished by common usage to such a degree that the author fails to get his or her ideas across to the intended readership. As long as authors succeed in this, however, we cannot fault them merely for unorthodoxy. The crucial test, then, is the pragmatic one—do they succeed in making language do what they want it to do (rather than do they show proper respect for its conventions)? And, of course, successful novel use has the effect of setting further precedents, which other writers and speakers may well follow— so that what seems virtually unintelligible to one generation may come to seem straightforward enough, and even commonplace, to another.

Our old-style skeptic may thus, with some reason, maintain that language is not really so restrictive or such a powerful agent of conservatism as Wittgensteinian philosophy (or some influential parts of it) would make it appear. He cannot be silenced, like a member of some very hidebound social circle, merely by being told that what he proposes to do with words is just "not done." But, more specifically and positively, he may claim that he is also calling attention to important features of our ordinary uses of language, features usually ignored by the layman and undervalued by the ordinary language philosopher.

What the skeptic is pointing out is, in essence, that our ordinary use of the relevant terms permits—indeed, requires—us to take risks and to overcommit ourselves. We habitually finance our intellectual enterprises, as it were, on overdrafts. Thus, for example, convention may sanction induction and absolve it from the requirement to satisfy the standards of deductive arguments; it may permit or require us to accept the fruits of some such inductions as instances of knowledge or truth. But it can do nothing to alter the fact that what satisfies the criterion for saying that all Xs are Ys—say, an unbroken run of observed Xs that are Ys—is less than what would meet the commitment made in saying it, which is nothing less than that every X whatsoever is a Y. Convention may license us to ignore the logical gap, but it cannot eliminate it. Or, we may imagine Descartes saying to the Wittgensteinian: Yes, I take your point about how we use and learn to use words like "dream" or "illusion." I am as familar as you are with the circumstances in which "I dreamt that X but in reality Y," or "This appears to be X but is really Y" are conventionally appropriate things to say; and I quite agree that without such shared conventions between myself and my readers the whole discussion would be impossible. But, nonetheless, when I say of something "This is really a tree, or a tower, and not merely a dream-image or an illusion," I am claiming much more than that our accepted criteria for saying such things—an experience of a distinctive kind, certain tests passed, or whatever—have been satisfied. I am making predictions about the contents of an indefinite variety of experiences, the results of an indefinite number of tests, my own and those of other observers. Such claims or predictions may be correct; but I have not, and cannot have, logically adequate grounds for saying so. There remain a plurality of overall pictures of the situation consistent with the satisfaction of our criteria, and not one of them has been (logically, as opposed to conventionally) established as the right one. Again, I may learn that it is appropriate to say of someone "He is depressed" or "He is angry" if I notice that he has a certain facial expression or is speaking in a certain tone of voice. But, when I say these things about him, I clearly commit myself to—and authorize my hearers to expect—a good deal more than merely my having made certain observations. Hence, while the skeptic needs to appreciate the force of his opponent's warnings about advancing too far beyond his linguistic base, may he not reply "But you still haven't answered my complaint that *you* habitually advance far beyond your evidential base"?

In reply to such a comeback from the skeptic, we may point out that it is futile to harp on the risks that we take, since there is no practicable way of avoiding them. The nearest we could get, presumably, to matching commitments to criteria would be to speak in some kind of sense-datum language, the whole point of which is to be as noncommittal as possible and thereby minimize the risk of error. For example, if I say "I am getting a treelike impression from that location," rather than "There is a tree over there," I merely record my immediate experience and do not commit myself as to what I or anyone else would find on examining the location in question. But the price of such safety is an utterance of minimal interest and utility. (To go back to our earlier analogy, if we refuse on principle to borrow capital, we are never likely to get any worthwhile business off the ground.) We may grant that in all or almost all our normal statements, whether in science, mathematics, or everyday affairs, there is a logical possibility of error. But, surely, as a quite general rule, to let ourselves be troubled or deterred by mere logical possibilities is neurotic and indeed, if carried to extremes, paralyzing. Take, for example, the phenomenon of a compulsion to keep washing one's hands or testing the lock on a door, over and over again, without ever being able to rest assured that the hands are properly clean or the door properly secured. It is, of course, logically possible that even after x washings there are still specks of dirt on the hands, that even after x tests the door is still unlocked; and no matter how high we raise the value of x, this remains true. In any situation where there is a question of performing an action rightly or wrongly, it is always possible that, whatever our efforts to get it right, we have in fact gone wrong; and the same applies to checking, to rechecking, and so on. But either we ignore such possibilities, and check only where there is positive reason to suspect error or we resign ourselves to endless and futile repetition or we abandon the activity altogether. Thus, in attempting to construct a sentence, say, either we assume, in the absence of positive indications to the contrary, that we have mastered the correct use of the requisite vocabulary and syntax or we embark on an endless sequence of checks and rechecks on our first word or, as some of the old Greek skeptics are said to have done, we retire into permanent silence. Obviously, whether or not our modern skeptic is prepared to follow such examples of heroic consistency or heroic folly, he cannot consistently *advocate* such self-paralysis. It is a necessary condition of saying meaningfully "We may be wrong," and a fortiori of giving any valid reasons for saying so, that sometimes we should be right.

Yet, even if skepticism proves in the end to be self-defeating—though it is notably resilient, and we are far from having silenced it—it still has its value. At the least, in making us think about the relations between what we say and our grounds for saying it, it makes us appreciate how complex and varied such relations are. Say of what is that it is and of what is not that it is not, as the old Greek formula for truth instructs us; tell it like it is, as the modern idiom has it. Admirable advice no doubt, so far as it goes; but it tells us very little of what is actually involved in saying of what is that it is, or telling it like it is, in any particular instance. Obviously, we have to abandon any simplistic idea of "holding a mirror up to nature," of in any strict or literal sense, *re-presenting* in words what is presented to us in experience. Even a statement as simple and commonplace as "This paper is white" is not *given* to me, or thrust upon me, in the way my immediate visual experience is. Like any other statement it is, perforce, something that we *make,* and into the making of it goes not only the experience that prompts it, but also the conceptual equipment that we bring to the task of organizing and classifying our experience and that is embodied in our language. In this regard, we have no option but to "go beyond" the initial experience, if we are ever to say anything at all.

And the truth or falsity of our statement is determined by whether or not we have applied the relevant conceptual and linguistic equipment to the relevant experience in the correct (convention-sanctioned) way. What the correct way is will obviously vary according to a number of factors—the subject matter, the concepts we elect to bring to it, the purpose of the exercise and the degree of accuracy this purpose requires, and no doubt other things as well. Hence, whereas we learn, it is to be hoped, early in life and once and for all, the importance of speaking the truth, we cannot learn once and for all, at any stage in our lives, *how* to speak it. This is something we can only learn piecemeal, as we enter new fields, acquire new concepts, master new techniques of inquiry. For example, we may take up a new branch of science—chemistry, perhaps, or biology—and become familiar with its characteristic technical and conceptual apparatus, learning how to make the appropriate inquiries and formulate our results in the appropriate terms. And this is what is needed, and all that is needed, to enable us to state and recognize truths in the field in question. There is no role for a concept or a criterion of truth independent of the correct conduct of our inquiry and statement of results; if we take care of these, then the truth takes care of itself. (If we have learnt how to do long division, then ipso facto, we have learnt how to tell whether a piece of long division has been done correctly or not; nothing extra is required.)

According to another time-honored formula, of course, a statement is true "when it corresponds to the facts." And there is no reason for us to disagree; as J. L. Austin said, simply "as a piece of standard English this can hardly be wrong."[12] But again, it affords only minimal help to anyone trying to tell, or to recognize, the truth in a particular instance. "Correspond" is a blanket term, covering a great many different relationships of matching, resembling, complementing, and so forth. There is no single clear-cut model of correspondence that we can bring to the elucidation of the concept of truth. Notoriously, we get into serious trouble if we try to assimilate the relation between a true statement and its subject matter to any specific model, for example, that of a naturalistic picture to the landscape pictured. "Correspondence" here can mean only doing successfully whichever of the indefinitely various jobs of formulating the results of inquiry the statement in question is designed to do. Thus it is unexceptionable, if unenlightening, to say of my statement "This paper is white" that it corresponds to the facts about the paper now before me. But obviously it is a very different kind of correspondence from that between the paper and a picture or photograph thereof. Here the correspondence consists simply in the fact that an inspection of the paper under standard conditions of light, eyesight of observer, etcetera, and a conventional use of English in formulating the result of this inspection yield this statement. Other statements—either more complex or more abstract, say, assessments of character or mental capacity or statements of scientific theories or theological doctrines—may equally be said to be true and hence to correspond to the facts. But clearly the correspondence relation is going to vary importantly from one statement to another, and it is futile to try to impose any single pattern on them all.

Accordingly, we may say, it is pointless to ask the skeptic's question "How do you know that that is true?" of any given statement, unless we appreciate what a truth claim amounts to in this particular instance, what connection is supposed to hold between it and its subject matter. Without such appreciation—without an awareness of what the statement undertakes to do and, hence, of what tests or checks are relevant to determining whether or not it fulfills its promise—the question is merely trivial and time wasting. And yet, if it is sufficiently irritating to provoke such awareness, to prompt us to explicate just how our words relate to the world in this or that particular field, then something important is gained. Thus, we may sympathize with the irritation of the physicist if a skeptical philosopher insists on treating his theories as though they were all generalizations of the "All crows are black" variety and makes a fuss because no such statement can be conclusively verified. But, nonetheless, such skepticism has undeniably been one of the factors that has stimulated Sir Karl Popper and others into fundamental reassessments of the true functions of science and of scientific discourse, reassessments that have influenced not only the philosophy of science but also science itself. Again, the theologian may find his forbearance taxed by the positivist who rejects his doctrines out of hand on the grounds that they are not empirically verifiable. But the positivist critique, however wrongheaded, has led many modern theologians and philosophers into radical rethinking about the nature of such doctrines—granted that they are not quasiscientific hypotheses and should not be treated as such—and about the whole character and function of theological and religious discourse.

The apparently destructive question "How do you know?" can, as it were, be made constructive by a shift of emphasis, that is, by responding to the claim "I know that S" not with "How do you *know*?" but, rather, with "*How* do you know?" In other words, the question is not so much whether you know or not but how you have come by your purported knowledge and hence what relationship you claim holds between S and its subject matter. A serious attempt to answer such questions is likely to prove instructive, not only to the philosophers, but also to the first-level practitioners of any field of interest. And if the skeptic's endeavors to show us what cannot be achieved lead to a better understanding of what can be and is achieved in science, theology, or whatever it may be, then we owe him at least a measure of gratitude.

Notes

1. L. Wittgenstein, *Philosophical Investigations*, G. E. M. Anscombe (trans.), Blackwell, Oxford, 1963, Pt. I., para. 43.

2. R. Descartes, *Meditations on the First Philosophy*, Med. I.

3. P. Strawson, *Individuals*, Methuen, London, 1959, p. 63.

4. Wittgenstein, *Philosophical Investigations*, especially Pt. I, para. 258 ff.

5. Ibid., Pt. I, para. 202.

6. Ibid., Pt. I, para. 199.

7. Ibid., Pt. I, para. 303.

8. J. L. Austin, *Philosophical Papers*, Oxford University Press, Oxford, 1970, p. 113.

9. Wittgenstein, *Philosophical Investigations*, Pt. I, para. 124.

10. K. Popper, *Conjectures and Refutations*, 5th ed., Routledge and Kegan Paul, London, 1974, p. 70.

11. Ibid., p. 71.

12. Austin, *Philosophical Papers*, p. 121.

TAKING LEAVE

We have toured the edges of the possible world. It has been little more than a two-week excursion. We might have arranged to visit more of the sites where interesting work is going on; we ought to have talked with a historian, a theologian, and many others, but enough would have been too much. One thing that has become clear to us is that the border is so convoluted, so long, winds its way through the countryside in so many places that almost everyone is its neighbor. We, the editors, also live nearby and have written of our experiences, but as editors we played the innocent tourists, asking simple questions. What did we find out? First, that everybody, *everybody* we talked to likes the idea of impossibility, feels close to it, is challenged by it, is to a certain extent guided by it, and wanted to write about it. No anthology was ever so easy to compile.

Nobody wanted to take the word at face value: the things and actions that are truly, totally, mathematically impossible pose no challenge, gird no loins, nobody had anything to say about them—except, of course, the mathematician among us, whose meat this is.

(And even he, believe it or not, hedged a bit!) But such impossibility does not suggest any personal limitation; it does not depend on any circumstance of the world or of humanity that might, just might, be transcended. In artificial intelligence there is such a huge gap between what one longs for, a thinking machine, and what has so far been made, a machine that makes calculations which may or may not be regarded as weak little thoughts. But is the machine impossible? No—compact, inexpensive, self-maintaining, there it is, inside the skull of each of us. Impossibility is a neighbor, not an enemy.

Circumstances arise that render a contract impossible to fulfill. At once the lawyer sees possibilities that arise out of the impasse: life must go on, a way out will be found. The impossibility of holding a concert in a hall that has just burned down is of the same order as that of jumping up to the moon. That isn't the interesting part of the case. The interesting part is: What shall we do about it?

The technologist finds that statements of impossibility call for a specially large grain of salt—impossibility lurks almost everywhere in that world. More often than not, the real impossibility lies in getting a project approved, funded, and continued. Optimism, robust even if occasionally shallow, is required for progress and change. There is no record that the Wright brothers conducted extensive feasibility studies before they started assembling parts.

Most impossibilities in this book have been lodged in the structure of the physical world and of the societies in which we live. They are limitations that we really can't do much to change; so we smile and adapt. Every adult, however, several times a day, must face the impossibilities that arise from the limitations of his own nature: the things that the person next door can do and he can't. To be an adult is to know these limitations, to try to overcome them, and finally to come to terms with them. Of the papers collected here, perhaps it is only the one on psychology that faces this issue.

In other areas, people interact with one another, or imagination reigns, or philosophies of "what is" and "how do I know" are forged. (The three overlap, of course.) As viewed from each, the impossible looks different, mountains that nobody needs or wants to climb, admired from a distance as we ply our boats in the rivers of possibility below.

Imagine a world of justice and equity, of peace and mental tranquillity, a world that balances the claims of individual and society. Imagine it. Does it lie beyond the wall? No question in history has been more important, or more debated. What is the answer? Plato's republic is an ideological monstrosity, and we should indeed be grateful that it lies on the other side of the border of impossibility.

In the creative arts, impossibility is encountered at many points. Is art possible only when we embrace the impossible? A novelist creates a character who exists and yet cannot exist, about whom everything that is said is both true and impossible—by so much do art and nature differ. Who can define the perfect biography? To reveal the main lines of character and motive, the biographer must carve away irrelevant details—but which are irrelevant? Who is to say? The visionary poet preaches a new Jerusalem in England's green and pleasant land; the simple words cause tears to flow (and blood, sometimes) for reasons that transcend verbal explanation.

We, the editors, have come to see that a grasp of the world's meaning requires a sober view of its impossibilities. A sense of the impossible leads to coherence and sanity; those who transcend impossibility are often deemed mad. Some of the most important lessons of childhood are those that teach what not to expect of the world or of ourselves. The world changes, of course, and so do our capacities. This, we think, is why everyone learns to be friends with impossibility, to be grateful for the lessons it teaches and the security it brings. Thus, while respectfully dismissing the impossible, we seriously require that it be there, and from the tension of these opposing frames of mind arises a part of man's creative power.

The philosopher also warms to impossibilities. When unstated assumptions have been removed, when logical tools have been sharpened and terms cleaned of their accumulated implications, what remains but mathematics in the abstract and skepticism as to the particular? Is this enough to repay an effort covering more than two millennia? As philosophers retreat from the extreme view of doubting everything, and perhaps lift up their eyes toward the East, they can at least point out that the stables of Augeas are a little cleaner than they were.

Most inhabitants of the United States live within one hundred miles of an ocean. It is not immediately obvious why this is true; people's choices today are hardly conditioned by the convenience of shipping. But perhaps we gravitate toward boundaries; at any rate, the editors were not surprised to find so many people living near the wall. What did surprise us is that they seem to like living there, and that so many of them live so close that they have actually built it into their houses.

ABOUT THE AUTHORS

SCOTT LANKFORD, a member of the 1985 American Everest Expedition, is a Ph.D. student in modern thought and literature at Stanford University.

MICHAEL J. KATZ teaches neuroanatomy in the medical school of Case Western Reserve University. His book *Templets and the Explanation of Complex Patterns* has just been published by the Cambridge University Press.

MICHAEL YARMOLINSKY is a microbiologist who has been associated with the Johns Hopkins University, the University of Paris VII, Frederick Cancer Research Facility, and the National Institutes of Health, Bethesda, Maryland, where he is currently employed. His contributions have been largely in the basic molecular biology of bacteriophages and plasmids, but he welcomes excursions of this sort. He is a brother to Adam.

JEAN M. GOODWIN obtained a B.A. in anthropology from Radcliffe College, an M.D. from Harvard University, and an M.P.H. from the

University of California, Los Angeles. She is currently professor of psychiatry at the Medical College of Wisconsin.

JAMES S. GOODWIN obtained a B.S. in psychology from Amherst College and an M.D. from Harvard University. He is currently professor and vice chairman of medicine at the Medical College of Wisconsin.

JEREMIAH A. BARONDESS is an internist involved in clinical care as well as undergraduate and postdoctoral medical education. A graduate of the Johns Hopkins University School of Medicine, he had his clinical training at the Johns Hopkins Hospital and the New York Hospital–Cornell Medical Center, and did research in clinical virology at the University of Pennsylvania School of Medicine. He is a past president of the American College of Physicians and a senior member of the Institute of Medicine of the National Academy of Sciences. He is professor of clinical medicine at the Cornell University Medical College.

WALTER J. GENSLER earned his doctoral degree in chemistry from the University of Minnesota in 1942 and subsequently taught and carried out research at Columbia University, Harvard University, and Boston University. Recently, after more than thirty years at Boston University, he retired as emeritus professor. He has published over one hundred original research papers.

ERNEST S. DAVIS received his Ph.D. in computer science from Yale University. He is assistant professor at New York University–Courant Institute of Mathematical Sciences and specializes in artificial intelligence.

MICHAEL D. STURGE is an experimental physicist working on the interaction of light with solids. He is a professor of physics at Dartmouth College and editor of the *Journal of Luminescence*. He obtained his B.A. in engineering in 1952 and his Ph.D. in physics in 1957, both from Cambridge University. With his wife and four sons, he emigrated from England to the United States in 1961. He was a member of the Solid State Electronics Laboratory of Bell Labs until 1983, when he joined Bell Communications Research, newly created in the break-up of the Bell System. He moved to Dartmouth in 1986.

DAVID PARK is Webster Atwell–Class of 1921 Professor of Physics at Williams College, Williamstown, Massachusetts. He has written numerous papers and some books on various branches of theoretical physics. His book *The Image of Eternity* won the Phi Beta Kappa Science Book Award for 1980.

PHILIP J. DAVIS is professor of applied mathematics at Brown University, Providence, Rhode Island. He has written numerous papers and books on mathematical research. He is Chauvenet Award Winner of the Mathematical Association of America. His book *The Mathematical Experience,* coauthored with Reuben Hersh, won an American Book Award in 1983.

THOMAS E. FOSTER received his B.A. from Williams College in 1969 and his J.D. from Harvard Law School in 1977. He is currently employed in the Office of General Counsel, Burroughs Corporation, Detroit, Michigan. He is married, has two children, and is working on a book entitled *Shakespeare's Judges.*

ADAM YARMOLINSKY served in the Kennedy and Johnson administrations in the Pentagon and the White House and in the Carter administration in the Arms Control Agency. He has taught at the Harvard Law School and the John F. Kennedy School of Government and was Ralph Waldo Emerson University Professor at the University of Massachusetts. He is currently teaching public policy at the University of Maryland and practicing law in Washington.

JUERGEN G. BACKHAUS received his J.S.D. and Ph.D. from the University of Konstanz, West Germany, and is an associate professor of economics at Auburn University. He has published books on the law of public enterprise, the microeconomics of unemployment, and the economics of firms with labor participation, as well as numerous articles and reviews in scholarly journals, spanning such research fields as applied economics, the history of economic thought, law, and politics.

SOPHIE FREUD, ACSW, Ph.D., is professor of social work at the Simmons College School of Social Work in Boston. She teaches courses on and has written about growth and development though the life cycle, psychological theories, and the psychology of women. She continues to be an imperfect mother to three adult children.

RICHARD P. IANO is professor in the College of Education at Temple University. He works with students who are preparing to become teachers of the handicapped and with students preparing to teach in the elementary and secondary schools. He received his Ed.D. from Syracuse University.

KINERETH GENSLER, B.A. University of Chicago, M.A. Columbia University, is a poet who teaches in the Radcliffe Seminars, Radcliffe College. Her books of poetry are *Without Roof* and *Threesome Poems*. She is coauthor of a textbook, *The Poetry Connection,* and wrote *Writing Guide for Chemists* with her husband, Walter J. Gensler.

EVERETT HAFNER is adjunct professor at Hampshire College, where he teaches optics and holography. He is also a composer and teacher of electronic music at the University of Massachusetts, Amherst.

T. E. BURKE is a graduate of Trinity College, Dublin, and lectures in philosophy at the University of Reading. He has written *The Philosophy of Popper* (Manchester University Press, 1983) and papers on epistemology and philosophy of religion in collections and in journals including *Mind, The Philosophical Quarterly,* and *Inquiry.*

INDEX